ALSO BY ROBERT W. BLY

*Secrets of a Freelance Writer*

*Selling Your Services*

*Business-to-Business Direct Marketing*

*The Elements of Business Writing*

*The Elements of Technical Writing*

*How to Promote Your Own Business*

*How to Get Your Book Published*

*Write More, Sell More*

*Direct Mail Profits*

*Ads That Sell*

*Careers for Writers*

*Creating the Perfect Sales Piece*

*Targeted Public Relations*

*Keeping Clients Satisfied*

# THE COPYWRITER'S HANDBOOK

# THE COPYWRITER'S HANDBOOK

3RD EDITION

A Step-by-Step Guide to
Writing Copy that Sells

## Robert W. Bly

A Holt Paperback
Henry Holt and Company
New York

Holt Paperbacks
Henry Holt and Company, LLC
*Publishers since 1866*
175 Fifth Avenue
New York, New York 10010
www.henryholt.com

A Holt Paperback® and ®® are registered trademarks of
Henry Holt and Company, LLC.

Distributed in Canada by H. B. Fenn and Company Ltd.

Library of Congress Cataloging-in-Publication Data

Bly, Robert W.
    The copywriter's handbook : a step-by-step guide to writing copy that sells /
Robert W. Bly.
        p. cm.
    Includes bibliographical references and index.
    ISBN-13: 978-0-8050-7804-6
    ISBN-10: 0-8050-7804-5
    1. Advertising copy. 2. Business writing. I. Title.
HF5825.B55 2006
808'.066659—dc22                                          2005050345

Henry Holt books are available for special promotions and
premiums. For details contact: Director, Special Markets.

Originally published in hardcover in 1985
by Dodd, Mead & Company

First Holt Paperbacks Edition 1990

Designed by Kelly S. Too

Printed in the United States of America
5  7  9  10  8  6  4

**For Fred Gleeck**

On writing—a matter of exercise. If you work out with weights for fifteen minutes a day over the course of ten years, you're gonna get muscles. If you write for an hour and a half a day for ten years, you're gonna turn into a good writer.

—Stephen King,
*Time* (October 6, 1986)

No one writes as well as he ought. He is fortunate if he has written as well as he could.

—Bliss Perry,
*Bedside Book of Famous British Stories* (1940)

# CONTENTS

Appendices:

# PREFACE TO THE THIRD EDITION

At a meeting of the Direct Marketing Club of New York held a few years after publication of the first edition of *The Copywriter's Handbook*, the club awarded a certificate to me declaring the book to be a "mini-classic of direct marketing."

I don't claim that this book is a classic, but over the years I have had hundreds of businesspeople—from entrepreneurs and Fortune 500 executives, to novice copywriters and some of the world's top direct-marketing pros—tell me they read and were influenced by the book.

So when my publisher, Henry Holt, asked me to prepare a revised third edition, I was conflicted: I'd already messed once with a "classic." But at the same time, there were new techniques I wanted to add. And of course, the first two editions, published in 1985 and 1990, respectively, had nothing in them about the Internet—and the Web has transformed marketing.

So here's the approach I took to preparing the updated new edition:

1. In those chapters containing copywriting techniques that have, for the most part, withstood the test of time, I kept

revisions to a minimum—deleting some extraneous text, cleaning up language, updating old data.

2. Where appropriate, I've selectively and judiciously added important new copywriting techniques. Example: the "4 U's" for writing headlines in chapter 2.

3. I've added two new chapters to cover electronic marketing: chapter 11 on writing Web site copy and chapter 12 on e-mail marketing.

And that's it. So if you've read or own the first or second edition, you know what to expect. And if you haven't—welcome to *The Copywriter's Handbook*. For decades, thousands of copywriters and other marketing professionals have relied on this book to help them produce more powerful, compelling, and persuasive copy. Now you can, too.

# PREFACE TO THE FIRST EDITION

This is a book for everyone who writes, edits, or approves copy—ad agency copywriters, freelancers, ad managers, account executives, creative directors, publicists, entrepreneurs, sales and marketing managers, product and brand managers, Internet marketers, marcom professionals, and business owners. It is largely a book of rules, tips, techniques, and ideas.

Many big agency copywriters and creative directors will tell you that advertising writers don't follow rules, and that "great" advertising breaks the rules.

Maybe so. But before you can break the rules, you have to know the rules.

This book is written to give you guidelines and advice that can teach you to write effective copy—that is, copy that gets attention, gets its message across, and convinces the customer to buy the product.

Beginners will learn all the basics they need to know: what copy is, what it can do, how to write copy that gets results.

For people who have been in the business a few years, *The*

*Copywriter's Handbook* will serve as a welcome refresher in writing clear, simple, direct copy. And, the book contains some new ideas, examples, and observations that can help these folks increase the selling power of their copy. Even "old pros" will get some new ideas—or some old ideas that they can use profitably for their own clients.

My approach is to teach through example. Numerous case histories and sample ads, commercials, mailers, and brochures illustrate the principles of effective copy. Guidelines are presented as short, easy-to-digest rules and hints.

Perhaps the copywriters who don't know the rules do produce great advertising—one time out of one thousand. But the rest of the time they create weak, ineffectual ads—ads that look pretty and read pretty but don't sell the product. (And the reason they produce bad ads is that they don't know what makes for a good ad!)

If you master the basics presented in this book, I can't guarantee that you'll go on to write "great" advertising or win prestigious advertising awards. But I can be fairly certain that you'll be writing good, clean, crisp, hardworking copy—copy that gives your customers reasons to dig into their wallets and buy your product . . . and not someone else's!

As you read *The Copywriter's Handbook*, you'll discover what you've suspected all along—that copywriters aren't "literary people" or creative artists. Copywriters are salespeople whose job is to convince people to buy products.

But don't be disappointed. When you begin to write copy that sells, you'll discover, as I have, that writing words that persuade can be just as challenging—and exciting—as writing a poem, magazine article, or short story. And it pays a lot better, too.

I do have one favor to ask: if you have a copywriting technique that has worked particularly well for you, why not send it to me so I can share it with readers of the next edition? You will receive full credit, of course. I can be reached at:

Robert W. Bly
Copywriter
22 E. Quackenbush Avenue
Dumont, NJ 07628
Phone: 201-385-1220
Fax: 201-385-1138
E-mail: rwbly@bly.com
Web site: www.bly.com

# ACKNOWLEDGMENTS

I'd like to thank the following people and companies for contributing samples of their work for publication in this book:

Jim Alexander, Alexander Marketing
Len Kirsch, Kirsch Communications
Wally Shubat, Chuck Blore & Don Richman Incorporated
Brian Cohen, Technology Solutions
Len Stein, Visibility PR
Sig Rosenblum
Richard Armstrong
Herschell Gordon Lewis
John Tierney, The DOCSI Corporation
Sandra Biermann, Masonry Institute of St. Louis

I'd also like to thank my editors, Cynthia Vartan and Flora Esterly, for their patient and dedicated work on this project; my agent, Dominick Abel, for his usual fine job in finding a home for the book; and Kim Stacey, for her valuable editorial assistance.

# 1

# AN INTRODUCTION TO COPYWRITING

"A copywriter is a salesperson behind a typewriter."*

That quote comes from Judith Charles, president of her own retail advertising agency, Judith K. Charles Creative Communication. And it's the best definition of the word *copywriter* I've ever heard.

The biggest mistake you can make as a copywriter is to judge advertising as laypeople judge it. If you do, you'll end up as an artist or an entertainer—but not as a salesperson. And your copy will be wasting your client's time and money.

Let me explain a bit. When ordinary folks talk about advertising, they talk about the ads or commercials that are the funniest, the most entertaining, or the most unusual or provocative. Geico commercials with the talking lizard, Budweiser's "real men of genius" radio spots, and the annual creative TV commercial extravaganza broadcast during the Super Bowl are the ads people point to and say, "I really like that!"

*Yes, I know you use a PC, not a typewriter. But we were using typewriters when Judith said this back in 1982 or so, and I've decided to let the quote stand as is. Substitute "PC" for "typewriter" in your own mind, if you like.

But the goal of advertising is not to be liked, to entertain, or to win advertising awards; it is to sell products. The advertiser, if he is smart, doesn't care whether people like his commercials or are entertained or amused by them. If they are, fine. But commercials are a means to an end, and the end is increased sales—and profits—for the advertiser.

This is a simple and obvious thing, but the majority of copywriters and advertising professionals seem to ignore it. They produce artful ads, stunningly beautiful catalogs, and commercials whose artistic quality rivals the finest feature films. But they sometimes lose sight of their goals—more sales—and the fact that they are "salespeople behind typewriters," and not literary artists, entertainers, or filmmakers.

Being artistic in nature, advertising writers naturally like ads that are aesthetically pleasing, as do advertising artists. But just because an ad is pretty and pleasant to read doesn't necessarily mean it is persuading people to buy the product. Sometimes cheaply produced ads, written simply and directly without a lot of fluff, do the best job of selling.

I'm not saying that all your ads should be "schlock" or that schlock always sells best. I am saying that the look, tone, and image of your advertising should be dictated by the product and your prospects—and not by what is fashionable in the advertising business at the time, or is aesthetically pleasing to artistic people who deliberately shun selling as if it were an unwholesome chore to be avoided at all costs.

In a column in *Direct Marketing* magazine, freelance copywriter Luther Brock gave an instructive example of creativity versus salesmanship in advertising. Brock tells of a printing firm that spent a lot of money to produce a fancy direct-mail piece. The mailing featured an elaborate, four-color, glossy brochure with a "pop-up" of a printing press. But, reports Brock, the mailing was less than effective:

They got plenty of compliments on "that unique mailing." But no new business. That's a pretty expensive price to pay for knocking 'em dead. The next mailing the firm sent was a simple two-page sales letter and reply card. It pulled a hefty 8 percent response. Same pitch but no frills.

As a creative person, you naturally want to write clever copy and produce fancy promotions. But as a professional, your obligation to your client is to increase sales at the lowest possible cost. If a classified ad works better than a full-page ad, use it. If a simple typewritten letter gets more business than a four-color brochure, mail the letter.

Actually, once you realize the goal of advertising is selling (and Luther Brock defines selling as "placing 100 percent emphasis on how the reader will come out ahead by doing business with you"), you'll see that there is a creative challenge in writing copy that sells. This "selling challenge" is a bit different than the artistic challenge: Instead of creating aesthetically pleasing prose, you have to dig into a product or service, uncover the reasons why consumers would want to buy the product, and present those sales arguments in copy that is read, understood, and reacted to—copy that makes the arguments so convincingly the customer can't help but want to buy the product being advertised.

Of course, Judith Charles and I are not the only copywriters who believe that salesmanship, not entertainment, is the goal of the copywriter. Here are the thoughts of a few other advertising professionals on the subjects of advertising, copywriting, creativity, and selling:

My definition says that an ad or commercial has a purpose other than to entertain. That purpose is to conquer a sale by persuading a logical prospect for your product or service, who

is now using or is about to use a competitor's product or service, to switch to yours. That's basic, or at least, it should be. In
order to accomplish that, it seems to me, you have to promise
that prospect an advantage that he's not now getting from his
present product or service and it must be of sufficient importance in filling a need to make him switch.

—Hank Seiden, Vice President, Hicks & Greist, New York

For years, a certain segment of the advertising industry has been
guilty of spinning ads out of whole cloth; they place a premium
on advertising's appearance, not on the reality of sales. The
result: too many ads and commercials that resemble third-rate
vaudeville, desperately trying to attract an audience with stale
jokes and chorus lines. On its most basic level, [the advertising]
profession involves taking a product, studying it, learning what's
unique about it, and then presenting that "uniqueness" so that
the consumer is motivated to buy the product.

—Alvin Eicoff, Chairman, A. Eicoff & Company

Those of us who read the criticisms leveled at advertising
around the world are constantly struck by the fact that they
are not really criticisms of advertising as such, but rather of
advertisements which seem to have as a prime objective finding their way into creative directors' portfolios, or reels of film.
Possibly the best starting discipline for any creative man in
any country is the knowledge that the average housewife does
not even know that an advertising agency, creative director, art
director, or copywriter even exists. What's more, she couldn't
care less if they do. She's interested in buying products, not
creative directors.

—Keith Monk, Nestlé, Vevey, Switzerland

Of course, I have never agreed that creativity is the great contri-
bution of the advertising agency, and a look through the pages

of the business magazines should dramatize my contention that much advertising suffers from overzealous creativity— aiming for high readership scores rather than for the accomplishment of a specified communications task. Or, worse, creativity for self-satisfaction.

—Howard Sawyer, Vice President, Marsteller, Inc.

When your advertising asks for the order right out front, with a price and a place to buy and with "NOW" included in the copy, that's hard-sell advertising, and it should invariably be tried before any other kind. Advertising is usually most beautiful when it's least measurable and least productive.

—Lewis Kornfeld, President, Radio Shack

Viewers are turned off by commercials that try so hard to be funny, which is the present product of so many agencies. The question that comes to mind is, "Why do these people have to have characters acting like imbeciles for thirty seconds or more just to get the product name mentioned once or twice?"

Are they afraid to merely show the product and explain why the viewer should buy it instead of another like product? Possibly the most stupid thing advertisers do is allow their agency to have background music, usually loud, rock-type music, played while the person is trying to explain the features of the product.

Frequently the music is louder than the voice, so the commercial goes down the drain. More and more people are relying on print ads for information to help them decide which product to purchase. The entertainment-type ads on TV are ineffective.

—Robert Snodell, "Why TV Spots Fail," *Advertising Age*

Humorous ads are troubling because you have to create a link to the product and its benefit. Often, people remember a funny ad but they don't remember the product.

—Richard Kirshenbaum, Co-Chairman,
Kirshenbaum Bond & Partners

Direct marketing . . . is the only form of accountable advertising. It's the only kind of advertising you can ever do where you can trace every dollar of sales to every dollar of costs. Major corporations using traditional advertising have no idea which advertising is effective. If you employ direct marketing you can tell exactly what works.

—Ted Nicholas, *How to Turn Words into Money*
(Nicholas Direct, 2004)

Copy cannot create desire for a product. It can only take the hopes, dreams, fears, and desires that already exist in the hearts of millions of people, and focus those already-existing desires onto a particular product. This is the copywriter's task: not to create this mass desire—but to channel and direct it.

—Eugene Schwartz, *Breakthrough Advertising*
(Boardroom, 2004)

Ads are not written to entertain. When they do, these entertainment seekers are little likely to be the people whom you want. This is one of the greatest advertising faults. Ad writers abandon their parts. They forget they are salesmen and try to be performers. Instead of sales, they seek applause.

—Claude Hopkins, *Scientific Advertising*
(Bell Publishing, 1960)

The advertisements which persuade people to act are written by men who have an abiding respect for the intelligence of their readers, and a deep sincerity regarding the merits of the goods they have to sell.

—Bruce Barton, Co-Founder,
Batten, Barton, Durstine & Osborn (BBDO)

A good advertisement is one which sells the product without drawing attention to itself. It should rivet the reader's attention on the product. It is the professional duty of the advertising agent to conceal his artifice.

—David Ogilvy, *Confessions of an Advertising Man*
(Atheneum, 1963)

The "literary quality" of an advertisement, per se, is no measure of its greatness; fine writing is not necessarily fine selling copy. Neither is its daring departure from orthodoxy, nor its erudition, nor its imaginative conceits, nor its catchiness.

—James Woolf, *Advertising Age*

I contend that advertising people are too tolerant of fluff copy, too eager to produce the well-turned phrase to bother with the hard-fought sale.

—Eleanor Pierce, *Printer's Ink*

If there are two "camps" in advertising—hard-sell versus creative—then I side with the former. And so do the experts quoted above.

*The Copywriter's Handbook* is written to teach you how to write copy that sells. For copy to convince the consumer to buy the product, it must do three things:

1. Get attention.
2. Communicate.
3. Persuade.

Chapter 2 shows you how to write copy that gets attention. You'll learn to use both headlines and pictures as attention-getting tools. (And you'll learn to make them work together.)

Chapter 3 is a primer on writing to communicate. It provides rules for writing clear, concise, simple copy that gets your message across to the reader.

Chapter 4 presents guidelines on persuasive writing. It will teach you to be a salesperson as well as a writer.

Chapter 5 presents step-by-step instructions that can help you prepare effectively for any copywriting assignment.

In chapters 6 through 12, you learn how to apply these copywriting principles to a variety of media both online and offline.

In chapters 13 and 14, we discuss the copywriting business, both how to get a job as a copywriter, as well as how to work with copywriters if you are a client.

And in chapter 15, we discuss the role of the copywriter in graphic design and layout.

## HAS THE INTERNET CHANGED COPYWRITING?

The major event that has taken place since the publication of the first edition of *The Copywriter's Handbook* is the rise of the Internet as a marketing medium and channel of commerce.

Many readers of the first edition have asked me, "Are the copywriting techniques *The Copywriter's Handbook* teaches still applicable in the Internet era in general, and particularly to writing for the Web?"

The answer is a resounding "Yes." The Internet has revolutionized marketing because of its speed, accessibility, ease, and low cost: sending an e-mail marketing campaign is faster, easier, and far less costly than distributing the same promotional material through the mail or running it as magazine ads or on TV.

But the important point is that the Internet has not changed human nature, nor does people's buying psychology change simply because they are reading your message online instead of offline. As Claude Hopkins wrote in his classic book *Scientific Advertising* (see appendix D):

Human nature is perpetual. In most respects it is the same today as in the time of Caesar. So the principles of psychology are fixed and enduring. You will never need to unlearn what you learn about them.

The good news for you is that virtually all of the copywriting techniques and selling principles you've learned throughout your career, including all of the ones in this book, are still as relevant as ever.

Has the Internet changed *anything*? Yes, and here are the changes I see. They are minor, but important, and where necessary, I have modified advice in this book to reflect them:

1. The Internet, computers, video games, and other electronic media have caused a reduction in the human attention span. Being concise has always been a virtue in writing, but now it is even more important. This does not mean that long copy doesn't work, that people don't read anymore (as some erroneously claim), or that all copy should be minimal. It does mean you must follow the wise advice of Strunk and White in *The Elements of Style* and "omit needless words," keeping your copy clean and concise.

2. Readers are bombarded by more ad messages and information overload than at any time in human history. As Yale librarian Rutherford D. Rogers has stated, "We are drowning in information and starving for knowledge." That means you must strive to make your copy relevant to the reader, understand what keeps him or her up at night, and address that need, desire, want, or fear in your ad.

3. The Internet has made consumers more savvy, training them to shun promotion, more easily detect hype, become increasingly skeptical, and prefer educational-type advertising material: advertising that respects their intelligence, does not talk down to them, and conveys information they perceive

as valuable in solving their problem or making a purchasing decision.

4. Your prospects are busier and have less time than ever. Convenience and speed of delivery are big selling points today, as is time saving.

5. Marketers now have the option of putting their product information in print material, online, or a combination of the two.

In modern society, copywriting is a more critical skill to master than ever before—both online and offline. Why? Consumers today are better educated and more skeptical. Thanks in part to the Internet, they have easier, faster access to product facts and pricing for comparative shopping. There are more products and brands to choose from than ever before, and also more advertising messages—commercials, e-mail, pop-up ads, mailers—competing for our attention.

Take direct mail, for example. With postage, printing, and list costs continually climbing, and response rates down, it is more difficult than ever to get a strong control in the mail— one generating a good return on investment (ROI) and likely to last a year, two years, or longer.

Worse, our prospects are bombarded by more communications than ever. There are literally millions of Web sites they can visit, and over eight hundred channels of television they can watch. Not to mention all the pop-up ads and spam they receive each day.

With all that information competing for the prospect's attention, you have to work extra hard to make your mailing— whether print or online—stand out and grab the prospect's attention. And of course that means one thing primarily: strong copy.

Yes, lists and offers are tremendously important. But you can identify, fairly quickly and easily, those lists and offers that work best for your product. Once you've found the right lists and offers, then the only additional leverage you have for boosting response is through—you guessed it—copy.

Writing is critical to success on the Web, too. As Nick Usborne points out in his book *Net Words*, "Go to your favorite Web site, strip away the glamour of the design and technology, and you're left with words—your last, best way to differentiate yourself online." In marketing, whether on the Internet or the printed page, copy is still king.

# 2

# WRITING TO GET ATTENTION:
# THE HEADLINE

When you read a magazine or a newspaper, you ignore most of the ads and read only a few. Yet, many of the ads you skip are selling products that may be of interest to you.

The reason you don't read more ads is simple: There are just too many advertisements competing for your attention. And you don't have the time—or the inclination—to read them all.

This is why you, as a copywriter, must work hard to get attention for your ad or commercial. Wherever you turn—the Web, magazines, television, or the mail basket of a busy executive—there are just too many things competing for your reader's attention.

For example, a single issue of *Cosmopolitan* magazine contained 275 advertisements. And one issue of the *New York Times* ran 280 display ads and 4,680 classified ads. Each year, American companies spend more than $20 billion to advertise in popular magazines, newspapers, and trade publications.

Even worse, your ad competes with the articles published in these newspapers and magazines, as well as with all other reading material that crosses the reader's desk or is piled in her mail basket.

Let's say you're writing an ad to sell laboratory equipment to scientists. Your ad will compete with the dozens of other ads in the scientific journal in which it is published. And the scientist probably receives a dozen or more such journals every month. Each is filled with articles and papers he should read to keep up to date in his field. But John Naisbitt, author of *Megatrends,* estimates that 6,000 to 7,000 scientific articles are written daily; the total amount of technical information in the world doubles every five and a half years.

This increased amount of information makes it difficult for any single piece of information to be noticed. According to Dr. Leo Bogart of the Newspaper Advertising Bureau, consumers are exposed to more than twice as many ads today as fifteen years ago, but pay attention to only 20 percent more.

Obviously, those ads that don't do something special to grab the reader's attention are not noticed and not read. Bob Donath, former editor of *Business Marketing,* says the successful ad is one that is able to "pop through the clutter."

Direct-mail advertisers know that a sales letter has only five seconds in which to gain the reader's attention. If the reader finds nothing of interest after five seconds of scanning the letter, she will toss the letter in the trash. Similarly, an ad or commercial has only a few seconds to capture the prospect's interest before the prospect turns the page or goes to the refrigerator.

In advertising, getting attention is the job of the headline. "If you can come up with a good headline, you are almost sure to have a good ad," writes John Caples in his book *How to Make Your Advertising Make Money.* "But even the greatest writer can't save an ad with a poor headline."

## HOW HEADLINES GET ATTENTION

In all forms of advertising, the "first impression"—the first thing the reader sees, reads, or hears—can mean the difference between success and failure. If the first impression is boring or irrelevant, the ad will not attract your prospect. If it offers news or helpful information or promises a reward for reading the ad, the first impression will win the reader's attention. And this is the first step in persuading the reader to buy your product.

What, specifically, is this "first impression"?

- In a print advertisement, it is the headline and the visual. In a brochure, it's the cover.
- In a radio or TV commercial, it's the first few seconds of the commercial.
- In a direct-mail package, it's the copy on the outer envelope or the first few sentences in the letter.
- In a press release, it's the lead paragraph.
- In a sales brochure or catalog, it's the front cover.
- In a sales presentation, it's the first few slides or flip charts.
- On a Web site, it's the first screen of the home page.
- In an e-mail marketing message, it's the From line and the Subject line.

No matter how persuasive your body copy or how great your product, your ad cannot sell if it does not attract your customer's attention. Most advertising experts agree that an attention-getting headline is the key ingredient in a successful advertisement.

Here's what David Ogilvy, author of *Confessions of an Advertising Man*, says about headlines:

The headline is the most important element in most advertisements. It is the telegram which decides whether the reader will read the copy.

On average, five times as many people read the headline as read the body copy. When you have written your headline, you have spent eighty cents out of your dollar.

If you haven't done some selling in your headline, you have wasted 80 percent of your client's money.

Ogilvy says that putting a new headline on an existing ad has increased the selling power of the ad tenfold. What is it that makes one headline a failure and the other a success?

Many copywriters fall into the trap of believing that clever wordplay, puns, and "cute" copy make for a good headline. But think a minute. When you make a purchase, do you want to be amused by the salesclerk? Or do you want to know that you're getting quality merchandise at a reasonable price?

The answer is clear. When you shop, you want products that satisfy your needs—and your budget. Good copywriters recognize this fact, and put sales appeal—not cute, irrelevant gimmicks and wordplay—in their headlines. They know that when readers browse ad headlines, they want to know: "What's in it for *me*?"

The effective headline tells the reader: "Hey, stop a minute! This is something that you'll want!" As mail-order copywriter John Caples explains, "The best headlines appeal to people's self-interest, or give news."

Let's look at a few examples:

• A classic appeal to self-interest is the headline "How to Win Friends and Influence People," from an ad for the Dale

Carnegie book of the same name. The headline promises that you will make friends and be able to persuade others if you read the ad and order the book. The benefit is almost irresistible. Who but a hermit doesn't want more friends?

• An ad for Kraft Foods appeals to the homemaker with the headline, "How to Eat Well for Nickels and Dimes." If you are interested in good nutrition for your family but must watch your budget carefully, this ad speaks directly to your needs.

• The headline for a Hellmann's Real Mayonnaise ad hooks us with the question, "Know the Secret to Moister, Richer Cake?" We are promised a reward—the secret to moist cake—in return for reading the copy.

Each of these headlines offers a benefit to the consumer, a reward for reading the copy. And each promises to give you specific, helpful information in return for the time you invest in reading the ad and the money you spend to buy the product.

## THE FOUR FUNCTIONS OF THE HEADLINE

Headlines do more than get attention. The Dale Carnegie headline, for example, lures you into the body copy of the ad by promising useful information. The Hellmann's ad also gets you interested in reading more. And it selects a specific type of reader—those people who are interested in baking cakes.

Your headline can perform four different tasks:

1. Get attention.
2. Select the audience.
3. Deliver a complete message.
4. Draw the reader into the body copy.

Let's take a look at how headlines perform each of these jobs.

## 1. Getting Attention

We've already seen how headlines get attention by appealing to the reader's self-interest. Here are a few more examples of this type of headline:

| | |
|---|---|
| "Give Your Kids a Fighting Chance" | Crest |
| "Why Swelter Through Another Hot Summer?" | GE air conditioners |
| "For Deep-Clean, Oil-Free Skin, Noxzema Has the Solution" | Noxzema moisturizer |

Another effective attention-getting gambit is to give the reader news. Headlines that give news often use words such as *new, discover, introducing, announcing, now, it's here, at last,* and *just arrived.*

| | |
|---|---|
| "New Sensational Video Can Give You Thin Thighs Starting Now!" | Exercise videotape |
| "Discover Our New Rich-Roasted Taste" | Brim decaffeinated coffee |
| "Introducing New Come 'N Get It. Bursting With New Exciting 4-Flavor Taste." | Come 'N Get It dog food |

If you can legitimately use the word *free* in your headline, do so. Free is the most powerful word in the copywriter's vocabulary. Everybody wants to get something for free.

A *TV Guide* insert for Silhouette Romance novels offers

"free love" in its headline, "Take 4 Silhouette Romance Novels FREE (A $9.80 Value) . . . And Experience the Love You've Always Dreamed Of." In addition, the word *FREE* is used twenty-three times in the body copy and on the reply card.

Other powerful attention-getting words include *how to, why, sale, quick, easy, bargain, last chance, guarantee, results, proven,* and *save*. Do not avoid these words because other copywriters use them with such frequency. Other copywriters use these words because they work. You should, too. Grade your performance as a copywriter on sales generated by your copy, not on originality.

Headlines that offer the reader useful information are also attention-getters. The information promised in the headline can be given in the copy or in a free booklet the reader can send for. Some examples:

| | |
|---|---|
| "Free New Report on 67 Emerging Growth Stocks" | Merrill Lynch |
| "Three Easy Steps to Fine Wood Finishing" | Minwax Wood Finish |
| "How to Bake Beans" | Van Camp's |

Many advertisers try to get attention with headlines and gimmicks that don't promise the reader a benefit or are not related to the product in any way. One industrial manufacturer features a photo of a scantily clad woman in his ads, with an offer to send a reprint of the photo to readers who clip the coupon and write in for a brochure on the manufacturer's equipment.

Does this type of gambit get attention? Yes, but not attention that leads to a sale or to real interest in the product. Attention-getting for attention-getting's sake attracts a lot of curious bystanders but precious few serious customers.

When you write a headline, get attention by picking out an important customer benefit and presenting it in a clear, bold, dramatic fashion. Avoid headlines and concepts that are cute, clever, and titillating but irrelevant. They may generate some hoopla, but they do not sell.

## 2. Selecting the Audience

If you are selling life insurance to people over 65, there is no point in writing an ad that generates inquiries from young people. In the same way, an ad for a $65,000 sports car should say, "This is for rich folks only!" You don't want to waste time answering inquiries from people who cannot afford the product.

The headline can select the right audience for your ad and screen out those readers who are not potential customers. A good headline for the life insurance ad might read, "To Men and Women Over 65 Who Need Affordable Life Insurance Coverage." One possible headline for the sports car ad is, "If You Have to Ask How Many Miles to the Gallon It Gets, You Can't Afford to Buy One."

Here are a few more headlines that do a good job of selecting the right audience for the product:

| | |
|---|---|
| "We're Looking for People to Write Children's Books" | The Institute of Children's Literature |
| "A Message to All Charter Security Life Policyholders of Single Premium Deferred Annuities" | Charter Security life insurance |
| "Is Your Electric Bill Too High?" | Utility ad |

## 3. Delivering a Complete Message

According to David Ogilvy, four out of five readers will read the headline and skip the rest of the ad. If this is the case, it pays to make a complete statement in your headline.

That way, the ad can do some selling to those 80 percent of readers who read headlines only. Here are a few headlines that deliver complete messages:

"Caught Soon Enough, Early            Colgate toothpaste
Tooth Decay Can Actually Be
Repaired by Colgate!"

"Gas Energy Inc. Cuts Cooling         Hitachi chiller-heaters
and Heating Costs Up to 50%"

"You Can Make Big Money in            Century 21
Real Estate Right Now"

Ogilvy recommends that you include the selling promise and the brand name in the headline. Many effective headlines don't include the product name. But put it in if you suspect most of your prospects won't bother to read the copy underneath.

### 4. Drawing the Reader into the Body Copy

Certain product categories—liquor, soft drinks, and fashion, for example—can be sold with an attractive photo, a powerful headline, and a minimum of words.

But many products—automobiles, computers, books, records, home study programs, life insurance, and investments—require that the reader be given a lot of information. That information appears in the body copy, and for the ad to be effective, the headline must compel the reader to read this copy.

To draw the reader into the body copy, you must arouse his or her curiosity. You can do this with humor, or intrigue, or mystery. You can ask a question or make a provocative statement. You can promise a reward, news, or useful information.

A sales letter offering motivational pamphlets was mailed to business managers. The headline of the letter was, "What Do Japanese Managers Have That American Managers Sometimes Lack?" Naturally, American managers wanted to read on and find out about the techniques the Japanese use to manage effectively.

A headline for an ad offering a facial lotion reads: "The $5 Alternative to Costly Plastic Surgery." The reader is lured into the ad to satisfy her curiosity about what this inexpensive alternative might be. The headline would not have been as successful if it said, "$5 Bottle of Lotion Is an Inexpensive Alternative to Costly Plastic Surgery."

PFS Software begins its ad with the headline, "If You're Confused About Buying a Personal Computer, Here's Some Help." If you are confused about computers, you will want to read the ad to get the advice offered in the headline.

## EIGHT BASIC HEADLINE TYPES

It's only natural for a creative person to avoid formulas, to strive for originality and new, fresh approaches. To the creative writer, many of the headlines in this chapter might seem to follow rigid formulas: "How to . . ," "Three Easy Ways . . . ," "Introducing the New . . ." And to an extent, copywriters do follow certain rules, because these rules have been proven effective in thousands of letters, brochures, ads, and commercials.

Remember, as a copywriter, you are not a creative artist; you are a salesperson. Your job is not to create literature; your job is to persuade people to buy the product. As the late John Francis Tighe, a top direct-mail copywriter, pointed out, "We are not in the business of being original. We are in the business of reusing things that work."

Of course, John doesn't mean copywriters spend their time deliberately copying the work of other writers. The challenge is to take what works and apply it to your product in a way that is compelling, memorable, and persuasive. Certainly, the best copywriters succeed by breaking the rules. But you have to know the rules before you can break them effectively.

Here, then, are eight time-tested headline categories that have helped sell billions of dollars' worth of products and services. Study them, use them well, and then go on to create your own breakthroughs in headline writing.

### 1. Direct Headlines

Direct headlines state the selling proposition directly, with no wordplay, hidden meanings, or puns. "Pure Silk Blouses—30 Percent Off" is a headline that's about as direct as you can get. Most retailers use newspaper ads with direct headlines to announce sales and bring customers into their stores.

### 2. Indirect Headlines

The indirect headline makes its point in a roundabout way. It arouses curiosity, and the questions it raises are answered in the body copy.

The headline for an ad for an industrial mixing device reads, "Ten Million to One, We Can Mix It." At first, this sounds like a wager; the company is betting ten million to one that its mixer can handle your mixing applications. But when you read the copy, you discover that the real significance of "ten million to one" is the mixer's ability to mix two fluids where one fluid is as much as ten million times thicker than the other. The headline has a double meaning, and you have to read the copy to get the real message.

### 3. News Headlines

If you have news about your product, announce it in the headline. This news can be the introduction of a new product, an improvement of an existing product ("new, improved Bounty"), or a new application for an old product. Some examples of headlines that contain news:

| | |
|---|---|
| "Introducing the New Citation II" | Chevrolet |
| "Finally, a Caribbean Cruise as Good as Its Brochure" | Norwegian Cruise Line |
| "The Greatest Market Discovery Ever Made" | Commodities trading newsletter |

The Norwegian Cruise Line headline, in addition to containing news, has added appeal because it empathizes with the reader's situation. We've all been disappointed by fancy travel brochures that promise better than they deliver. Norwegian gains credibility in our eyes by calling attention to this well-known fact.

### 4. How-to Headlines

The words *how to* are pure magic in advertising headlines, magazine articles, and book titles. There are more than 7,000 books in print with *how to* in their titles. Many advertising writers claim if you begin with *how to*, you can't write a bad headline. They may be right.

How-to headlines offer the promise of solid information, sound advice, and solutions to problems: "How to Turn a Simple Party Into a Royal Ball." "How to Write Better and Faster." "How to Stop Smoking in 30 Days . . . Or Your Money Back."

Whenever I'm stuck for a headline, I type "How to" on the page, and what follows those words is always a decent, hardworking headline: good enough to use until something better comes along.

### 5. Question Headlines

To be effective, the question headline must ask a question that the reader can empathize with or would like to see answered. Some examples:

| | |
|---|---|
| "What in the World Is Wrong With Me?" | *Prevention* magazine |
| "When an Employee Gets Sick, How Long Does It Take Your Company to Recover?" | Pilot Life Insurance |
| "Is Your Pump Costing You More to Operate Than It Should?" | Gorman-Rupp pumps |
| "Do You Close the Bathroom Door Even When You're the Only One Home?" | *Psychology Today* |
| "Have You Any of These Decorating Problems?" | Bigelow carpets |
| "What Do Japanese Managers Have That American Managers Sometimes Lack?" | *Bits & Pieces* |

Question headlines should always focus on the reader's self-interest, curiosity, and needs, and not on the advertiser's. A typical self-serving question headline used by many companies reads something like, "Do You Know What the XYZ Company Is Up to These Days?" The reader's response is "Who cares?" and a turn of the page.

### 6. Command Headlines
Command headlines generate sales by telling your prospects what to do. Here are a few command headlines:

| | |
|---|---|
| "Try Burning This Coupon" | Harshaw Chemical |
| "Put a Tiger in Your Tank" | Esso |
| "Aim High. Reach for New Horizons." | U.S. Air Force |

Note that the first word in the command headline is a strong verb demanding action on the part of the reader.

### 7. Reason-Why Headlines

One easy and effective way of writing body copy is to list the sales features of your product in simple 1-2-3 fashion. If you write your ad this way, you can use a reason-why headline to introduce the list.

Examples of reason-why headlines include "Seven Reasons Why You Should Join the American Institute of Aeronautics and Astronautics" and "120 to 4,000 Reasons Why You Should Buy Your Fur During the Next Four Days."

Reason-why headlines need not contain the phrase "reason why." Other introductory phrases such as "6 ways," "7 steps," and "here's how" can do just as well.

### 8. Testimonial Headlines

In a testimonial advertisement, your customers do your selling for you. An example of a testimonial is the Publishers Clearinghouse commercial in which past winners tell us how they won big prize money in the sweepstakes. Testimonials work because they offer proof that a business satisfies its customers.

In print ad testimonials, the copy is written as if spoken by the customer, who is usually pictured in the ad. Quotation marks around the headline and the body copy signal the reader that the ad is a testimonial.

When writing testimonial copy, use the customer's own words as much as possible. Don't polish his statements; a natural, conversational tone adds believability to the testimonial.

## 38 MODEL HEADLINES FOR YOUR "SWIPE FILE"

A "swipe file" is a collection of promotions that you turn to for reference when creating your own marketing materials. The best way to get ideas for headlines when you are stuck is to keep a swipe file and consult it for inspiration when you sit down to write a new ad or mailing.

As a shortcut, here's a partial collection of such headlines from my vast swipe file, organized by category so as to make clear the approach being used:

1. *Ask a question in the headline.*
   "What Do Japanese Managers Have That American Managers Sometimes Lack?"
2. *Tie-in to current events.*
   "Stay One Step Ahead of the Stock Market Just Like Martha Stewart—But Without Her Legal Liability!"
3. *Create a new terminology.*
   "New 'Polarized Oil' Magnetically Adheres to Wear Parts in Machine Tools, Making Them Last Up to 6 Times Longer."
4. *Give news using the words "new," "introduction," or "announcing."*
   "Announcing a Painless Cut in Defense Spending."
5. *Give the reader a command—tell him to do something.*
   "Try Burning This Coupon."
6. *Use numbers and statistics.*
   "Who Ever Heard of 17,000 Blooms from a Single Plant?"
7. *Promise the reader useful information.*
   "How to Avoid the Biggest Mistake You Can Make in Building or Buying a Home."
8. *Highlight your offer.*
   "You Can Now Subscribe to the Best New Books—Just as You Do to a Magazine."
9. *Tell a story.*
   "They Laughed When I Sat Down at the Piano, But When I Started to Play. . . ."

10. *Make a recommendation.*
   "The 5 Tech Stocks You Must Own NOW."
11. *State a benefit.*
   "Managing UNIX Data Centers—Once Difficult, Now Easy."
12. *Make a comparison.*
   "How to Solve Your Emissions Problems—at Half the Energy Cost of Conventional Venturi Scrubbers."
13. *Use words that help the reader visualize.*
   "Why Some Foods 'Explode' in Your Stomach."
14. *Use a testimonial.*
   "After Over Half a Million Miles in the Air Using AVBLEND, We've Had No Premature Camshaft Failures."
15. *Offer a free special report, catalog, or booklet.*
   "New FREE Special Report Reveals Little-Known Strategy Millionaires Use to Keep Wealth in Their Hands—and Out of Uncle Sam's."
16. *State the selling proposition directly and plainly.*
   "Surgical Tables Rebuilt—Free Loaners Available."
17. *Arouse reader curiosity.*
   "The One Internet Stock You MUST Own Now. Hint: It's NOT What You Think!"
18. *Promise to reveal a secret.*
   "Unlock Wall Street's Secret Logic."
19. *Be specific.*
   "At 60 Miles an Hour, the Loudest Noise in This New Rolls-Royce Comes from the Electric Clock."
20. *Target a particular type of reader.*
   "We're Looking for People to Write Children's Books."
21. *Add a time element.*
   "Instant Incorporation While U-Wait."

22. *Stress cost savings, discounts, or value.*
    "Now You Can Get $2,177 Worth of Expensive Stock
    Market Newsletters for the Incredibly Low Price of
    Just $69!"

23. *Give the reader good news.*
    "You're Never Too Old to Hear Better."

24. *Offer an alternative to other products and services.*
    "No Time for Yale—Took College At Home."

25. *Issue a challenge.*
    "Will Your Scalp Stand the Fingernail Test?"

26. *Stress your guarantee.*
    "Develop Software Applications Up to 6 Times Faster
    or Your Money Back."

27. *State the price.*
    "Link 8 PCs to Your Mainframe—Only $2,395."

28. *Set up a seeming contradiction.*
    "Profit from 'Insider Trading'—100% Legal!"

29. *Offer an exclusive the reader can't get elsewhere.*
    "Earn 500+% Gains With Little-Known 'Trader's Secret
    Weapon.'"

30. *Address the reader's concern.*
    "Why Most Small Businesses Fail—and What You Can
    Do About It."

31. *"As Crazy as It Sounds . . ."*
    "Crazy as It Sounds, Shares of This Tiny R&D
    Company, Selling for $2 Today, Could Be Worth as
    Much as $100 in the Not-Too-Distant Future."

32. *Make a big promise.*
    "Slice 20 Years Off Your Age!"

33. *Show ROI (return on investment) for purchase of your
    product.*
    "Hiring the Wrong Person Costs You Three Times Their
    Annual Salary."

34. *Use a reasons-why headline.*
   "7 Reasons Why Production Houses Nationwide Prefer Unilux Strobe Lighting When Shooting Important TV Commercials."
35. *Answer important questions about your product or service.*
   "7 Questions to Ask Before You Hire a Collection Agency . . . and One Good Answer to Each."
36. *Stress the value of your premiums.*
   "Yours Free—Order Now and Receive $280 in Free Gifts With Your Paid Subscription."
37. *Help the reader achieve a goal.*
   "Now You Can Create a Breakthrough Marketing Plan Within the Next 30 Days . . . for FREE!"
38. *Make a seemingly contradictory statement or promise.*
   "Cool Any Room in Your House Fast—Without Air Conditioning!"

## THE 4 U'S FORMULA FOR WRITING EFFECTIVE HEADLINES

When prospects see your ad, they make a quick decision, usually in a couple of seconds, to read it or turn the page, based largely on the subject line. But given the flood of commercial messages today, how can you convince a busy prospect—in just a few words—that your ad is worthy of attention?

The "4 U's" copywriting formula—which stands for urgent, unique, ultra-specific, and useful—can help.

Developed by my colleague Michael Masterson for writing more powerful headlines, the 4 U's formula states that strong headlines are:

*1. Urgent.* Urgency gives the reader a reason to act now instead of later. You can create a sense of urgency in your headline by incorporating a time element. For instance, "Make $100,000 working from home this year" has a greater sense of urgency than "Make $100,000 working from home." A sense of urgency can also be created with a time-limited special offer, such as a discount or premium if you order by a certain date.

2. *Unique.* The powerful headline either says something new, or if it says something the reader has heard before, says it in a new and fresh way. For example, "Why Japanese women have beautiful skin" was the headline in an e-mail promoting a Japanese bath kit. This is different than the typical "Save 10% on Japanese Bath Kits."

3. *Ultra-specific.* Boardroom, a newsletter publisher, is the absolute master of ultra-specific bullets, known as "fascinations," that tease the reader into reading further and ordering the product. Examples: "What never to eat on an airplane," "Bills it's okay to pay late," and "Best time to file for a tax refund."

4. *Useful.* The strong subject line appeals to the reader's self-interest by offering a benefit. In the headline, "An Invitation to Ski & Save," the benefit is saving money.

When you have written your headline, ask yourself how strong it is in each of the 4 U's. Use a scale of 1 to 4 (1 = weak, 4 = strong) to rank it in each category.

Rarely will a headline rate a 3 or 4 on all four U's. But if your headline doesn't rate a 3 or 4 on at least *three* of the U's, it's probably not as strong as it could be—and can benefit from some rewriting.

A common mistake is to defend a weak headline by pointing to a good response. A better way to think is as follows: If the ad generated a profitable response despite a weak headline, imagine how much more money you could have made by applying the 4 U's.

A marketer wrote to tell me he had sent out a successful

e-mail marketing campaign with the subject line "Free Special Report." How does this stack up against the 4 U's?

• *Urgent.* There is no urgency or sense of timeliness. On a scale of 1 to 4, with 4 being the highest rating, "Free Special Report" is a 1.

• *Unique.* Not every marketer offers a free special report, but a lot of them do. So "Free Special Report" rates only a 2 in terms of uniqueness.

• *Ultra-specific.* Could the marketer have been less specific than "Free Special Report"? Yes, he could have just said "Free Bonus Gift." So we rate "Free Special Report" a 2 instead of a 1.

• *Useful.* I suppose the reader is smart enough to figure the report contains some helpful information. On the other hand, the usefulness is in the specific information contained in the paper, which isn't even hinted at in the headline. And does the recipient, who already has too much to read, really need yet another "free special report"? I rate it a 2. Specifying the topic would help, e.g., "Free special report reveals how to cut training costs up to 90% with e-learning."

I urge you to go through this exercise with every headline you write. You can also apply the formula to other copy, both online and offline, including e-mail subject lines, direct mail envelope teasers, letter leads, Web page headlines, subheads, and bullets.

Rate the headline you've written in all 4 U's. Then rewrite it so you can upgrade your rating on at least two and preferably three or four of the categories by at least 1 point. This simple exercise can increase readership and response rates substantially with very little effort.

## MORE HEADLINE TIPS

Here are a few points to consider when evaluating headlines:

- Does the headline promise a benefit or a reward for reading the ad?
- Is the headline clear and direct? Does it get its point across simply and quickly?
- Is the headline as specific as it can be? ("Lose 19 Pounds in Three Weeks" is a better headline than "Lose Weight Fast.")
- Does the headline reach out and grab your attention with a strong sales message, dramatically stated in a fresh new way?
- Does the headline relate logically to the product? (Avoid "sensationalist" headlines that lure you with ballyhoo and then fail to deliver what they promise.)
- Do the headline and visual work together to form a total selling concept?
- Does the headline arouse curiosity and lure the reader into the body copy?
- Does the headline select the audience?
- Is the brand name mentioned in the headline?
- Is the advertiser's name mentioned in the headline?
- Avoid blind headlines—the kind that don't mean anything unless you read the copy underneath. ("Give It a Hand" is a blind headline used in a recent ad for facial powder.)
- Avoid irrelevant wordplay, puns, gimmicks, and other copywriter's tricks. They may make for amusing advertising, but they do not sell products.
- Avoid negatives. (Instead of "Contains No Sodium," write "100% Sodium-Free.")

## A TECHNIQUE FOR PRODUCING HEADLINES

No two copywriters have identical methods for producing headlines. Some writers spend 90 percent of their writing time coming up with dozens of headlines before they write one word of body copy. Others write the body copy first and extract the headline from this copy. Many copywriters keep swipe files of published ads and use headlines from these ads as inspiration for their own advertisements (I gave you 38 of these from my personal collection earlier).

Copywriters who work at big agencies often rely on art directors to help them develop the concept. But I believe professional copywriters should be able to generate headlines, concepts, and ideas on their own.

Let me tell you how I go about writing a headline. You may find these techniques useful in your own work. First, I ask three questions:

1. Who is my customer?
2. What are the important features of the product?
3. Why will the customer want to buy the product? (What product feature is most important to him?)

When I have my answer to question number 3, I know the key selling proposition I want to feature in the headline. Then it's simply a matter of stating this benefit in a clear, compelling, interesting fashion, in a way that will make the reader take notice and want to know more about the product.

Sometimes I'll use a how-to headline. Sometimes I'll use a question or a reason-why format. Other times I do something that doesn't fit in any of these categories. The point is, I don't try to force-fit the selling proposition into a formula. I start with a sales message and write headlines that do the best job of illuminating this message.

I usually come up with the right headline on the second or third try. Other copywriters I know write a dozen or more headlines for a single ad. If writing a lot of headlines works best for you, fine. You can always use the discarded headlines as subheads or sentences in your body copy.

When writing a new ad for an existing product, I go through the file of previous ads to see what sales points were covered in these ads. Often, the sales message for my headline will be buried in the body copy of one of the existing ads.

Sometimes when I am unable to produce a lively headline I make a list of words that relate to the product. I then mix and match the words from this list to form different headlines.

For instance, a client asked me to write an ad on a new type of dental splint used to keep loose teeth in place. The old-type splints were made of stiff strips of metal; the new splint was made of braided wire that could more easily twist to fit the patient's teeth.

My word list looked something like this:

| | |
|---|---|
| Twist | Easy |
| Splint | Technology |
| Teeth | Invented |
| New | Revolutionary |
| Developed | Contour |
| Dental | Bend |
| Braided | Dentist |
| Wire | Introducing |
| Steel | Flexible |
| Fit | Loose |

Mixing and matching words from this list produced half a dozen good headlines. The one I liked best was "Introducing a New Twist in Splint Technology." The client liked it and used it in a successful ad.

If you cannot come up with a headline, don't let it result in writer's block. Put it aside and begin to write the body copy. As you write the copy and go over your notes, ideas for headlines will pop into your head. Write them down as they come and go back to them later. Much of this material will be inadequate, but the perfect headline might just be produced this way.

## A FINAL WORD ON HEADLINES

The headline is the part of the ad that gets attention. And getting attention is the first step in persuading your reader to buy your product.

Showmanship, clever phrases, and ballyhoo do not, by themselves, make for a good headline. Creating headlines that are wonderfully clever is worthwhile only if the cleverness enhances the selling message and makes it more memorable. Unfortunately, many copywriters engage in creativity for creativity's sake, and the result is cleverness that obscures the selling message.

If you have to choose between being clever and obscure or simple and straightforward, I advise you to be simple and straightforward. You won't win any advertising awards. But at least you'll sell some merchandise.

Jim Alexander, president of Alexander Marketing Services, also believes that headlines should sell. Here are a few of Jim's thoughts on the subject:

> We believe in dramatizing a product's selling message with flair and excitement. Those are important ingredients of good salesmanship in print. But simple statements and plain-Jane graphics often make powerful ads.
>
> For example, the headline "Handling Sulfuric Acid" might sound dull or uncreative to you. To a chemical engineer who's

forever battling costly corrosion, that simple headline implies volumes. And makes him want to read every word of the problem-solving copy that follows.

So before we let our clients pronounce an ad dull, we first ask them, "Dull to whom?" Dull to you, the advertiser? Or dull to the reader, our potential customer? It's easy to forget that the real purpose of an ad is to communicate ideas and information about a product. Too many ads are approved because of their entertainment value. That's a waste of money.

# 3 ✒

# WRITING TO COMMUNICATE

In an article published in the *Harvard Business Review*, Charles K. Ramond described experiments designed to measure advertising effectiveness. The experiments showed, not surprisingly, that advertising is most effective when it is easy to understand. In other words, you sell more merchandise when you write clear copy.

In theory, it sounds easy. Advertising deals, for the most part, with simple subjects—clothing, soda, beer, soap, records. But in practice, many advertisements don't communicate as effectively as they could. Here's an example from an ad that appeared in *Modern Bride* magazine:

> **THEY LOVED MY DRESS ON QUIRIUS 3**
> They smiled politely when Harry showed them our late model telestar, but when he opened the hood of our auto-drive one of their children burst into a shrill laugh and was boxed on his starfish-shaped ears. . . .

The students in my copywriting seminars call this one "What did she say?" This is an example of a "borrowed interest" ad: The writer didn't have faith in her ability to make the product interesting, so she hid behind a made-up scenario involving a conversation on the planet Quirius 3. The result? Maximum confusion and minimum communication.

"Borrowed interest" is a major cause of confusing copy. There are others: lengthy sentences, clichés, big words, not getting to the point, a lack of specifics, technical jargon, and poor organization, to name a few.

The following tips will help you write copy that gets its message across to the reader.

## 11 TIPS FOR WRITING CLEAR COPY

### 1. Put the Reader First

In his pamphlet, "Tips to Put Power in Your Business Writing," consultant Chuck Custer advises executives to think about their readers when they write a business letter or memo.

"Start writing to people," says Custer. "It's okay that you don't know your reader! Picture someone you do know who's like your reader. Then write to him."

Think of the reader. Ask yourself: Will the reader understand what I have written? Does he know the special terminology I have used? Does my copy tell her something important or new or useful? If I were the reader, would this copy persuade me to buy the product?

One technique to help you write for the reader is to address the reader directly as "you" in the copy, just as I am writing to *you* in this book. Copywriters call this the "you-orientation." Flip through a magazine, and you'll see that 90 percent of the ads contain the word "you" in the body copy.

The column at left shows examples of copy written without regard to the reader's interests. The column at right gives revisions that make the copy more you-oriented.

| *Advertiser-Oriented Copy* | *You-Oriented Copy* |
|---|---|
| Bank Plan is the state-of-the-art in user-friendly, sophisticated financial software for small-business accounts receivable, accounts payable, and general ledger applications. | Bank Plan can help you balance your books. Manage your cash flow. And keep track of customers who haven't paid their bills. Best of all, the program is easy to use—no special training is required. |
| The objective of the daily cash accumulation fund is to seek the maximum current income that is consistent with low capital risk and the maintenance of total liquidity. | The cash fund gives you the maximum return on your investment dollar with the lowest risk. And, you can take out as much money as you like—whenever you like. |
| To cancel an order, return the merchandise to us in its original container. When we have received the book in salable condition, we will inform our Accounting Department that your invoice is cancelled. | If you're not satisfied with the book, simply return it to us and tear up your invoice. You won't owe us a cent. What could be fairer than that? |

## 2. Carefully Organize Your Selling Points

The Northwestern National Bank in Minneapolis wanted to know if people read booklets mailed by the bank. So they included an extra paragraph in a booklet mailed to a hundred customers. This extra paragraph, buried in 4,500 words of technical information, offered a free ten-dollar bill to anyone who asked for it.

So, how many bank customers requested the free money? None. Obviously, the organization of your material affects how people read it. If the bank had put "FREE $10!" on the brochure cover and on the outside of the mailing envelope, many customers would have responded to the offer.

When you write your copy, you must carefully organize the points you want to make. In an ad, you might have one primary sales message ("This car gets good mileage") and several secondary messages ("roomy interior," "low price," "$500 rebate").

The headline states the main selling proposition, and the first few paragraphs expand on it. Secondary points are covered later in the body copy. If this copy is lengthy, each secondary point may get a separate heading or number.

The organization of your selling points depends on their relative importance, the amount of information you give the reader, and the type of copy you are writing (letter, ad, commercial, or news story).

Terry C. Smith, a communications manager with Westinghouse, has a rule for organizing sales points in speeches and presentations. His rule is: "Tell them what you're going to tell them. Tell them. And then, tell them what you told them." The speechwriter first gives an overview of the presentation, covers the important points in sequence, and then gives a brief summary of these points. Listeners, unlike readers, cannot refer to a printed page to remind them of what was said, and these overviews and summaries help your audience learn and remember.

Burton Pincus, a freelance copywriter, has developed a unique organizational pattern for the sales letters he writes. Pincus begins with a headline that conveys a promise, shows how the promise is fulfilled, and gives proof that the product is everything the copy says it is. Then he tells the reader how to order the product and explains why the cost of the product is insignificant compared to its value.

Before you create an ad or mailer, write down your sales points. Organize them in a logical, persuasive, clear fashion. And present them in this order when you write your copy.

### 3. Break the Writing into Short Sections

If the content of your ad can be organized as a series of sales points, you can cover each point in a separate section of copy. This isn't necessary in short ads of 150 words or less. But as length increases, copy becomes more difficult to read. Breaking the text into several short sections makes it easier to read.

What's the best way to divide the text into sections? If you have a series of sections where one point follows logically from the previous point, or where the sales points are listed in order of importance, use numbers.

If there is no particular order of importance or logical sequence between the sales points, use graphic devices such as bullets, asterisks, or dashes to set off each new section. If you have a lot of copy under each section, use subheads (as I've done in this book).

Paragraphs should also be kept short. Long, unbroken chunks of type intimidate readers. A page filled with a solid column of tiny type says, "This is going to be tough to read!"

When you edit your copy, use subheads to separate major sections. Leave space between paragraphs. And break long paragraphs into short paragraphs. A paragraph of five sentences can usually be broken into two or three shorter paragraphs by finding places where a new thought or idea is introduced and beginning the new paragraph with that thought.

### 4. Use Short Sentences

Short sentences are easier to read than long sentences. All professional writers—newspaper reporters, publicists, magazine writers, copywriters—are taught to write in crisp, short, snappy sentences.

Long sentences tire and puzzle your readers. By the time they have gotten to the end of a lengthy sentence, they don't remember what was at the beginning.

D. H. Menzel, coauthor of *Writing a Technical Paper*, conducted a survey to find the best length for sentences in technical papers. He found that sentences became difficult to understand beyond a length of about 34 words. And the consumer has far less patience with wordiness and run-on sentences than does the scientist studying an important report.

Rudolf Flesch, best known for his books *Why Johnny Can't Read* and *The Art of Plain Talk*, says the best average sentence length for business writing is 14 to 16 words. Twenty to 25 words is passable, he adds, but above 40 words, the writing becomes unreadable.

Because ad writers place a premium on clarity, their sentences are even shorter than Flesch's recommended 14- to 16-word average. Here's a list showing the average sentence length of some ads and promotions:

| Ad | Average sentence length (number of words) |
| --- | --- |
| Velveeta cheese spread | 6.7 |
| Lanier dictaphone | 8.3 |
| IBM PC software | 10.6 |
| Porsche 944 | 10.6 |
| 3M/Audio-Visual Division | 13.6 |
| IBM PC database communication | 14.5 |
| Jack Daniels | 16.2 |

The average sentence length in these and dozens of other ads I measured ranges from 6 to 16 words. The average sentence length of your copy should also fall in this range.

Now, let's take a look at how you can reduce sentence length. First, you should break large sentences into two or more separate sentences whenever possible:

| | |
|---|---|
| Today every penny of profit counts and Gorman-Rupp wants your pumps to work for all they're worth. | Today every penny of profit counts. And Gorman-Rupp wants your pumps to work for all they're worth. |
| This article presents some findings from surveys conducted in Haiti in 1977 that provide retrospective data on the age at menarche of women between the ages of 15 and 49 years. | This article presents some findings from surveys conducted in Haiti in 1977. These surveys provide retrospective data on the age at menarche of women between the ages of 15 and 49 years. |

Another method of breaking a long sentence is to use punctuation to divide it into two parts.

| | |
|---|---|
| One purpose is to enable you to recognize and acknowledge the importance of people who handle people from the company president right down to the newest foreman. | One purpose is to enable you to recognize and acknowledge the importance of people who handle people—from the company president right down to the newest foreman. |
| The outcome is presentations that don't do their job and make others wonder whether you're doing yours. | The outcome is presentations that don't do their job . . . and make others wonder whether you're doing yours. |

Copy becomes dull when all sentences are the same length. To make your writing flow, vary sentence length. By writing an occasional short sentence or sentence fragment, you can reduce the average sentence length of your copy to an acceptable length even if you frequently use lengthy sentences.

| | |
|---|---|
| Over thirty thousand aerospace engineers are members now. To join them, send your check for $146 with the coupon below and become a member today. | Over thirty thousand aerospace engineers are members now. Join them. Send your check for $146 with the coupon below and become a member today. |
| Now, discover the Splint-Lock System, a simply beautiful, effective, and versatile chair-side splinting technique that helps you stabilize teeth quickly, easily, and economically. | Now, discover the Splint-Lock System . . . a simply beautiful, effective, and versatile chair-side splinting technique that helps you stabilize teeth. Quickly. Easily. And economically. |

Train yourself to write in crisp, short sentences. When you have finished a thought, stop. Start the next sentence with a new thought. When you edit, your pencil should automatically seek out places where a long string of words can be broken in two.

### 5. *Use Simple Words*

Simple words communicate more effectively than big words. People use big words to impress others, but they rarely do. More often, big words annoy and distract the reader from what the writer is trying to say.

Yet big words persist, because using pompous language makes the reader or speaker feel important. Some recent examples of big words in action:

In his sermon, a Unitarian minister says: "If I were God, my goal would be to maximize goodness, not to eternalize evil."

In a cartoon appearing in *Defense News*, a publication of the Westinghouse Defense Center, a manager tells his staff: "I want you to focalize on your optionalizations, prioritize your parametrics, budgetize your expendables, and then schedualize your throughput." Fred Danzig, writing in *Advertising Age*, asks why an E. F. Hutton executive says the market might "whipsaw back and forth" when he could have said it "will go up and down."

In advertising copy, you are trying to communicate with people, not impress them or boost your own ego. Avoid pompous words and fancy phrases. Cecil Hoge, the mail-order expert, says the words in your copy should be "like the windows in a storefront. The reader should be able to see right through them and see the product."

The column at left lists some big words that have appeared in recent ads, brochures, and articles. The column at right offers simpler—and preferable—substitutions.

| Big Word | Substitute Word or Phrase |
| --- | --- |
| assist | help |
| automobile | car |
| container | bottle, jar, package |
| database | information |
| diminutive | small |
| eliminate | get rid of |
| employ | use |
| facilitate | help |
| facility | building, factory, warehouse |
| finalize | finish, complete, conclude |
| garment | suit, shirt, dress |
| indicate | tell, say, show |

| | |
|---|---|
| obtain | get |
| operate | run, use |
| optimum | best |
| parameters | factors |
| prioritize | set priorities, rank |
| procure | get |
| perspiration | sweat |
| purchase | buy |
| substantiate | prove |
| select | pick |
| superior | best |
| utilize | use |
| terminate | end, finish |
| visage | face |

Small words are better than big words whether you're writing to farmers or physicists, fishermen or financiers. "Even the best-educated people don't resent simple words," says John Caples. "But [simple words] are the only words many people understand."

And don't think your copy will be ignored because you write in plain English. In Shakespeare's most famous sentence—"To be or not to be?"—the biggest word is three letters long.

### 6. Avoid Technical Jargon

Industrial copy isn't the only writing that uses technical jargon. Here's a sample from a Porsche ad that ran in *Forbes*:

The 944 has a new 2.5-liter, 4-cylinder, aluminum-silicon alloy Porsche engine—designed at Weissach, and built at Zuffenhausen.

It achieves maximum torque of 137.2 ft-lbs as early as 3,000 rpm, and produces 143 hp at 5,500 rpm.

The 944 also has the Porsche transaxle design, Porsche aerodynamics, and Porsche handling.

Like many *Forbes* readers, I'm not an automotive engineer. I didn't know that torque is achieved in ft-lbs, or that 3,000 rpm is considered early for achieving it. I know hp is "horsepower" and rpm "revolutions per minute," but I don't know whether 143 hp at 5,500 rpm is good, bad, or mediocre.

The point is: Don't use jargon when writing to an audience that doesn't speak your special language. Jargon is useful for communicating within a small group of experts. But used in copy aimed at outsiders, it confuses the reader and obscures the selling message.

Computer people, for example, have created a new language: bits and bytes, RAMS and ROMs, CRTs and CPUs. But not everybody knows the vocabulary.

A business executive may know the meaning of "software" and "hardware," but not understand terms like "interprocess message buffer," "asynchronous software interrupt," and "four-byte integer data type." When you use jargon, you enjoy an economy of words, but you risk turning off readers who don't understand this technical shorthand.

Computer experts aren't the only technicians who baffle us with their lingo. Wall Streeters use an alien tongue when they speak of downside ticks, standstills, sideways consolidation, and revenue enhancements. Hospital administrators, too, have a language all their own: cost outliers, prospective payments, catchment areas, diagnostic-related groups, and ICD-9 codes.

Because advertisers are specialists, it is they—not their copywriters—who most often inflict jargon on the readers.

One of my clients rewrote some brochure copy so that their storage silo didn't merely dump grain; the grain was "gravimetrically conveyed."

When is it okay to use technical terms, and when is it best to explain the concept in plain English? I have two rules:

RULE #1: Don't use a technical term unless 95 percent or more of your readers will understand it. If your client insists you use jargon that is unfamiliar to your readers, be sure to explain these terms in your copy.

RULE #2: Don't use a technical term unless it precisely communicates your meaning. I would use *software* because there is no simpler, shorter way to say it. But instead of using *deplane*, I would just say, "Get off the plane."

## 7. Be Concise

Good copy is concise. Unnecessary words waste the reader's time, dilute the sales message, and take up space that could be put to better use.

Rewriting is the key to producing concise copy. When you write your first draft, the words just flow, and you can't help being chatty. In the editing stage, unnecessary words are deleted to make the writing sparkle with vigor and clarity.

One copywriter I know describes her copy as a "velvet slide"—a smooth path leading the prospect from initial interest to final sale. Excess words are bumps and obstacles that block the slide.

For example, a writing consultant's brochure informs me that his clients receive "informed editorial consideration of their work." As opposed to *uninformed*? Delete *informed*.

Another such brochure refers to "incomplete manuscripts still in progress." Obviously, a manuscript still in progress is incomplete.

Make your writing concise. Avoid redundancies, run-on sentences, wordy phrases, the passive voice, unnecessary adjectives, and other poor stylistic habits that take up space but add little to meaning or clarity. Edit your writing to remove unnecessary words, phrases, sentences, and paragraphs.

Here are some examples of wordy phrases and how to make them more concise.

| *Wordy Phrase* | *Concise Substitute* |
| --- | --- |
| at first glance | at first |
| the number 20 | 20 |
| free gift | gift |
| whether or not | whether |
| a general principle | a principle |
| a specific example | an example |
| he is a man who | he |
| they managed to use | they used |
| from a low of 6 to a high of 16 | from 6 to 16 |
| a wide variety of different models | a variety of models |
| approximately 17 tons or so | approximately 17 tons |
| expert specialists | specialists |
| simple and easy to use | easy to use |
| can help you | helps you |
| can be considered to be | is |
| most unique | unique |
| the one and only | the only |
| comes to a complete stop | stops |
| the entire issue | the issue |
| dull and boring | boring |
| on an annual basis | yearly |
| in the form of | as |
| exhibits the ability to | can |

| | |
|---|---|
| as you may or may not know | as you may know |
| a substitute used in place of | a substitute for |
| features too numerous to mention | many features |
| John, Jack, Fred, Tom, etc. | John, Jack, Fred, and Tom |
| feminine hygiene products for women | feminine hygiene products |
| children's toys | toys |
| where you were born originally | where you were born |
| your own home | your home |
| a product that you can use | a product you can use |
| RAM memory* | RAM |

## 8. Be Specific

Advertising persuades us by giving specific information about the product being advertised. The more facts you include in your copy, the better. Copywriters who don't bother to dig for specifics produce vague, weak, meaningless copy.

"If those who have studied the art of writing are in accord on any one point," write Strunk and White in *The Elements of Style*, "it is this: the surest way to arouse and hold the attention of the reader is by being specific, definite, and concrete. The greatest writers—Homer, Dante, Shakespeare—are effective largely because they deal in particulars and report the details that matter."

When you sit down at the PC, your file of background information should have at least twice as much material as you will end up using in the final version of your ad. When you have a warehouse of facts to choose from, writing copy is easy: You

---

*RAM stands for *random access memory*. So a RAM memory is a "random access memory memory."

just select the most important facts and describe them in a clear, concise, direct fashion.

But when copywriters have little or nothing to say, they fall back on fancy phrases and puffed-up expressions to fill the empty space on the page. The words sound nice, but say nothing. And the ad doesn't sell because it doesn't inform.

Here are some examples of vague versus specific copy.

| Vague Copy | Specific Copy |
| --- | --- |
| He is associated in various teaching capacities with several local educational institutions. | He teaches copywriting at New York University and technical writing at Brooklyn Polytech. |
| Adverse weather conditions will not result in structural degradation. | The roof won't leak if it rains. |
| *Good Housekeeping* is one of the best-read publications in America. | Each month, more than five million readers pick up the latest issue of *Good Housekeeping* magazine. |

## 9. Go Straight to the Point

If the headline is the most important part of an ad, then the lead paragraph is surely the second most important part. It is this lead that either lures the reader into the text by fulfilling the promise of the headline, or bores the reader with uninteresting, irrelevant, unnecessary words.

The first piece of copy I ever wrote was a brochure describing an airport radar system. Here's the lead:

Times change. Today's airports handle a far greater volume of traffic than the airports of the late 1960s.

The radars of that era were not built with an eye toward the future and could not handle the rapidly increasing demands placed upon terminal air traffic control systems.

The air traffic handled by today's airports continues to increase at a tremendous rate. An airport surveillance radar must be built to handle not only today's airport traffic but also the more complex air traffic control requirements of tomorrow's airports.

All this is true, and as a layman, I found it interesting. But the person reading the brochure is in charge of air traffic control at a large or medium-size airport. Doesn't he already know that air traffic volume is increasing? If so, I am wasting his time by repeating the obvious. Many novice copywriters fall into this trap. They spend the first few paragraphs "warming up" before they get to the sales pitch. By the time they do start talking about the product, most readers have fled.

Start selling with the very first line of copy. Here's how I should have written the lead to that radar brochure:

The X-900 radar detects even the smallest commercial aircraft out to a range of 145 miles. What's more, the system's L-band operating efficiency makes it 40 times more efficient than S-band radars.

If you feel the need to "warm up" as you set your thoughts on paper, do so. But delete these warm-ups from your final draft. The finished copy should sell from the first word to the last.

Here's another example of copy that fails to get to the point:

**AIM HIGH. REACH FOR NEW HORIZONS**
It's never easy. But reaching for new horizons is what aiming high
is all about. Because to reach for new horizons you must have the
vision to see things not only as they are, but as they could be. . . .

Why write vague copy like this? The ad tries to be dramatic,
but the result is empty rhetoric; the copy does not give a clue
as to what is being advertised.

This copy appeared in a U.S. Air Force recruitment ad. The
benefits of joining the air force are travel, vocational training,
and the chance to fly jets. Why not feature these points right off?

### 10. Write in a Friendly, Conversational Style

Ann Landers was one of the most widely read columnists in
the country. Why was she so popular? Said Ann, "I was taught
to write like I talk."

People enjoy reading clear, simple, easy-to-understand writing. And the simplest, clearest style is to write the way you
talk. (The writing experts call this "conversational tone.")

Conversational tone is especially important in advertising,
where the printed page is an economical substitute for a salesperson. (The only reason companies advertise is that advertising can reach more people at less cost than a traveling
salesperson can.) A light, conversational style is much easier to
read than the stiff, formal prose of business, science, and aca-
demia. And when you write simply, you become the reader's
friend. When you write pompously, you become a bore.

For example, IBM's famous Charlie Chaplin ads and commercials launched IBM's first PC and helped make it a best-
seller. This ad series was a model of friendly, helpful,
conversational copy. Here's a sample:

There's a world of information just waiting for you. But to use
it, study it, enjoy it and profit from it, you first have to get at it.

Yet the facts can literally be right at your fingertips—with your own telephone, a modem, and the IBM Personal Computer.

Note the use of colloquial expressions ("a world of information," "at your fingertips") and the informal language ("just waiting for you," "you first have to get at it"). IBM seems to want to help us on a person-to-person level, and their copy has the sound of one friend talking to another.

But here's how the copy might read if written in strictly technical terms:

> Thousands of databases may be accessed by individuals. These databases provide information for business, educational, and leisure activities.
>
> To access these databases from your home, a telephone, modem, and IBM Personal Computer are required.

See the difference? When you write copy, you'll want to use conversational tone to make your ads glow with warmth, as IBM's do.

So how do you go about it? In an article in the *Wall Street Journal*, John Louis DiGaetani recommends this simple test for conversational tone: "As you revise, ask yourself if you would ever say to your reader what you are writing. Or imagine yourself speaking to the person instead of writing."

My former boss once wrote a sales letter that began, "Enclosed please find the literature you requested." I asked him, "If you were handing this envelope to me instead of mailing it, what would you say?"

"Well, I'd say, 'Here is the information you asked for' or 'I've enclosed the brochure you requested' or something like that."

"Then why not write it that way?" I replied. He did.

And to help you write the way you talk, here are some tips for achieving a natural, conversational style:

• Use pronouns—*I, we, you, they.*
• Use colloquial expressions—*a sure thing, turn-on, rip-off, OK.*
• Use contractions—*they're, you're, it's, here's, we've, I'm.*
• Use simple words.
• If you must choose between writing naturally and being grammatically correct, write naturally.

## 11. Avoid Sexist Language

The day of the advertising man, salesman, and Good Humor man are over. Now it's the advertising *professional*, sales*person*, and Good Humor *vendor*.

Copywriters must avoid sexist language. Like it or not, sexist language offends a large portion of the population, and you don't sell things to people by getting them angry at you.

Handling gender in writing is a sensitive, as yet unresolved issue. Do we change manpower to *person*power? His to *his/her*? Foreman to fore*person*?

Fortunately, there are a few techniques for handling the problem:

• *Use plurals.* Instead of "the doctor receives a report on his patients," write, "the doctors receive reports on their patients."
• *Rewrite to avoid reference to gender.* Instead of "the manager called a meeting of his staff," write, "the manager called a staff meeting."
• *Alternate gender references.* In the past, I used *his* and *he* throughout my copy. Now, I alternate *he* with *she* and *his* with *her*.
• *Use "he and she" and "his and her."* This works in simple sentences. But it can become cumbersome in such sentences as, "When he or she punches his or her time-card, he or she is automatically switched to his or her overtime pay rate." When

you use *he and she* and *his and her*, alternate these with *she and he* and *her and his*.

• *Do not use the awkward constructions he/she or his/her.* Instead, write "he or she" or "his or her."

• *Create an imaginary person to establish gender.* For example: "Let's say Doris Franklin is working overtime. When she punches her time-card, she is automatically switched to her overtime pay rate."

Finally, here's a helpful list of sexist terms and non-sexist substitutes:

| Sexist Term | Nonsexist Substitute |
| --- | --- |
| anchorman | anchor |
| advertising man | advertising professional |
| chairman | chairperson |
| cleaning woman | domestic |
| Englishmen | the English |
| fireman | firefighter |
| foreman | supervisor |
| a man who | someone who |
| man the exhibit | run the exhibit |
| man of letters | writer |
| mankind | humanity |
| manpower | personnel, staff |
| man-made | artificial, manufactured |
| man-hours | work hours |
| Mrs., Miss | Ms. |
| newsman, newspaper man | reporter |
| postman | mail carrier |
| policeman | police officer |
| salesman | salesperson |

| | |
|---|---|
| self-made man | self-made person |
| stewardess | flight attendant |
| weatherman | meteorologist |
| workman | worker |

## A FEW TRICKS OF THE TRADE

Copywriters use a number of stylistic techniques to pack a lot of information into a few short paragraphs of smooth-flowing copy. Here are a few tricks of the trade:

### End with a Preposition

Ending a sentence with a preposition adds to the conversational tone of the copy. And it's a perfectly acceptable technique endorsed by Zinsser, Flesch, Fowler, and most other authorities on modern writing. Some examples:

| | |
|---|---|
| He's the kind of fellow with whom you love to have a chat. | He's the kind of fellow you love to have a chat with. |
| Air pollution is something of which we want to get rid. | Air pollution is something we want to get rid of. |
| For what are we fighting? | What are we fighting for? |

### Use Sentence Fragments

Sentence fragments help keep your average sentence length to a respectable number of words. And sentence fragments can add drama and rhythm to your copy.

Basic Eye Emphasizer does it all. It's the one eye makeup everyone needs. The only one.

Not one of the Fortune 1000 companies even comes close to our rate of growth. And no wonder. Computers are the hottest product of the 1980s, with no end to demand in sight.

It doesn't take much to block the door to success. A flash of an idea that slips your mind. A note that never gets written.

### Begin Sentences with Conjunctions

Beginning a sentence with *and, or, but,* or *for* makes for a smooth, easy transition between thoughts.

Use these simple words instead of more complex connectives. *But* is a shorter, better way of saying *nevertheless, notwithstanding,* and *conversely.* And don't use such antiquated phrases as *equally important, moreover,* and *furthermore* when *and* will do just as well.

The first lesson is free. But I can't call you. You have to take the first step.

The choice is simple. Be a pencil pusher. Or get the Messenger. And move ahead at the speed of sound.

ECS phones the first two numbers you've selected until someone answers. It announces the emergency. Gives your address. And repeats it.

### Use One-Sentence Paragraphs

An occasional one-sentence paragraph provides a change of pace that can liven up a piece of copy. When all sentences and paragraphs are pretty much the same, the reader is lulled into a stupor, just as a driver can be hypnotized by a long stretch of straight road. A one-sentence paragraph is like a sudden curve in the road—it can shock your reader to wakefulness again. Here's an example from a sales letter pitching freelance copywriting services:

For many ad agency people, industrial advertising is a difficult chore. It's detailed work, and highly technical. To write the copy, you need someone with the technical know-how of an engineer and the communications skills of a copywriter.

That's where I can help.

### Use Graphic Techniques To Emphasize Words or Phrases in the Copy

College students use yellow markers to highlight sentences in their textbooks. This saves time in studying, since the highlights allow them to reread only the important material and not the entire book.

Highlighting and underlining can make words and phrases stand out in print advertising and promotion as well as in schoolbooks. Many readers skim copy without reading it carefully, so an underline or highlight can be useful in calling out key words, phrases, paragraphs, and selling points.

Of course, underlines and other mechanical devices should be used sparingly. If you underline every other word in your sales letter, nothing stands out. On the other hand, if you underline only three words in a one-page letter, you can be sure most readers will read those words. Here is a list of mechanical techniques copywriters use to call attention to key words and phrases:

underlines
capital letters
indented paragraphs
boldface type
italics
colored type
fake handwriting
arrows and notes in margins
yellow highlighting

reverse type (white type on black background)
boxed copy
call-outs
P.S. (in letters)

## Use Bullets

One of the most effective techniques for writing subscription copy is to present the publication's content as a list of bulleted items, e.g., "7 ways to reduce your heating bill this winter." Many copywriters rattle off the bullets quickly—and as a result settle for bullets that are ordinary and therefore not engaging.

It takes a bit more energy and creativity to come up with a bullet item that is as strong and compelling as this classic from Boardroom: "What Never to Eat on an Airplane."

One of the most common mistakes with bullets is not including the right level of information. "Tell too much, and you give away the information free, and there is no need to order the product to find the answer," says copywriter Parris Lampropolous. "For example, if your bullet says 'how to erase pain by using an over-the-counter lotion called capsaicin,' no curiosity is generated because you've already told the secret."

On the other hand, says Parris, if your bullet contains too little information, or not enough specific information, it fails to grab attention. "If you say 'why B vitamins are an absolute must for people predisposed to this disease,' you fail to hook me, because I don't know what 'this disease' is," says Parris.

His rule of thumb for writing strong bullets: Be specific about the *problem*; be vague and mysterious about the solution. Plus, do it with a twist, hook, or unusual angle.

Parris gives as an example a copywriter who had to write a promotion for a book on natural health. One of the tips in the book was that sitting on bulky objects can cause back pain. So if you have a big, bulging wallet, take it out of your back pocket and keep it in your front pocket to prevent back stress. The bullet that the copywriter came up with: "How a pickpocket can make your back pain better." He is specific about the problem (back pain), but mysterious about the solution (how can a pickpocket help with back pain?).

## A COPYWRITER'S CHECKLIST

Before you release copy to the client or the art department, ask yourself these questions:

• *Does the copy fulfill the promise of the headline?* If the headline is "How to Win Friends and Influence People," the copy should tell you how to win friends and influence people. Copy that doesn't fulfill the promise of the headline cheats the reader—and the reader knows it.

• *Is the copy interesting?* Your copy can't generate enthusiasm for the product if the reader yawns as she reads it. Tell a story, give news, improve the reader's life. Make it *interesting*. You can't bore people into buying your product.

• *Is it easy to read?* When a person reads your copy, it is not his job to try to figure out what you mean. It is your job to explain what you mean in plain, simple English. Use short sentences, short paragraphs, small words. Be clear.

• *Is it believable?* Once a teacher said of a phrase I had written, "Bob, this has all the sincerity of a three-dollar bill." People mistrust advertising and advertising professionals. You must work hard to convince the reader that what you say is true. One way to establish credibility is to include testimonials from satisfied customers. Another is to offer a demonstration or scientific evidence that proves your claim. But the best way to get people to believe you is to tell the truth.

• *Is it persuasive?* Clear, readable prose is not enough. Your copy must sell as well as communicate. To sell, your copy must get attention . . . hook the reader's interest . . . create a desire for the product . . . prove the product's superiority . . . and ask for action. (Chapter 4 covers the basics of salesmanship in print.)

• *Is it specific?* To persuade people to buy, you have to give them specifics—facts, features, benefits, savings—reasons why they should buy the product. The more specific you are, the more informative and believable your copy.

• *Is it concise?* Tell the whole story in as few words as possible. When you are finished, stop.

• *Is it relevant?* Freelance copywriter Sig Rosenblum explains: "One of the rules of good copy is: Don't talk about yourself. Don't tell the reader what you did, what you achieved, what you like or don't like. That's not important to him. What's important to him is what he likes, what he needs, what he wants." Make sure your copy discusses facts that are relevant to the reader's self-interest.

• *Does it flow smoothly?* Good copy flows smoothly from one point to the next. There are no awkward phrases, no confusing arguments, and no strange terms to jar the reader and break the flow.

• *Does it call for action?* Do you want the consumer to switch to your brand, send for a free brochure, call your sales representative, send you a check? Find the next step in the buying process and tell the reader to take it. Use coupons, reply cards, toll-free numbers, and other such devices to increase response.

# 4

# WRITING TO SELL

"The object of advertising is to sell goods," said Raymond Rubicam of Young & Rubicam. "It has no other justification worth mentioning."

For the beginning copywriter, this may be a new idea. If you've done other kinds of writing—magazine articles, news reporting, fiction, technical writing—you know how to express yourself in clear, simple English. You know how to write words that inform, and maybe even words that amuse or entertain. But now, you're faced with a new challenge: writing words that convince the reader to *buy your product*.

This puts most writers on uncertain ground. There are many choices you have to make, and unless you're experienced in sales or advertising, you don't know how to make them.

For example, should you write a lot of copy, or is it better to write short copy? (If you write a lot of copy, will people read it? Or is it true that people won't read ads with more than a couple of paragraphs?)

Do you need some clever gimmick, slogan, or sexy model to get the reader's attention? Or should you concentrate on the product when you write?

If your product has a minor advantage over the competition, should you focus on that advantage? Or should you concentrate on the general benefits of using the product (which the reader gets from both your product and your competitor's)? What do you do if there is no difference between your product and the competition's?

How do you know whether what you're writing will be convincing or interesting to the reader? If you think of two or three ideas for an ad, how do you pick the best one?

Let's start finding out the answers to these questions.

## FEATURES AND BENEFITS

The first step in writing copy that sells is to write about benefits and not about features.

A *feature* is a descriptive fact about a product or service; it's what the product is or has. A *benefit* is what the product does; it's what the user of the product or service gains as a result of the feature.

For example, I'm writing this book on a PC. A feature of the machine is that it allows me to edit and revise what I'm typing electronically, so I can move a sentence or add a word without retyping the whole page. The benefit of this feature is that I save a lot of time and can increase my productivity (and make more money) as a result.

Another example: A second feature of my PC is that it has a detachable keyboard connected to the main unit with a coil cable. The benefit is that I can position the keyboard for maximum typing comfort.

In their pamphlet "Why Don't Those Salespeople Sell," Learning Dynamics Incorporated, a sales training firm, cites poor ability to present benefits as one of ten reasons why salespeople fail to make the sale. "Customers don't buy products or services," the firm explains. "They buy what these products and services are going to do for them. Yet many salespeople describe only the features, assuming the customer knows the benefits. Salespeople need to know how to translate features into benefits, and then present them in a customer-centered language."

The same goes for copywriters. Novices tend to write about features: the facts, figures, and statistics at hand. Experienced copywriters turn those features into customer benefits: reasons why the reader should buy the product.

Here's a simple technique for digging out a product's benefits: divide a sheet of paper into two columns. Label the left-hand column "Features" and the right-hand column "Benefits."

In the left-hand column write down all the features of the product. Some of these you'll find in the background material you've collected on the product (chapter 5 tells you what background material to collect). The rest you can learn by examining and using the product or by talking with people involved with the product: customers, salespeople, distributors, engineers.

Then, go down the list of features and ask yourself, "What benefit does this feature provide to the customer? How does this feature make the product more attractive, useful, enjoyable, or affordable?"

When you complete the list, the right-hand column will contain all the benefits the product offers the customer. These are the sales points that should be included in your copy.

Try this exercise with a common household product that you have nearby. Below is my features/benefits checklist for a No. 2 pencil. Can you add to this list or think of a stronger way to state the benefits?

| Features | Benefits |
|---|---|
| Pencil is a wooden cylinder surrounding a graphite core. | Can be resharpened as often as you like to ensure clean, crisp writing. |

| | |
|---|---|
| Cylinder is hexagonal. | Won't roll off your desk. |
| One end is capped by a rubber eraser. | Convenient eraser lets you correct writing errors cleanly and quickly. |
| Eraser is attached with a tight-fitting metal band. | Holds eraser snugly in place; no pencils ruined by eraser coming loose. |
| Pencil is 7½ inches long. | 7½-inch graphite core ensures long writing life. |
| Pencil is ¼ inch in diameter. | Slender shape makes it easy to hold and comfortable to write with. |
| Pencil is No. 2. | Graphite core is blended for just the right hardness—writes smoothly yet crisply. |
| Yellow exterior. | Bright, attractive exterior—stands out in a pencil holder or desk drawer. |
| Sold by the dozen. | One stop to the store gives you enough pencils to last for months. |
| Also available in a box containing a gross. | Easier purchasing and lower price per unit for large-volume users such as business offices and schools. |
| Made in the U.S.A. | A quality product. (Also, buying American-made strengthens U.S. economy.) |

Now that you have a list of customer benefits, you must decide which sales point is the most important, the one you will feature in your headline as the "theme" of the ad. You also have to decide which of the other points you will include and which you will not use. And, you have to arrange these points in some sort of logical order.

Let's take a look at a handy five-step sequence that can help you put your sales points in an order that will lead the reader from initial interest to final sale.

## THE MOTIVATING SEQUENCE

Over the years, many advertising writers have developed "copy formulas" for structuring ads, commercials, and sales letters.

The best known of these formulas is AIDA, which stands for Attention, Interest, Desire, Action.

According to AIDA, the copy must first get the reader's *attention*, then create an *interest* in the product, then turn that interest into a strong *desire* to own the product, and finally ask the reader to buy the product or take some other *action* that will eventually lead to a sale.

A second well-known formula is ACCA: Awareness, Comprehension, Conviction, Action. In ACCA, consumers are first made *aware* that the product exists. Then they must *comprehend* what the product is and what it will do for them. After comprehension, the readers must be *convinced* to buy the product. And finally, they must take *action* and actually make the purchase.

A third famous formula is the 4 P's: Picture, Promise, Prove, Push. The copywriter creates a *picture* of what the product can do for the reader, *promises* the picture will come true if the reader buys the product, *proves* what the product has done for others, and *pushes* for immediate action.

Lately, others have come up with their own versions, and I

might as well join the crowd. The "motivating sequence" presented below is a five-step formula for writing copy that sells.

### 1. Get Attention

This is the job of the headline and the visual. The headline should focus on the single strongest benefit you can offer the reader.

Some copywriters try to hook the reader with clever phrases, puns, or irrelevant information, then save the strongest benefit for a big windup finish. A mistake. If you don't hook the reader with the strongest benefit—the most important reason why he or she should be interested in what you're selling—the reader won't get past the headline. (For a quick refresher on headline writing, go back and reread chapter 2.)

### 2. Show a Need

All products, to some degree, solve some problem or fill a need. A car solves the problem of getting to and from work. An air conditioner prevents you from sweltering in summer heat. Toothpaste with fluoride keeps your teeth from getting holes in them. And mouthwash saves you the embarrassment of having bad breath.

However, with most products, the need for the product may not be obvious or it may not be ingrained in the reader's mind. The second step of writing copy that sells, then, is to show the reader why she needs the product.

For example, many small-business owners do their own taxes and haven't thought about hiring an accountant. But an accountant, with his superior knowledge of taxes, can take advantage of the latest tax regulations and shelters and save the business owner hundreds or even thousands of dollars in income tax.

So an accountant seeking small businesses as clients might run an ad with the headline, "Would You Pay $1,000 to Save

$5,500 a Year or More on Your Taxes?" This headline does double duty by grabbing attention with a provocative question and hinting at the need for professional help at tax time. Body copy could go on to explain how an accountant can save you enough money to justify his fee several times over.

### 3. Satisfy the Need and Position Your Product as a Solution to the Problem

Once you've convinced the reader that he has a need, you must quickly show him that your product can satisfy his need, answer his questions, or solve his problems.

The accountant ad might begin like this:

**WOULD YOU PAY $1,000 TO SAVE $5,500?**
Last year, a local flower shop decided to hire an accountant to do their income tax returns. They worried about the seemingly high fee, but realized they didn't have the time—or the expertise—to do it themselves.

You can imagine how delighted they were when they hired an accountant who showed them how they could pay thousands of dollars less in income tax than they originally thought they would owe.

I am their accountant, and I'd like to tell you how the flower shop—and dozens of other firms whose taxes I prepare—have saved $1,000 . . . $2,500 . . . even $5,500 a year or more by taking advantage of legitimate tax regulations, deductions, and shelters.

This copy isn't perfect. It needs some work. But it does get attention, shows a need (the need to save money!), and shows that the service being advertised can satisfy the need.

### 4. Prove Your Product Can Do What You Say It Can Do

It isn't enough to say you can satisfy the reader's needs—you've got to prove you can. You want the readers to risk their hard-earned money on your product or service. You want them to buy from or hire you instead of your competitors. How do you demonstrate your superiority over the competition? How do you get the reader to believe what you say?

Here are a few proven techniques for convincing the readers that it's to their advantage to do business with you:

• Talk about the benefits of your product or service (use the features/benefits list as the source of your discussion). Give the reader reasons to buy by showing the benefits she'll get when she owns your product.

• Use testimonials. In testimonials, others who have used the product praise the product in their own words. This third-party endorsement is much more convincing than a manufacturer praising his own product.

• Compare your product to the competition's. Show, benefit for benefit, how you are superior.

• If you have conducted studies to prove your product's superiority, cite this evidence in the copy. Offer a free reprint of the study to interested readers.

• Show that your company is reliable and will be in business a long time. Talk about number of employees, size of distributor network, annual sales, number of years in business, growth rate.

## 5. Ask for Action

The last step in any piece of copy should always be a call for action. If the product is sold by mail, ask the reader to mail in an order. If the product is sold retail, ask the reader to clip the ad and bring it into the store.

If your ad doesn't sell the product directly, then find out the next step in the buying process and tell the reader about it. For example, you might offer a free brochure on the product, a demonstration, or a sample. At the very least, encourage the reader to look for the product in the future if he is not going to buy it today.

Make it easy for the reader to take action. Include your company name, address, and phone number in every piece of copy you write.

If you're writing retail copy, include store hours and locations.

If you're writing copy for a hotel or tourist attraction, include easy-to-follow instructions on how to get there, along with a clearly drawn map of the area.

If you want the reader to send in an order or write for a free brochure, include a handy coupon she can clip and mail.

If you want the reader to call, highlight your toll-free number in large type. And, if you take credit-card orders, be sure to say so and indicate which cards you accept.

Put order forms in catalogs, reply cards in mailers, dealer lists in industrial sales literature. Make it easy for your reader to respond.

And, if possible, give the reader an incentive for responding now: a price-off coupon, a time-limited sale, a discount to the first 1,000 people who order the product. Don't be afraid to try for immediate action and sales as well as long-range "image building." Ask for the order, and ask for it right away.

## USE "FALSE LOGIC" TO MAKE THE FACTS SUPPORT YOUR SALES ARGUMENTS

False logic, a term coined by my friend, master copywriter Michael Masterson, is copy that, through skillful writing, manipulates (but does not lie about or misrepresent) existing facts. The objective: to help readers come to conclusions that these facts, presented without the twists of the copywriter's pen, might not otherwise support.

A catalog for Harry & David says of its pears, "Not one

person in 1,000 has ever tasted them." The statistic, as presented by the catalog writer, makes the product sound rare and exclusive—and that's how the average reader interprets it, just as the copywriter intended.

But a logician analyzing this statement might say that it simply indicates the pears are not very popular—almost no one buys them.

It's possible to argue that some false logic borders on deception, but the marketer has to make that call for himself. A metals broker advertised "95 percent of orders shipped from stock" to indicate ready availability. But he ran his business out of an office and had no warehouse. How could he claim he shipped from stock?

"We do ship 95 percent of orders from stock," the marketer explains. "But not from *our* stock—from the *metal supplier's stock*. We are just a broker. But we do not advertise that, since being a broker is perceived as a negative."

A promotion selling a stock market newsletter to consumers compares the $99 subscription price to the $2,000 the editor would charge if he were managing your money for you, based on a 2 percent fee and a minimum investment of $100,000.

The copy implies that the subscriber is getting Mr. Editor to give him $2,000 worth of money management services for $99, and quickly glosses over the fact that the newsletter is not precisely the same as a managed account.

A similar example is the promotion done by my friend Don Hauptman for *American Speaker*, a loose-leaf service for executives on how to give good speeches. In his promotion, he points out that this product can help you with your speeches all year long (it has periodic supplements), in contrast to the $5,000 it costs to have a professional speechwriter write just one speech. Of course, *American Speaker* is not actually writing your speech for you.

There is an ongoing debate over whether people buy for

emotional or for logical reasons, but most successful marketers know that the former is more dominant as a buying motive than the latter. It is commonly said, "People buy based on emotion, then rationalize the purchase decision with logic."

"Only five percent of our thought processes are fully conscious," writes Dan Hill, president of Sensory Logic. "There's neurological evidence that we make an emotional response—in effect, a decision—about a product or service within three seconds. So businesses need to make an emotional connection with consumers."

Because buying decisions are based on strong feelings and ingrained beliefs, marketers should provide justification and support for what the consumer already wants to do. Therefore, as long as the logical argument seems credible and sensible, your readers will accept it. They do not probe into it as scientifically or deeply as would, say, Ralph Nader or an investigative reporter for *Consumer Reports*.

Some critics view direct marketing as a step below general marketing in respectability, ethics, and honesty. And perhaps they might reason that my advocating the use of false logic adds fuel to their argument. But in fact, false logic is not just the purview of direct marketers: General marketers use it routinely, some with great success.

For years, McDonald's advertised "billions sold" to promote their hamburger—leading customers to the false conclusion that just because something is popular, it is necessarily good. Publishers use similar logic when they trumpet a book as "a *New York Times* best-seller."

Is all this unethical? You can draw your own conclusion, but in my opinion, no.

Copywriters, like lawyers, are advocates for the client (or employer). Just as lawyers use all the arguments at their disposal to win cases, so do copywriters use all the facts at their disposal to win consumers over to the product.

Certainly, we should market no products that are illegal, dangerous, or immoral, although one man's *Victoria's Secret* catalog is another man's soft porn. But to not use all the tools at our disposal to persuade the buyer is either incompetence, failure to discharge fiduciary duties, or both—and false logic is among the most effective of those tools.

## THE UNIQUE SELLING PROPOSITION

Samuel Johnson said, "Promise, large promise, is the soul of an advertisement."

But how do you make a big promise in your advertising that is powerful enough to convince the consumer to buy your product instead of competing brands?

One way is to develop a compelling USP, or Unique Selling Proposition.

What is a USP? Rosser Reeves, author of *Reality in Advertising*, coined this term to describe the major advantage of your product over the competition. The idea is this: If your product is no different from or better than other products of the same type, there is no reason for consumers to choose your product over someone else's. Therefore, to be promoted effectively, your product must have a Unique Selling Proposition: a major benefit that other products in its category don't offer.

According to Reeves, there are three requirements for a USP (and I am quoting, in the italics, from *Reality in Advertising*):

*1. Each advertisement must make a proposition to the consumer. Each must say, "Buy this product, and you will get this specific benefit."* Your headline must contain a benefit—a promise to the reader.

*2. The proposition must be one that the competition either cannot, or does not, offer.* Here's where the *unique* in Unique

Selling Proposition comes in. It is not enough merely to offer a benefit. You must also *differentiate* your product from other, similar products.

3. *The proposition must be so strong that it can move the mass millions, i.e., pull over new customers to your product.* The differentiation cannot be trivial. It must be a difference that is very important to the reader.

Why do so many advertisements fail? One reason is that the marketer has not formulated a strong USP for his product and built his advertising upon it. Formulating a USP isn't difficult, but it does take some thinking, and many people don't like to think. But when you start creating direct mail and advertising without first thinking about what your USP is, your marketing is weak because there is nothing in it to compel the reader to respond. It looks and sounds like everyone else, and what it says isn't important to the reader.

In general advertising for packaged goods, marketers achieve differentiation by building a strong brand at a cost of millions or even billions of dollars.

Coca-Cola has an advantage because of its brand. If you want a cola, you can get it from a dozen soda makers. But if you want a Coke, you can only get it from Coca-Cola.

Intel has achieved a similar brand dominance, at an extraordinary cost, with its Pentium line of microprocessors.

Most businesses are too small, and have too strong a need to generate an immediate positive return on investment (ROI) from their marketing, to engage in this kind of expensive brand building. So we use other means to achieve the differentiation in our USP.

One popular method is to differentiate your product or service from the competition based on a feature that your product or service has and they don't.

The common error here is building the USP around a feature

that, while different, is unimportant to the prospect, and therefore unlikely to move her to try your product or service.

For example, in the chemical equipment industry, it is common for pump manufacturers to attempt to win customers by advertising a unique design feature. Unfortunately, these design twists often result in no real performance improvement, no real advantage that the customer cares about. Realizing that they could not differentiate based on a concrete design principle, Blackmer pump took a different tack: to create a USP based upon *application* of the product.

Their trade ads showed a Yellow Pages ripped out of an industrial buying guide, full of listings for pump manufacturers, including Blackmer. Their company name was circled in pen. The headline of the ad read, "There are only certain times you should call Blackmer for a pump. Know when?"

Body copy explained (and I am paraphrasing here), "In many applications, Blackmer performs no better or worse than any pump, so we are not a particularly advantageous choice."

But, the ad went on, for certain applications (viscous fluids, fluids containing abrasives, slurries, and a few other situations) Blackmer has been proven to outperform all other pumps, and is the logical brand of choice. Blackmer closed the ad by offering a free technical manual proving the claim.

My old friend Jim Alexander of Alexander Marketing in Grand Rapids, Michigan, created this campaign and tells me it worked extremely well.

The easiest situation in which to create a strong USP is when your product has a unique feature—one that competitors lack—that delivers a strong benefit. This must be an advantage the customer really cares about. Not one that, though a difference, is trivial.

But what if such a proprietary advantage does not exist?

What if your product is basically the same as the competition, with no special features?

Reeves has the answer here, too. He said the uniqueness can either stem from a strong brand (already discussed as an option 95 percent of marketers can't use) or from "a claim not otherwise made in that particular form of advertising"—that is, other products may also have this feature, but advertisers haven't told consumers about it.

An example from packaged goods advertising: "M&Ms melt in your mouth, not in your hand." Once M&M established this claim as their USP, what could the competition do? Run an ad that said, "We *also* melt in your mouth, not in your hand!"?

To be successful marketers, we must create advertising that generates net revenues in excess of its cost. Reeves believed all advertising had to do this. He defined advertising as "the art of getting a USP into the heads of the most people at the lowest possible cost." If I were to modify his definition, I would change it to "getting a USP into the heads of the people *most likely to buy the product*, at the lowest possible advertising cost."

Herb Ahrend, founder of Ahrend Associates, Inc., once said, "A copywriter has to create perceived value. He has to ask, 'What is the nature of the product? What makes the product different? If it isn't different, what attribute can you stress that hasn't been stressed by the competition?'"

Malcolm D. MacDougall, former president and creative director of SSC&B, says there are four ways to advertise seemingly similar products:

1. *Stress an underpublicized or little-known benefit.* Once a copywriter visited a brewery in the hopes of learning something that could set the brewery's beer apart from other beers.

He was fascinated to discover that beer bottles, like milk containers, are washed in live steam to kill the germs. Although all brands of beer are purified this way, no other manufacturer had stressed this fact. So the copywriter wrote about a beer so pure that the bottles are washed in live steam, and the brew's Unique Selling Proposition was born.

Study your list of product features and benefits. Then look at the competition's ads. Is there an important benefit that they have ignored, one you can embrace as the Unique Selling Proposition that sets your product apart from all others?

2. *Dramatize a known benefit in a compelling fashion.* Radio Shack once ran a commercial showing two people using walkie-talkies, with each person standing on a different side of the Grand Canyon. Although most walkie-talkies work effectively over this distance, the Radio Shack commercial aimed to call attention to its product by demonstrating the walkie-talkie's range in a unique and dramatic fashion.

3. *Dramatize the product name or package.* Remember "Pez," the candy that came in plastic dispensers made to resemble Mickey Mouse, Pluto, and other cartoon characters? Pez was an ordinary candy, but the package made it special.

In the same way, the most unusual feature of L'Eggs pantyhose is not its design, fabric, or style but the egg-shaped package it is sold in.

And those old Maypo commercials never proved that Maypo was any better than other hot cereals. They simply made the name—"I want my Maypo!"—a household word.

Making your product name or package famous is one sure way to move merchandise off the shelves. But it's also expensive. Unless your client is a major marketer with a million-dollar budget, this tactic will be tough to pull off.

4. *Build long-term brand personalities.* Another tactic used by the manufacturers of major national brands is to create advertising that gives their brand a "personality."

Thousands of Marlboro-man commercials once made Marlboro a "macho" cigarette.

The old Don Meredith spots drummed into the consumer's mind that Lipton Tea is "brisk" and "dandy tasting."

If you have millions to spend, you can use advertising to give your product a unique "personality" in the mind of the consumer. But even if your advertising budget is more modest, you can still use features and benefits to create a Unique Selling Proposition that sets your product apart from the rest.

## THE SECONDARY PROMISE

Samuel Johnson was right: To break through the clutter and generate a profitable response, direct marketing must make a big promise. Some examples of big promises from recent direct-mail packages:

"Retire overseas on $600 a month."

"Free money reserved for you."

"John F. Kennedy had it. So did Princess Diana. Michael Jordan has it now. It's the reason why millions of people adore them. Look inside to find out what it is and how you can get it."

Testing shows that, at least in consumer direct marketing, small promises don't work. To get attention and generate interest, you have to make a large, powerful promise.

But there's a problem: What happens if the reader is skeptical . . . because the big promise is so fantastic, it sounds too good to be true? In that case, use a *secondary promise*.

The secondary promise is a lesser benefit that the product also delivers. Although not as large as the big promise, the secondary promise should be big enough so that, by itself, it is reason enough to order the product—yet small enough so that it is easily believed.

This way, even if the reader is totally skeptical about the big promise, she can believe the secondary promise and order on that basis alone.

For instance, a recent investment promotion had a big promise in its headline: "Crazy as It Sounds, Shares of This Tiny R&D Company, Selling for $2 Today, Could Be Worth as Much as $100 in the Not-Too-Distant Future."

That's a really big promise—having a stock go from $2 to $100 is a gain of 4,900 percent. On a thousand shares, your profit would be $98,000.

The problem is, in a bear market, this gain may, to some readers, be too high to be believable. Yet, in this case, it was the truth: If the company's medical device won FDA approval, a fifty-fold increase in share price was not out of the question.

The solution: A subhead, placed directly under the big promise in the headline, made a secondary promise:

> I think this new technology for treating liver disease is going to work. And if it does, the stock price could easily increase 50-fold or more.
>
> But even if it doesn't . . . and the company's treatment is a total failure . . . the stock could still earn early-stage investors a 500% gain on their shares within the next 24 months.

The catch was this: Even if the treatment did not win FDA approval, the company would still make a lot of money (though not as much as with the treatment being approved) using the same technology in a different application. So even if the big promise didn't pan out, the secondary promise was enough to make the stock worth owning.

There are many techniques you can use to prove your big promise when your reader is skeptical. These include testimonials, case studies, test results, favorable reviews, superior product design, track record, system or methodology, reputation of the manufacturer.

All are good. But the trouble is this: If the big promise is so strong that readers are inclined to dismiss it as false, you find yourself arguing with them and going against their ingrained belief when you introduce all this proof.

I would still present the proof, but an easier way to overcome doubt concerning the big promise is always to accompany it with a secondary promise that is also desirable yet smaller and more credible.

The secondary promise is your "backup" promise. In a package with both a big promise and a secondary promise, the big promise will attract readers because it is so large—and if you offer enough proof, many of those readers will believe it.

What about those prospects who are not convinced? Without a secondary promise, they simply toss your ad or mailing without responding.

But when you add a secondary promise and make it prominent (which means featuring it in the headline or the lead), many of those who reject the big promise as being unbelievable will find the secondary promise credible—and appealing enough to sell them all on its own.

Actually, with a secondary promise, prospects who don't fully believe your big promise can still be sold by it. They think: "Hey, if this big promise happens to be true, this is a good product to buy; but even if it isn't true, the product is more than worth the price just for the secondary promise— which I am sure *is* true—by itself. So either way, I can't lose."

And if you use both a big promise and a secondary promise in your next promotion, neither can you. And that's a promise.

## KNOW YOUR CUSTOMER

*Psychology Today* reported on a study designed to uncover the characteristics of successful salespeople.

"The best salespeople first establish a mood of trust and rapport by means of 'hypnotic pacing'—statements and gestures that play back a customer's observations, experience, or behavior," wrote the author of the study. "Pacing is a kind of mirror-like matching, a way of suggesting: 'I am like you. We are in sync. You can trust me.'"

In other words, successful salespeople empathize with their customers. Instead of launching into a canned sales pitch, the successful salesperson first tries to understand the customer's needs, mood, personality, and prejudices. By mirroring the customer's thoughts and feelings in their sales presentations, successful salespeople break down resistance to sales, establish trust and credibility, and highlight only those product benefits that are of interest to the customer.

Copywriters, too, must get to know the customer. Of course, as a copywriter, you can't create a separate ad or brochure for each individual prospect. But by understanding the needs of the marketplace, you can tailor your presentation to specific groups of buyers—segments of the total market.

Understanding the customer and her motivation for buying the product is the key to writing copy that sells. Too much advertising is created in a vacuum. The advertiser and the agency write copy based on the product features that catch their fancy, not on the features that are important to the customer. The result is copy that pleases the agency and the advertiser, but leaves the customer cold.

In a survey published in *Mainly Marketing*, advertising

agencies and buyers of high-tech products were asked which product features they considered important. The results showed that advertising agencies stressed features that were not important to buyers. The agencies also omitted information that was vital to the buyers. For example, both purchasing agents and engineers ranked price as the number-two consideration when buying high-tech equipment. But the agencies said price was unimportant as a copy point. Agencies said high-tech ads should stress how the product saves the buyer time. But engineers and purchasing agents said this is far less important than product specifications and limitations.

When you write copy, don't write in a vacuum. Don't just sit down at the typewriter and pick the features and benefits that suit your fancy. Instead, find out which benefits and features your readers care about—and write about the sales points that will motivate readers to buy the product.

A good example of copy that "hits home" with the reader is a subscription letter I received from *INC.* magazine. Here's the opening of the letter:

A special invitation to the hero of American business

Dear Entrepreneur:
You're it!

You're the kind of person free enterprise is built on. The ambition, vision, and guts of small business people like yourself have always been the driving force behind the American economy.

Unfortunately, that's a fact which the general business press seems to have forgotten. In their emphasis on everything big, like conglomerates, multinationals, oil companies the size of countries, most business publications pay very little attention to the little guy.

The letter is effective because it speaks directly to the pride entrepreneurs feel in being "self-made." The letter writer has done a good job of empathizing with the reader and understanding how an entrepreneur thinks of himself.

You, too, must get to know your reader. One way of doing this is to start paying close attention to your own behavior as a consumer.

The next time you start to write a TV commercial that uses dancing soup cans to sell canned soup, ask yourself if you want to be entertained when you buy soup . . . or if you're more interested in how the soup tastes, what it costs, its nutritional value, and where to find it in the supermarket.

Once you start thinking as a consumer rather than a writer, you'll have more respect for your reader. And you'll write copy that provides useful product information and sales appeals rather than empty hype and ballyhoo.

Another way to understand your prospect is to observe consumers and be an active student of the marketplace. When you're in the supermarket, watch other buyers. Which type of person picks the sale items and which type goes for the name brand?

When you visit an automobile dealer, observe how the successful salespeople deliver their pitches and handle their customers. Listen to the pitch you receive and think about why it did or didn't sway you.

Take an active interest in the world of commerce. When you receive a telephone solicitation, listen to the entire call to see what techniques you can use in your own copy. Attend trade shows to find out the nature of buyers in the various industries your clients deal in.

And talk to the businesspeople you trade with—store owners, the plumber, your lawyer, the gardener, the person who repairs your hot-water heater—to find out the techniques they use to promote their services and products. People who are close to their customers—and most small business people are—know more about the reality of selling than most ad agency account executives or corporate brand managers do. Listen to these people, and you'll learn what makes the customer tick. (Chapter 5 provides additional tips on getting to know your reader.)

There's an old saying: "You can't be all things to all people." And it certainly applies to advertising and selling. You can't create one ad or commercial that appeals to everybody, because different groups of buyers have different needs. So, as a copywriter, you must first identify your audience—the segment of the market you are selling to—and then learn which product benefits interest these buyers.

You will tailor both the content and the presentation of your information to the group of customers you're selling to. Take frozen foods as an example. When you sell frozen foods to a homemaker, he or she is most interested in nutrition and price. But a young, single professional person is primarily interested in convenience: He or she doesn't want to spend too much time in the kitchen. Price is not as much of a factor because the young professional has more disposable income than the homemaker.

Take photocopiers as another example. The large corporation buying a copier wants a machine that is fast and offers a variety of features such as color copies, collating, and two-sided copying. But the self-employed professional who works at home has different needs. His budget is limited, so the copier must be inexpensive. And, since he's working from home, space is at a premium, so compactness is an important feature. But speed and capacity are not as crucial, since the work-at-home professional makes fewer copies than the corporate user.

Sometimes, the benefits to stress to various groups of buyers are obvious. In other cases, you must ask the advertiser or his customers which features should be stressed. I once had the assignment of selling a water purification system to two different types of customers: marine users (mostly commercial fishing vessels) and chemical industry users (chemical plants). Same product, two different buyers.

By talking with a few customers in each group, I discovered that marine users put a premium on reliable operation, since they can't afford to be without fresh water while at sea. Weight is also important, because the larger the equipment, the more fuel the boat consumes in hauling the equipment around.

Chemical industry buyers, on the other hand, don't care about weight, because the machine is placed on the plant floor. And, because they have many sources of water, reliability is not as crucial. The chemical industry buyers—all engineers by training—were more interested in technical features. They wanted to know every product specification down to the last nut, bolt, pump, and pipeline. I wouldn't have known these differences existed unless I asked. Which is why it's vital that you get to know your buyer.

But how well do you really know your customers? Knowing that you are writing to farmers, information technology (IT) professionals, or plumbers is just the start. You have to dig deeper. But how?

To write powerful copy, you have to go beyond the demographics to understand what really motivates these people: who they are, what they want, how they feel, and what their biggest problems and concerns are that your product can help solve. Your copy should reach prospects on three levels: *intellectual, emotional*, and *personal*.

*Intellectual* is the first level and, while effective, not as strong as the other two. An intellectual appeal is based on logic, for example, "Buy the stocks we recommend in our investment newsletter and you will beat the market by 50 to 100 percent."

More powerful is to reach the prospect on an *emotional* level. Emotions that can be tapped include fear, greed, love, vanity, and, for fund-raising, benevolence. Going back to our example of a stock market newsletter, the emotional appeal might be, "Our advice can help you cut your losses and make much more money, so you become much wealthier than your friends and neighbors. You'll be able to pay cash for your next car—a Lexus, BMW, or any luxury automobile you care to own—and you'll sleep better at night."

The most powerful way you can reach people is on a *personal* level. Again, from our example of a stock market newsletter: "Did you lose a small fortune in the April 2000 tech stock meltdown? So much that it put your dreams of retirement or financial independence on hold? Now you can gain back everything you lost, rebuild your net worth, and make your dream of early retirement or financial independence come true. A lot sooner than you think."

## THE BFD FORMULA

To reach your prospects on all three levels—intellectual, emotional, and personal—you must understand what copywriter Michael Masterson calls the buyer's "Core Complex." These are the emotions, attitudes, and aspirations that drive them, as represented by the BFD formula, which stands for *beliefs*, *feelings*, and *desires*.

• *Beliefs*. What does your audience believe? What is their attitude toward your product and the problems or issues it addresses?
• *Feelings*. How do they feel? Are they confident and brash? Nervous and fearful? What do they feel about the major issues in their lives, businesses, or industries?
• *Desires*. What do they want? What are their goals? What change do they want in their lives that your product can help them achieve?

For instance, a company did this exercise using IT people, for a company that gives seminars in communication and interpersonal skills for IT professionals. Here's what they came up with in a group meeting:

• *Beliefs*. IT people think they are smarter than other people, technology is the most important thing in the world, users are stupid, and management doesn't appreciate them enough.

• *Feelings*. IT people often have an adversarial relationship with management and users, both of whom they service. They feel others dislike them, look down upon them, and do not understand what they do.

• *Desires*. IT people want to be appreciated and recognized. They also prefer to deal with computers and avoid people whenever possible. And they want bigger budgets.

Based on this analysis, particularly the feelings, the company created a direct-mail letter that was its most successful ever to promote a seminar "Interpersonal Skills for IT Professionals." The rather unusual headline: "Important news for any IT professional who has ever felt like telling an end user, 'Go to hell.'"

Before writing copy, write out in narrative form the BFD of your target market. Share these with your team and come to an agreement on them. Then write copy based on the agreed-upon BFD.

Occasionally insights into the prospect's desires and concerns can be gleaned through formal market research. For instance, a copywriter working on a cooking oil account was reading a focus group transcript and came across this comment from a user: "I fried chicken in the oil and then poured the oil back into a measuring cup. All the oil was there except one teaspoon."

This comment, buried in the appendix of a focus group report, became the basis of a successful TV campaign dramatizing the selling point that food did not absorb the oil and therefore was not greasy when cooked in it.

Veteran ad man Joe Sacco once had an assignment to write a campaign for a new needle used by diabetics to inject insulin. What was the key selling point?

The diabetics Sacco talked to all praised the needle because it was sharp. A non-user would probably view being sharp as a negative. But if you have ever given yourself or anyone else an injection, you know that sharper needles go in smoother, with no pain. Sacco wrote a successful ad campaign based on the claim that these needles were sharp, therefore enabling easier, pain-free insulin injections.

Copywriter Don Hauptman advises, "Start with the prospect, not the product." With BFD, you can quickly gain a decper understanding of your prospects before you attempt to sell them something. Stronger marketing campaigns usually follow.

## A CHECKLIST OF "COPY MOTIVATORS"

As I've pointed out, different people buy products for different reasons. If I buy a car, I buy reliable transportation to get me where I want to go, and a used economy car suits me just fine. But the buyer of a Porsche or Mercedes Benz is buying more than transportation—she's buying status and prestige as well.

Before you write your copy, it's a good idea to review the reasons why people might want to buy your product. To help you, I've compiled the following checklist of "copy motivators": 22 motivations people have for making purchases. This list is not comprehensive. But it will get you thinking about who you're writing to and why you're writing to them.

Here, then, are 22 reasons why people might buy your product. Don't just read the list; think about each of the reasons and how it might apply to the products you handle.

- ❏ To be liked
- ❏ To be appreciated
- ❏ To be right
- ❏ To feel important
- ❏ To make money
- ❏ To save money
- ❏ To save time
- ❏ To make work easier
- ❏ To be secure
- ❏ To be attractive
- ❏ To be sexy
- ❏ To be comfortable
- ❏ To be distinctive
- ❏ To be happy
- ❏ To have fun
- ❏ To gain knowledge
- ❏ To be healthy
- ❏ To gratify curiosity
- ❏ For convenience
- ❏ Out of fear
- ❏ Out of greed
- ❏ Out of guilt

Think about the things you buy—and why you buy them.

You buy cologne to smell nice. And you want to smell nice to attract a mate.

You buy sports equipment to have fun. You join a spa to become healthy. You buy a gold-plated money clip to be distinctive and feel important.

You buy insurance to be secure. You buy slippers to be comfortable. You buy a refrigerator with an ice maker for convenience.

Once you understand what makes people buy things, you know how to sell—and how to write copy. The rest is just organization and good editing and a few simple techniques.

## LONG COPY VS. SHORT COPY

The slogan from an old cigarette commercial was, "It's not how long you make it; it's how you make it long." And that's a good rule of thumb for determining the length of the copy you write.

In other words, the question isn't how many words you should write; it's how much information to include for the copy to accomplish its sales mission.

In general, the length will depend upon three things: the product, the audience, and the purpose of the copy. First, consider your product. Is there a lot you can say about it? And will giving these facts help convince the reader to buy it?

Some products have a lot of features and benefits you can highlight in your copy. These include computers, stereos, cars, books, insurance policies, investment opportunities, courses and seminars, resorts and vacation trips, video recorders, software, cameras, typewriters, and home-exercise equipment.

Many other products don't have a lot of features and benefits, and there isn't too much you can say about them. These include soft drinks, fast food, designer clothes, candy, chewing gum, beer, wine, liquor, jewelry, lingerie, cologne, perfume, soap, laundry detergent, cosmetics, linens, pet food, and shampoo.

For example, there isn't much you can say about a new ginger ale, other than it tastes good and costs less.

But an automatic food processor has a lot of benefits you can highlight: It saves time. It eliminates messy chopping and cutting. It makes cooking easier and more pleasant. It can slice, dice, mash, peel, whip, blend, chop, and crush virtually any food. You can use it for desserts, appetizers, salads, and main courses. It can process fruits, vegetables, meats, nuts, cheeses.

So, the length of the copy depends on the product and what there is to say about it.

Second, the length of the copy depends upon the audience. Some customers don't need a lot of information and are not accustomed to reading long text. Others seek out all the facts they can get and will devour as much as you can provide.

The Playboy Book Club wanted to know how much copy to include in the direct-mail package it used to get new members to join the club. They tested sales letters of various lengths: one, two, four, eight, and twelve pages. The twelve-page letter pulled the most orders. Why? One of the reasons is that people who will join a book club are readers—and they will read twelve pages of text if it interests them.

The third factor in determining copy length is the purpose of the copy. If you want your copy to generate a sales lead, then there's no need to go into complete detail because you'll get a chance to provide more information when people respond to the lead. On the other hand, an ad that asks for the order by mail must give all the facts the reader needs to make a buying decision and order the product.

"This is all very nice," you say, "but how do I determine the length that's best for my product, my audience, and my purpose?"

Fortunately, there's an answer. I've developed a tool, which I call the Copy Length Grid (see diagram), that can enable us to determine copy length in a somewhat more scientific and semi-quantitative fashion.

The Copy Length Grid says there are two major factors determining whether long or short copy will work best for your promotion: emotion and involvement.

*Emotion* refers to the degree to which the purchase is emo-

---

## DETERMINING COPY LENGTH

Audience: _____

Product: _____

|  | High | Long Copy | Medium Copy |
|---|---|---|---|
| INVOLVEMENT | Low | Medium Copy | Short Copy |

High      Low

**EMOTION**

---

tional. Buying a diamond engagement ring is a highly emotional purchase. But you are moved very little emotionally when deciding which brand of paper clips to buy.

*Involvement* refers to how much time, effort, and thought goes into the product purchase. As with most large purchases, a lot of consideration goes into the selection and purchase of a diamond engagement ring. But most of us grab the first box of paper clips on the shelf of the stationery store without giving it a second thought.

To use this system for determining copy length, rate these two criteria—emotion and involvement—as high or low. This dictates what quadrant of the Copy Length Grid you end up in, which in turn gives you at least a rough guideline for copy length.

For instance, the highly emotional purchase of a diamond engagement ring is a "considered purchase"—something you give a lot of thought to—so it rates high in involvement. As you can see in the diagram, this puts us firmly in the upper left quadrant of the grid, indicating that long copy is appropriate for this offer.

On the other hand, paper clips are more of an impulse purchase: We go to the store and pick up the first box we see, providing it's the right size. There's no emotion and very little thought that goes into this purchase.

This puts us in the lower right quadrant of the grid, which indicates that writing long, passionate copy about paper clips probably isn't going to sell more of them.

Of course, the Copy Length Grid is only a rough guide, not a precise analyzer. A number of other factors must also be taken into account when determining copy length. These factors include:

• *Price.* The more expensive a product is, the more copy you generally need to sell it. Lots of copy is needed to build the case for value before asking for the order, so that when the price is finally given, it seems like a drop in the bucket compared to what the buyer is getting in return.

• *Purpose.* Copy that sells the product directly off the printed page or screen (known as "one-step" or "mail-order" copy) usually has to be long, because it must present all product information and overcome all objections. Copy designed to generate a lead ("two-step copy") can be short, since a catalog, brochure, or salesperson will have the opportunity to present product details and overcome objections later.

• *Audience.* People who are pressed for time, such as busy executives and professionals, often respond better to short copy. Prospects with more time on their hands, such as retirees, as well as those with a keen interest in your offer, such as hobbyists, are more likely to read long copy.

• *Importance.* Products that people *need* (a refrigerator, a fax machine) can be sold with short copy because . . . well, the prospect *has* to buy them. Products that people *want* but don't *have* to buy (exercise videos, self-help audio programs, financial newsletters) must be "sold," and require long copy to do so.

• *Familiarity.* Short copy works well with products the prospect is already familiar with and understands. This is why vouchers and double postcards are used so frequently to sell subscriptions to popular, well-known magazines (*Newsweek, BusinessWeek*).

Based on the Copy Length Grid and these other factors, it's clear that long copy is not always better, and there are many instances when short or almost no copy works best. This is the case with items that "sell themselves," such as staplers or garden hoses.

But for items that have to be "sold"—life insurance policies, luxury automobiles, IT systems, collectibles, high-end jewelry, career training—long copy is often required because of the high degree of emotion and involvement.

Many studies confirm that, all else being equal, long-copy ads sell more effectively than short ones. For example, a survey of seventy-two retailers measured the "success ratio" of their ads against the number of merchandise facts each ad contained. Here are the results:

| Number of Merchandise Facts | Success Ratio |
| --- | --- |
| 4 | 1 |
| 5 | 1:1 |
| 6 | 1:3 |
| 7 | 1:4 |
| 8 or more | 1:5 |

As you can see, the more facts included, the more success-ful the ad. The study also revealed that whenever a store omit-ted any essential information from an advertisement, sales response was instantly reduced.

Don't be afraid of long copy. Include as many facts as it takes to make the sale.

## POSITIONING

Once, when I was shopping for a phone-answering machine, a salesperson told me that a certain model was "the Rolls-Royce of answering machines." The mention of "Rolls-Royce" con-notes excellence: quality, value, and high price. By comparing his product to a familiar brand, the answering-machine sales-person instantly created an image of the machine in my mind. This technique is called "positioning."

Jack Trout and Al Ries, authors of numerous articles and a book on positioning, write: "Today, positioning is used in a broader sense to mean what the advertising does for the prod-uct in the prospect's mind. In other words, a successful adver-tiser today uses advertising to position his product, not to communicate its advantages or features."

Here are examples Trout and Ries give of using advertising to position a product:

- Seven-Up's positioning is defined by something it is not—a cola. Seven-Up is the "Un-Cola."
- Schaefer is positioned as a beer for the heavy beer drinker: "The one beer to have when you're having more than one."
- Avis is positioned as a hardworking underdog: "We're number 2 so we try harder."
- Tide makes clothes "white." Cheer makes them "whiter than white." Bold makes them "bright."

Despite what Trout and Ries have written, positioning does not take the place of features and benefits and sales arguments; it *complements* them. If your product fills a special niche, positioning it against a well-known brand is a quick and effective way of establishing the product's identity in the consumer's mind.

But your copy must do more than get the consumer to think about the product; it must also persuade him to buy it. And you can't persuade consumers to buy unless you tell what the product can do for them and why the product does it better than other products can.

# 5

## GETTING READY TO WRITE

Helmut Krone, the art director who helped create such famous campaigns as Avis's "We Try Harder," Volkswagen's "Think Small," and Mennen's "Thanks, I Needed That," has a basic approach to tackling advertising assignments:

"I start with a blank piece of paper and try to fill it with something interesting."

But what exactly should the copywriter do to prepare himself for facing that blank piece of paper? What information do you need before you're ready to write your copy? How do you go about collecting this information? How do you develop advertising ideas?

This chapter provides answers to these questions and outlines specific techniques you can use to gain familiarity with a product and its market before you tackle your copywriting assignment.

### INTENSIVE RESEARCH GIVES YOU THE EDGE

Unnecessary, time-wasting meetings are probably the thing I hate most about the advertising business. But the smart copywriter can eliminate 95 percent of these meetings by working with clients primarily by e-mail and phone. Oh, you can have an occasional meeting to renew old acquaintances or discuss major ideas and strategies that aren't easily handled long distance. But with e-mail now an accepted method of rapid communication, the majority of assignments can be handled without long meetings that drag on and go nowhere.

Of course, convincing some clients to work this way takes time. You may have to educate them on the efficiency and economy of "copy by e-mail." You have to demonstrate that you can provide great copy and concepts without marathon meetings or the legendary three-martini lunches that Madison Avenue is famous for.

Most important, you need to establish a procedure for conducting research that will allow you to handle assignments by e-mail and phone, especially when working with out-of-state clients. My way of doing it is outlined below.

## HOW TO PREPARE FOR A COPYWRITING ASSIGNMENT

Here's a four-step procedure you can use to get the information you need to write persuasive, fact-filled copy for your clients:

*Step 1: Get All Previously Published Material on the Product*
For an existing product, there's a mountain of literature the client can send to the copywriter as background material. This literature includes:

- Tear sheets of previous ads
- Brochures
- Annual reports
- Catalogs
- Article reprints

- Technical papers
- Copies of speeches and presentations
- Audiovisual scripts
- Press kits
- Market research
- Advertising plans
- Web sites
- Letters from users of the product
- Back issues of promotional newsletters and e-zines
- Files of competitors' ads and literature

Did I hear someone say the client can't send such material because their product is new? Nonsense. The birth of every new product is accompanied by mounds of paperwork that you can ask the client to give you. This paperwork includes:

- Internal memos
- Letters of technical information
- Product specifications, blueprints, plans
- Illustrations and photos of product prototypes
- Engineering drawings
- Business and marketing plans
- Reports
- Proposals

Insist that the client provide this background material before you attend any briefings or write the copy. One way to simplify this request for information is to create a checklist of the background material you need.

And, of course, extract as much product information as you can from the Internet. You should spend a lot of time printing out and reading the client's Web site, or at least the pages pertaining to the product you are promoting.

Ask the client who their major competitors are, and study

the content on those Web sites as well. Finally, a Google search on key words related to the product can unearth a lot of valuable information that may find its way into your copy.

By studying this background material, the copywriter should have 90 percent of the information he or she needs to write the copy. The copywriter can get the other 10 percent by asking the right questions, either in a brief in-person conference or over the telephone. Steps 2 through 4 outline the questions the copywriter should ask about the product, the audience, and the objective of the copy.

### Step 2: Ask Questions About the Product

- What are its features and benefits? (Make a *complete* list.)
- Which benefit is the most important?
- How is the product different from the competition's? (Which features are exclusive? Which are better than the competition's?)
- If the product isn't different, what attributes can be stressed that haven't been stressed by the competition?
- What technologies does the product compete against?
- What are the applications of the product?
- What problems does the product solve in the marketplace?
- How is the product positioned against competing products?
- How does the product work?
- How reliable is the product? How long will it last?
- How efficient is the product?
- How economical?
- How much does it cost?
- Is it easy to use? Easy to maintain?
- Who has bought the product and what do they say about it?
- What materials, sizes, and models is it available in?
- How quickly does the manufacturer deliver the product?

- If they don't deliver, how and where can you buy it?
- What service and support does the manufacturer offer?
- Is the product guaranteed?

### Step 3: Ask Questions About Your Audience

- Who will buy the product? (What markets is it sold to?)
- What exactly does the product do for them?
- Why do they need the product? And why do they need it now?
- What is the customer's main concern when buying this type of product (price, delivery, performance, reliability, service, maintenance, quality, efficiency, availability)?
- What is the character of the buyer? What type of person is the product being sold to?
- What motivates the buyer?
- How many different buying influences must the copy appeal to? (A toy ad, for example, must appeal to both the parent and the child.)
- If you are writing an ad, read issues of the magazines in which the ad will appear.
- If you are writing direct mail, find out what mailing lists will be used and study the list descriptions.

### Step 4: Determine the Objective of Your Copy

This objective may be one or more of the following:

- To generate inquiries
- To generate sales
- To answer inquiries
- To qualify prospects
- To generate store traffic
- To introduce a new product or an improvement of an old product
- To keep in touch with prospects and customers

- To transmit news or product information
- To build brand recognition and preference
- To build company image
- To provide marketing tools for salespeople

Before you write the copy, study the product you're writing about: its features, benefits, past performance, applications, and markets. Digging for the facts will pay off, because in copywriting, specifics sell.

## USING INTERVIEWS TO GATHER FACTS

Of course, collecting background material doesn't always give you all the answers to the questions listed above. At times you must get additional facts from product experts employed by your client: engineers, designers, salespeople, product managers, and brand managers.

Journalists will tell you that a face-to-face interview is better than a phone interview. When you sit across the table from people, you can observe their manner, their dress, their appearance. And you can learn a lot about people from their surroundings.

But the kind of interview you conduct as a copywriter is different than the interview conducted by a reporter. You are not interested in the subject's colorful personality or history. You are only seeking straight facts and product information of an informational nature. Therefore, there's no need to get "up close" to the subject, and a telephone interview will serve your purpose just as well as an in-person conference.

Actually, there are a number of advantages to doing interviews by phone. First, although the experts have intimate knowledge of the product, advertising is usually not their area of responsibility and, since they are busy, they don't want to get involved with it. A phone interview takes less of their time and busy managers appreciate the efficiency of this method.

Second, it's easier to take notes by phone. Some people are made nervous by tape recorders; others get jittery when they see you scribbling on a pad or clicking away on your laptop. But these note-taking tools are invisible in a phone conference, and the subject can talk in a relaxed, natural manner without being aware that his words are being recorded.

Third, the copywriter eliminates a trip to and from the client's office. If you're billing by the job, this increases your profit on the assignment. If you're billing by the hour, the time saving is passed on to the client as less time spent on research. Either way, money is saved.

A frequent question beginning copywriters ask is, "Should I use a tape recorder or take notes by hand?" My answer is that it depends on the situation and on the assignment. By the way, if you do decide to tape the interview, be sure you let the subject know your intention before you begin.

At times, you will be forced to go to a briefing without much background material on the product or the market. In this case, new information will be given to you at a frantic rate. It's best to use a tape recorder in these situations, because you can't write fast enough to get it all down on paper. And when you tape the interview, it leaves your pen free to jot down questions as they occur to you.

If, on the other hand, you have been thoroughly briefed and are familiar with the product, you should go into the meeting or the phone conference with a list of specific questions: gaps in your product knowledge that the background material didn't fill. Here you are looking for short, specific answers, and taking notes with pen or pencil does the job. When in doubt about how much note taking you need to do, have both a notepad and a tape recorder handy.

The method of note taking also depends on whether you need quotations from the subject. In writing testimonial copy, feature articles, speeches, press releases, newsletters, and case histories, you want the information in the person's own words, and you need a tape recorder to get it right. But if the interview is just for collecting information that you'll rewrite as copy for an ad, mailer, commercial, brochure, or catalog, use a pencil and pad instead.

In an article in *The Writer,* author Dorothy Hinshaw Patent gives these tips for arranging and conducting a successful interview (the basic tips are Dorothy's, but I've added some elaboration to tailor them to the needs of the copywriter):

1. When you call a person to arrange an interview, immediately say who you are, who suggested you get in touch with the person, and why you want to interview him or her.

For example: "Jim Rosenthal? Good morning. My name is Bob Bly, and I'm handling the writing of the ground radar brochure for your ad agency, Anderson & Associates. Lansing Knight at the agency suggested I give you a call and says you know a lot about the design of the radar dish. I'd like to ask you a few questions, if that's convenient. . . ."

At times, you will encounter resistance from the person. Here are a few tactics to overcome this:

• *Explain that the interview won't take much time.* ("Well, I've got a small list of just six questions in front of me, and the interview will take but ten minutes to complete. I know you're busy, but do you think we might chat for just ten minutes sometime in the next few days?")

• *Flatter the subject, but be sincere.* ("I suppose I could talk to someone else in your department. But they told me you designed the antenna, and I'd really like to make sure I get the right information for this ad, since it's appearing in *Machine Design, Design News,* and *Electronic Digest.*")

• *Explain the importance of your assignment.* ("The article I'm putting together will be published in this year's annual report, so you can see why I'm trying to get the most accurate information possible.")

• *Use authority as leverage.* ("Shirley Parker, your department head, is working closely with the agency on this one and she felt it would be really important to get your input.")

2. Let the subject select the time and date for the interview. Offer to do the interview in the morning, during lunch, after work, in the evening, or any time that's convenient and comfortable for the person. Some people are too busy during office hours to talk with you, and would prefer to do it after 5 P.M., when they can relax. Others may find lunch to be the best time. Schedule the interview at the subject's convenience.

And, just as important, set a firm date and time for the interview, whether it's a face-to-face meeting or a phone call. If you're doing a phone interview, make sure the subject understands that you are setting aside time to be by your phone on that date; the phone interview should be considered as firm a commitment as a meeting.

3. Arrange for interviews well in advance of your deadline. With advertising's short deadlines, this isn't always possible. So it's best to arrange interviews the day you get the assignment. That way, if a key interview subject is out of town or unavailable to meet, you can notify your client and work around it (by extending the deadline or finding someone else to take the subject's place).

4. Do your homework. Come prepared. Read all the background information before the interview. Know in advance specifically what you want to find out during the interview. Prepare a written list of questions you want to ask.

The subject's time—and your time—is money spent by the client. Don't waste it by asking your subject to give you an education in the basics. Instead, use this valuable time with the expert to get specific, detailed product and marketing facts that the product literature and other background material didn't provide.

5. Be on time for the interview. Many businesspeople are impatient types, and if you miss your appointment, you may never get a second chance. If you can't avoid being late, call in advance and explain the situation.

6. If you are taking notes, write down only the information you need to get the facts straight. This saves time when you type up your notes later on.

7. Establish a rapport with the subject. You two may not have a lot in common, but by showing an interest in and understanding of the subject's problems, you win that person over as a friend. And friends give better interviews than hostile or indifferent subjects.

Maybe you really don't care how difficult it was to manufacture the world's first fiber-optic fishing pole. But the engineer you're interviewing does. So, when he turns to you and says, "Boy, you don't know the problems we had in adjusting tensile strength to the right length-to-diameter ratio," give an understanding nod and a smile. Maybe even say, "I can imagine the problems you've had. But it sure is a great fishing pole." This is just common courtesy, and it helps make the interview go smoothly.

8. Keep a list of the people you interviewed. Also save your notes until the copy is accepted and published. Refer to the list and notes if the client wants to know where you got your information or questions the accuracy of the copy.

9. Show your appreciation. You should always say "thank you" at the close of the interview. A short note in the mail is an even nicer way of showing your gratitude. A copy of the ad or brochure you've written (in its published form) is even better. You may not have time to do all these follow-ups, and it's not a necessity. But when you do follow up, it will always be appreciated.

## ORGANIZING YOUR INFORMATION

At this point, you've read mounds of product literature and have taken notes or underlined key passages, or both. You also have notes or tapes of interviews with product experts. The next step in getting ready to write copy is to type up your notes on your PC and print them out for quick and easy reference.

There are two benefits to this. First, by filtering the information through your brain, to your fingers, and onto the typewritten page, you gain more familiarity with your facts.

In elementary school, teachers often assigned simple reports that could be based entirely on articles found in the encyclopedia. Not much research was involved, and as students, we thought we were pulling the wool over the teacher's eyes by cribbing from the *World Book* or *Encyclopedia Britannica*.

But the teachers were smart. They knew that, by re-forming the encyclopedia essay in our own words, we would think through the ideas and come to our own conclusions about the subject.

So it is with the copywriter. As you retype interviews and

previous copy in your own words, you gain a perspective on the product and generate your own ideas on how to sell it.

Now, to be fair, I know many copywriters who don't go through this step. All I can tell you is that it works for me, and I wouldn't tackle an assignment without first reprocessing all the information I've collected through my brain and keyboard and onto the printed page.

The second advantage of typing up and printing out your notes is that you have clean, typewritten sheets to work from. By single spacing, you can reduce hours of interviews and mounds of old brochures and catalogs to three or four sheets of paper. Instead of searching through tapes and a pile of literature to find a key fact, you can quickly locate it in your typed notes.

You can also use the notes as a checklist, checking off facts you have used in your copy, circling those facts you must include but haven't yet, and crossing out information that will not be used in the copy. Also, looking at typed notes is a lot easier on the eye than trying to decipher page after page of your handwriting.

Convenient as these notes are, I must tell you that once you've gone through the process of typing them, the material will be so fresh in your mind that you will probably be able to write the copy with only an occasional glance at the pages to confirm a fact or search for a missing bit of data.

I've written complete ads and brochures without once looking at my notes. After the copy was finished, I used the notes as a checklist to make sure all important facts were included.

Some writers prefer index cards to 8½- by 11-inch pages of notes because cards are easily rearranged in different order. The advantage of pages over cards is that you can see more information at a glance. With experience, you'll choose the method that works best for you.

I use index cards if the project has many separate, distinct sections. This is the case with a catalog offering many products, a newsletter with many different articles, a press kit with four or five separate releases, or a product folder containing a number of inserts on different aspects or features of the same product.

Many copywriters debate the usefulness of preparing an outline before they write the copy. Again, this depends on your individual approach to writing, and you should make an outline only if it is helpful to you.

With most short pieces of copy—ads, sales letters, pamphlets—the number of separate sales points to be covered is small enough that I can hold the outline in my head. And so there's no need to commit it to paper. But if the copy has an unusually large number of sales points, or if an organizational scheme hasn't popped into my head (as it usually does), I will sit with pencil and paper and work up an outline.

For longer pieces—brochures, annual reports, feature articles, Web sites, white papers—an outline is always helpful to me. I pin the outline to the bookcase next to my computer and use it to guide me through the assignment. As first drafts of each section are completed, I check off the section on the outline. This gives me a sense of accomplishment and motivation to go on to the next step.

For over a decade now, I have made a practice of showing at least a rough outline of the promotion to the client and getting approval before I proceed to a first draft. The outline consists of a working headline and a description, either in a numbered or bullet list or in paragraph form, of the theme and contents I intend to cover in the body copy.

Known as a "copy platform," this type of outline ensures that the client agrees with your approach before you write. Without submitting a copy platform and getting it approved, you risk writing an entire promotion on a theme or concept that the client is going to reject, forcing you to write the whole thing over again. This is far less likely to occur when you are writing from an approved copy platform.

How do you organize your outline? The "motivating sequence" presented in chapter 4 is a general outline for all pieces of persuasive writing. Examples of organizational schemes for specific writing tasks—ads, brochures, catalogs, commercials, press releases, sales letters, Web sites, e-mails— are presented in subsequent chapters of this book.

## THE WRITING PROCESS

Now comes the hard part: the actual writing of the ad, letter, commercial, or brochure.

Each writer has his or her own way of putting the words on paper, and you should use the method that's most productive for you.

Some writers start with a headline and rough drawing of the visual, then fill in the body copy. They cannot write a word of body copy until they have a headline and visual concept that pleases them.

Others write the body copy first. Then they extract the headline from the body copy or from their rough notes. Some writers like to start with the longest or most difficult section of a brochure or annual report. Others prefer to "warm up" by typing up the easy sections first: the list of the board of directors; the company branch offices; the cover note.

However you approach copywriting, one thing you must realize is that you'll rarely get it right the first time. The key to writing great copy is rewriting two, three, four, five, six, seven drafts, or as many as it takes to get it right. Beginning copywriters tend to "freeze up" when faced with having to produce copy. They get nervous because they're afraid to write bad sentences or generate lousy ideas.

But nobody has to see your first efforts, and you don't have to get it right the first time. So don't be afraid to write down all the ideas, phrases, slogans, headlines, sentences, and fragments that come to you. You can always delete words that don't work. But once you have an idea or think of a way to say something, it is lost unless you write it down.

Many copywriters write much more copy than they will need in the final version. This lets them trim the fat and save only the prime cut. In the same way, you should collect much more information than you will use in the final version. This lets you be more selective in the facts you include in your copy.

Basically, copywriting can be divided into a three-stage process, although there may be several rewrites in each stage.

In the first stage, you "get it all down" on paper. Just let the ideas flow. Don't edit yourself; don't stop ideas from forming. Just write what comes to mind. Don't go back and fix up the words you've put on the page, but instead go on and keep writing as long as you have a flow of ideas and phrases you want to put down on paper.

Some writers have trouble letting their thoughts flow freely. They become inhibited and intimidated because they are "writing an ad," and that sounds like a difficult and challenging thing to do. If that's the case with you, try pretending you're writing a letter to a friend . . . a letter to convince this friend to buy a new product you've become excited about. This technique seems to work, perhaps because letter writing, unlike ad writing, is a familiar, everyday task.

In the second stage, you edit your work. You delete unnecessary words. You rewrite awkward phrases and sentences. You read the copy aloud to make sure that it flows smoothly. And you rearrange and reorder material into a more logical sequence.

Also, you read what you've written to see if it conforms to your criteria for effective, persuasive copy. If it doesn't, you rewrite to strengthen its selling power. This may involve more facts, a better headline, a stronger closing, or a different visual.

In the third stage, you "clean up" your copy by proofreading for spelling and grammar and checking the accuracy of your facts. Here's where you make sure you are consistent in your copy. For example, you don't want to write the company name as "GAF" in the headline and "G.A.F." in the body copy.

Skill in copywriting, and in any type of writing, comes only with practice. As you write copy, you will learn to overcome poor stylistic habits, become more comfortable with your writing, and gain greater control over the English language.

## DOCUMENTING YOUR SOURCES

As the copywriter, you are responsible for documenting the sources for all of the information you use in your copy. For instance, if you are writing a brochure for a fertility clinic and say, "one out of six couples in the U.S. is infertile," you need to document the source.

At the beginning of my manuscript, before I get to the actual copy, I put a key code documenting the sources I use:

References:

References are cited in squiggly brackets {} throughout the copy according to the key code below; these should be removed when the package goes to layout:

AO = Guner, A. B., "Can Overreaction Explain Part of the Size Premium," 10/04

MS = Morningstar, "Where and Why Asset Size Matters"

SS = Tran, Toan, "Finding Bargains in the Market's Dark Corners," *Stock Strategist*, 4/13/05

ML = "Sir John Templeton," www.meta-library.net

TS = Swarts, William, "Small-Cap Funds Max Out," TheStreet .com, 3/15/04

TW = "Capital Glut," *The Week*, 4/15/05, p. 36
RA = Mayer, Chris, "Advantage: Little Guy," *The Rude Awakening*,
  3/15/05

Whenever I use a fact other than what is common knowledge in my copy, I put the key code for the source in squiggly brackets at the end of that sentence as follows:

> "The individual investor, with a long-term focus and without the constraints of a big professional money manager, should always be willing to dig around and explore the small-cap arena to take advantage of possible discounts," advises my colleague Chris Mayer in *The Rude Awakening*. "It is the one area where the little guy has a decided edge." {RA}

Some copywriters document references only for facts taken from outside sources, such as articles or Web sites. I prefer to document everything, including facts taken from the client's own materials (brochures, ads, Web site) and even phone calls and e-mail correspondence with the client. This way, if a fact is ever questioned later, we know exactly where it came from.

After you write a promotion, keep copies of all the source documents on file for at least six to twelve months. You may even want to mail a set of these documents to the client for their own files.

## A TECHNIQUE FOR PRODUCING PROFITABLE ADVERTISING IDEAS

The copywriter's job is to come up with words and ideas that sell the product or service being advertised. Where do these ideas come from? They come from an understanding of the product, the market, and the mission of the copy—which is to generate sales.

However, even the best copywriters get stuck for ideas at times. Here is a proven 9-step procedure you can follow to come up with ideas for ads, headlines, marketing campaigns, or anything else under the sun:

## 1. Identify the Problem

The first step in solving a problem is to know what the problem is. But many of us forge ahead without knowing what it is we are trying to accomplish. Moral: Don't apply a solution before you have taken the time to accurately define the problem.

## 2. Assemble Pertinent Facts

In crime stories, detectives spend most of their time looking for clues. They cannot solve a case with clever thinking alone; they must have the facts. You, too, must have the facts before you can solve a problem or make an informed decision.

Professionals in every field know the importance of gathering specific facts. A scientist planning an experiment checks the abstracts to see what similar experiments have been performed. An author writing a book collects everything he can on the subject: newspaper clippings, photos, official records, transcripts of interviews, diaries, magazine articles, and so on. A consultant may spend weeks or months digging around a company before coming up with a solution to a major problem.

Keep an organized file of the background material you collect on a project. Review the file before you begin to formulate your solution. Use your PC to take notes on your research materials. This step increases your familiarity with the background information, and can give you a fresh perspective on the problem. Also, when you type up notes you condense a mound of material into a few neat pages that show all the facts at a glance.

### 3. Gather General Knowledge

In copywriting, specific facts have to do with the project at hand. They include the product, the market, the competition, and the media. General knowledge has to do with the expertise you've developed in business and in life, and includes your storehouse of information concerning life, events, people, science, technology, management, and the world at large.

Become a student in the many areas that relate to your job. Trade journals are the most valuable source of industry knowledge. Subscribe to the journals that relate to your field. Scan them all, and clip and save articles that contain information that may be useful to you. Organize your clipping files for easy access to articles by subject.

Read books in your field and start a reference library. If a copywriter with twenty-five years of experience writes a book on radio advertising, and you buy the book, you can learn in a day or so of reading what it took him twenty years to accumulate. Take some night school courses. Attend seminars, conferences, trade shows. Make friends with people in your field and exchange information, stories, ideas, case histories, technical tips.

Most of the successful professionals I know are compulsive information collectors. You should be one, too.

### 4. Look for Combinations

It has been said more than once, "There's nothing new in the world. It's all been done before." Maybe. But an idea doesn't have to be something completely new. Many ideas are simply a new combination of existing elements. By looking for combinations, for new relationships between old ideas, you can come up with a fresh approach.

The clock radio, for example, was invented by someone who combined two existing technologies: the clock and the radio. Niels Bohr combined two separate ideas—Rutherford's model of the atom as a nucleus orbited by electrons and Planck's quantum theory—to create the modern conception of the atom.

Look for synergistic combinations when you examine the facts. What two things can work together to form a third thing that is a new idea? If you have two devices, and each performs a function you need, can you link them together to create a new product?

### 5. Sleep on It

Putting the problem aside for a time can help you renew your idea-producing powers just when you think your creative well has run dry.

But don't resort to this method after only five minutes of puzzled thought. First, you have to gather all the information you can. Next, you need to go over the information again and again as you try to come up with that one big idea. You'll come to a point where you get bleary and punch-drunk, just hashing the same ideas over and over. This is the time to take a break, put the problem aside, sleep on it, and let your unconscious mind take over.

A solution may strike you as you sleep, shower, shave, or walk in the park. Even if it doesn't, when you return to the problem, you will find you can attack it with renewed vigor and a fresh perspective. I use this technique in writing—I put aside what I have written and read it fresh the next day. Many times the things I thought were brilliant when I wrote them can be much improved at second glance.

### 6. Use a Checklist

Checklists can be used to stimulate creative thinking and as a starting point for new ideas. There are several checklists in this book you can use. But the best checklists are those you create yourself, because they are tailored to the problems that come up in your daily routine.

For example, Jill is a technical salesperson well versed in the technical features of her product, but she has trouble when it comes to closing a sale. She could overcome this weakness by making a checklist of typical customer objections and how to answer them. (The list of objections can be culled from sales calls made over the course of several weeks. Possible tactics for overcoming these objections can be garnered from fellow sales-people, from books on selling, and from her own trial-and-error efforts.) Then, when faced with a tough customer, she doesn't have to reinvent the wheel, but will be prepared for all the standard objections because of her familiarity with the checklist.

However, no checklist can contain an idea for every situation that comes up. Remember, a checklist should be used as a tool for creative thinking, not as a crutch.

### 7. Get Feedback

Sherlock Holmes was a brilliant detective. But even he needed to bounce ideas off Dr. Watson at times. As a professional writer, I think I know how to write an engaging piece of copy. But when I show a draft to my wife, she can always spot at least half a dozen ways to make it better.

Some people prefer to work alone. I'm one of them, and maybe you are, too. But if you don't work as part of a team, getting someone else's opinion of your work can help you focus your thinking and produce ideas you hadn't thought of.

Take the feedback for what it's worth. If you feel you're right, and the criticisms are off base, ignore them. But more often than not, feedback will provide useful information that can help you come up with the best, most profitable ideas.

Of course, if you ask others to "take a look at this report," you should be willing to do the same for them when they solicit your opinion. You'll find that reviewing the work of others is fun; it's easier to critique someone else's work than create your own. And you'll be gratified by the improvements you come up with—things that are obvious to you but would never have occurred to the other person.

### 8. Team Up

Some people think more creatively when working in groups. But how large should the group be? My opinion is that two is the ideal team. Any more and you're in danger of ending up with a committee that spins its wheels and accomplishes nothing. The person you team up with should have skills and thought processes that balance and complement your own. For example, in advertising, copywriters (the word people) team up with art directors (the picture people).

In entrepreneurial firms, the idea person who started the company will often hire a professional manager from onc of the Fortune 500 companies as the new venture grows; the entrepreneur knows how to make things happen, but the manager knows how to run a profitable, efficient corporation.

As an engineer, you may invent a better microchip. But if you want to make a fortune selling it, you should team up with someone who has a strong sales and marketing background.

### 9. Give New Ideas a Chance

Many businesspeople, especially managerial types, develop their critical faculties more finely than their creative faculties. If creative engineers and inventors had listened to these people, we would not have personal computers, cars, airplanes, lightbulbs, or electricity.

The creative process works in two stages. The first is the idea-producing stage, when ideas flow freely. The second is the critical or "editing" stage, where you hold each idea up to the cold light of day and see if it is practical.

Many of us make the mistake of mixing the stages together,

especially during the idea-producing stage, when we are too eager to criticize an idea as soon as it is presented. As a result, we shoot down ideas and make snap judgments when we should be encouraging the production of ideas. Avoid making this mistake, as many good ideas are killed this way.

The tasks and procedures outlined in this chapter may seem like a tall order. But don't worry. You can do it. Heed this advice from Lou Redmond, a former Ogilvy & Mather copywriter: "Advertising is one of the minor arts, so don't be intimidated by it."

# 6

# WRITING PRINT ADVERTISEMENTS

Internet enthusiasts are telling us print advertising is dead, but don't you believe it for a second. According to the Census Bureau, $87 billion was spent in the United States on newspaper and magazine advertising in 2002, the most recent year for which figures are available.

All ad agency copywriters are expected to master print advertising before they are assigned work in television. Judging from the print ads appearing in the newspapers and magazines I read, many never do. This chapter will teach you to write print ads that build product awareness, generate sales leads, and bring in the orders.

## TYPES OF ADS

Are all print advertisements basically the same? Or are there different techniques for writing ads in different media or ads designed to achieve different goals?

The basics of good print advertising are the same in all media, and the next section of this chapter outlines the nine characteristics of the successful ad. But the tone, content, and focus of the ad can vary with the purpose and the place of publication. Let's take a look at the different kinds of print ads you will be called upon to write.

First, an ad can have one of four basic missions:

1. To sell products directly (mail-order advertising)
2. To generate sales leads (ads that invite you to send for a free brochure or pamphlet)
3. To build awareness of a product (ads for package goods and most consumer products of low unit cost)
4. To build the company's image (corporate advertising)

How do these four categories differ?

Ads that ask for the order—generate a sale directly—do a *complete* selling job. There is no salesperson, no showroom, no retail display, no explanatory brochure to add to the sales pitch. The ad must get attention, hook the reader, and then convince her to send in an order for a product she has never seen.

Mail-order ads are usually lengthy (800 words and up), because they must give complete information. They must answer all of the buyer's questions, lay his fears to rest, and overcome all his objections in order to close the sale. They must also devote space to the mechanism used in placing the actual order: a Web site link, coupon, toll-free number, or other device.

Ads appealing to buyers in business and industry usually try to generate a sales lead: a response from an interested buyer asking for more information. This is because most products sold to business and industry cannot be sold directly, but require a company salesperson to give a presentation and close the sale in person.

Ads that generate leads may give a lot of information or a little, but they never give the full story. To get complete information, the reader must respond to the ad by writing, phoning, or mailing in a coupon. To write a successful lead-generating ad, you must understand the steps in the buying process and where the ad fits in.

Most consumer products are not sold by mail or by salespeople; instead, you can buy them at supermarkets, department stores, in automobile showrooms, and at fast-food chains. And, you usually buy them only when you need them, not when you read an ad about them.

Therefore, the ads for these products don't sell them directly; they seek to generate an awareness of the product and a desire to use it. The ad campaign builds this awareness and desire over an extended period. Burger King knows you don't rush out to buy a Whopper after viewing a Burger King commercial. The goal of their advertising is to make Burger King the first place you think of when you do want a hamburger, so you will eat their product instead of McDonald's or Wendy's.

Some ads promote companies instead of products. This type of advertising, known as corporate advertising, seeks to create a certain image of the company in the mind of the reader. Sometimes these campaigns are aimed at the general public to clear up a misconception about a firm or promote the firm in a general sense. More often they are aimed at stockholders, investors, and the business community. You can find examples of corporate advertising in any issue of *Forbes, Fortune*, or *Business Week*.

Ads also differ according to the type of medium in which they appear: newspaper, magazine, directory, or online. Newspapers have long been the backbone of retail advertising campaigns. Retailers run what is called "price and where to buy" advertising—simple display ads that emphasize the price of the merchandise and then direct local consumers to a nearby retail outlet to make the purchase. Such ads usually center around a storewide sale or price-off deal for certain items.

Of course, newspapers attract many other advertisers

besides retailers: banks, insurance companies, real estate agents, theaters, restaurants, book publishers. Some use the simple price-and-where-to-buy format of retailers. Others run more sophisticated campaigns closer to magazine advertisements.

Magazines are different from newspapers in two important ways. First, newspapers are written for a general readership, while magazines are published for specialized audiences: women, teens, Christians, business executives, computer buffs, plumbing engineers, geologists, writers. As a result, magazines are effective for reaching small segments of the market, while newspapers are a medium of mass advertising.

Second, the reproduction quality of magazines is far superior to newspapers. Plus, magazines offer the advertiser the use of full color in their advertisements.

Manufacturers use magazines for campaigns that build product awareness and company image. Many consumer magazines also have special sections for mail-order advertisements.

There are several advertising options on the Internet. Years ago, the most prevalent was banner advertising, but the response to banner ads has been declining for years. A growing number of PC users have filters that prevent pop-up ads from cluttering their screens. In a 2004 survey of 605 Internet users, 95 percent said that they felt negatively about pop-ups blocking their window.

An alternative to banner advertising is to run small ads in online newsletters, also known as "e-zines." These ads consist of short text (50 to 100 words is typical) with a hyperlink to a Web site giving more information about the product being advertised.

Whether it is published in a newspaper or a magazine, on a Web site or in an online newsletter, your ad has to work hard to get the reader's attention. The reader, after all, bought the publication or clicked to the Web site for the articles and content, not for the ads. In most major newspapers, for example, your ad competes with hundreds of other ads. And most readers read only four ads in a typical magazine. So the headline and visual must stop the reader in her tracks with an attention-getting concept centered around a strong reader benefit or the promise of a reward.

Directory advertising is different. When the reader turns to the Yellow Pages or an industrial buyer's guide, he is searching for a supplier of a specific type of product or service. So, your ad doesn't have to convince him that he needs a limousine; it has to convince him to try your limousine service.

Naturally, the ads listed at the beginning of a category are the first ones read. But the order is alphabetical, so unless you change your company name, there is little chance of changing your position in the Yellow Pages.

*Thomas Register,* the major industrial product directory, did a study to show the effect of size on an ad's ability to generate response. The study showed that the biggest ad on the page gets forty times the response of an ordinary one-line directory listing. You may not be able to afford the biggest ad, but the bigger your ad, the more response it will generate. Even a boldface listing generates twice the response of a listing in ordinary type.

Directory ads should immediately flag the reader with the benefit or special service she is looking for. For example, most people ordering a late-night pizza will pick the place that delivers for free. The winning ad in this section of the phone book will have, in big, bold type, the headline, "CRISP, HOT PIZZA—*FREE* DELIVERY!"

Think about what your prospects have in mind when they turn to the Yellow Pages to look for a pizza, limousine, exterminator, or whatever your business offers. Then make this important item the theme of your ad.

A New Jersey insurance agent reasoned that people with something to insure will respond to an ad that specifically refers to that type of insurance. He placed an ad with the headline "INSURANCE" run across the top in large bold lettering. Underneath, he simply listed twenty-eight different types of insurance he offered: everything from aircraft and accident protection to trucks, trailers, and snowmobiles. His simple 4-by 5-inch ad pulls one or two phone calls every business day of the year.

The size of your ad also affects your approach to writing the copy. A full-page magazine or newspaper ad gives you great flexibility in the size of the illustrations and the amount of copy you use. (Although they are usually shorter, a full-page magazine ad consisting of solid text can contain more than a thousand words.) Smaller ads, of course, cannot contain as much artwork and copy.

As a result, advertisers frequently use full-page ads as the "core" of their campaign for building image and awareness; smaller ads are used for generating sales leads. Many mail-order advertisers have also had great success with smaller ads.

## HOW TO WRITE A GOOD ADVERTISEMENT

The techniques used in different advertising situations— magazines versus newspapers, mail order versus image, business versus consumer—are important, to be sure. But the basics of good print advertising are pretty much the same no matter what medium you're writing for.

Here are nine criteria that an ad must satisfy if it is to be successful as a selling tool:

**1. The headline contains an important consumer benefit, or news, or arouses curiosity, or promises a reward for reading the copy.**

An ad for RCA's satellite channel has the headline, "How to Cut Your Company's Long-Distance Phone Bill 50% Or More." The benefit and the reward are clear: You will find out how to cut your phone bill in half if you read the ad.

A savings or discount is one of the most powerful benefits you can feature in a headline. An example is the headline for a mail-order ad offering a set of cassette tapes on "assertiveness skills." The headline reads: "For $30 you can acquire the same Assertiveness Skills that are now being taught to Fortune 500 managers for up to $500 a day."

Never mind that tapes are different from live seminars; this headline creates the impression that you can acquire new knowledge for $470 less than others have paid for it: a good bargain, simply but powerfully stated.

Century 21's recruitment ad for real estate agents is also direct: "You Can Make Big Money in Real Estate Sales Right Now." No clever copy. No puns. No fancy photography or special effects. Just an irresistible promise stated in plain, straightforward language.

**2. The visual (if you use a visual) illustrates the main benefit stated in the headline.**

Note that I said "if you use a visual." Contrary to what some folks may tell you, it is the words, not the pictures, that do most of the selling in an advertisement. Hundreds of successful ads have used words alone to get their message across. Thousands of other successful ads are adorned only with simple photos, spot drawings, and plain-Jane graphics.

If possible, the visual should illustrate the benefit stated in the headline. One of the most effective visual techniques for doing so is the use of before-and-after photos.

DuPont's ad for TEFLON explains how coating industrial-process equipment with TEFLON protects it from acid. There are two photos. One shows an uncoated mixing blade reduced to scrap by industrial acids. The other shows a TEFLON-coated blade used in the same corrosive chemicals; the TEFLON blade is in perfect condition. What better way to illustrate and prove the benefit of using TEFLON?

A Johnson & Johnson ad headline contains a strong benefit: "Now, from Johnson & Johnson, Toys That Allow Babies to Master New Skills." The photo shows a toddler playing with and obviously enjoying one of the toys. The visual illustrates the benefit of the product and offers proof that babies like these toys.

A visual doesn't have to be elaborate to illustrate the benefit. An ad for a set of encyclopedias can show young children studying and using the books. An ad for homeowners insurance can show the safe, cozy home the insurance helped pay for after the family's first home burned down.

*3. The lead paragraph expands on the theme of the headline.* A few examples:

**THE WORSE YOUR CORROSION PROBLEMS, THE MORE YOU NEED DUPONT TEFLON**
In harsh, highly corrosive chemical process environments, fluid handling components lined or made with DuPont TEFLON resins and films consistently outlast other materials.

**YOU CAN MAKE BIG MONEY IN REAL ESTATE SALES RIGHT NOW**
Business is booming at CENTURY 21. And so are careers. CENTURY 21 offices have helped more people to achieve

rewarding careers in real estate than any other sales organization in the world.

## NOW, FROM JOHNSON & JOHNSON, TOYS THAT ALLOW BABIES TO MASTER NEW SKILLS

Your child is growing bigger. Brighter. More curious and eager to learn every day. That's why Johnson & Johnson Child Development Toys are designed to change and grow with your child. To encourage his skill development every step of the way.

**4. *The layout draws readers into the ad and invites them to read the body copy.***

Copywriters must consider the graphic elements of the ad and how these graphics will affect readership of their copy. Will the copy be broken up by subheads into many short sections? Will there be a coupon? Should the phone number be in larger type to encourage call-ins? Should the product or process be illustrated using a number of small secondary photos with captions? These are all the concerns of the writer.

The key to getting the ad read is a layout that is clean, uncluttered, and easy on the eyes. The layout should catch the reader's eye and move it logically from headline and visual to body copy to logo and address.

Chapter 15 covers graphics in detail. But here are some factors that enhance the readability and eye appeal of a layout:

- Use one central visual.
- Headline set in large, bold type.
- Body copy set underneath headline and visual.
- Body copy set in clear, readable type.
- Space between paragraphs increases readability.
- Subheads help draw the eye through the text.
- Copy should be printed black on a white background.

Copy printed in reverse, on a tint, or over a visual is difficult to read.

• Short paragraphs are easier to read than long ones.

• The lead paragraph should be very short—less than three lines of type, if possible.

• Simple visuals are best. Visuals with too many elements in them confuse the reader.

• The best layout is a simple layout: headline, large visual, body copy, logo. Additional elements—a subhead, a sidebar, secondary photos—can enhance the ad's readability, but too many make it cluttered and unappealing to the eye.

• Many art directors believe that ads must have a large amount of "white space" (blank space) or else they will look cluttered and people won't read them. But, if your typography is clean and readable, you can set a solid page of text and people will read every word of it.

In the same way, there are certain visual techniques that make ads unappealing to readers. These techniques give ads an "addy" look and should be avoided. They include:

• Headlines and blocks of copy set on a slant
• Reverse type (white letters on a black background)
• Tinting of black-and-white photographs with a second color (usually blue or red)
• Tiny type (smaller than eight-point)
• Long, unbroken chunks of text
• A long listing of company locations and addresses crammed in under the logo
• Type set in overly wide columns
• Poorly executed or reproduced artwork and photography

The look of your ad—its appearance, its layout, how the elements are set up on the page—won't make an ad with poor copy effective. But an unappealing layout can discourage interested consumers from reading brilliant copy that has a lot to offer them. Again, chapter 15 covers the basics of what copywriters need to know about designing ads.

### 5. The body copy covers all important sales points in logical sequence.

The effective ad tells an interesting, important story about the product. And, like a novel or short story, the copy must be logically organized, with a beginning, a middle, and an end.

If you are describing a product and its benefits, you will probably organize your sales points in order of importance, putting the most important point in the headline and taking the reader from the major benefits to minor features as you go through the body copy. In this format, the ad resembles the "inverted pyramid" style used by journalists in news stories.

If the sales points are not related in any way, you might prefer to use a list format, in which you simply list the sales points in simple 1-2-3 fashion.

If you are writing a case history or testimonial ad, you can use chronological order to relate the story as it happened. Or, you might use a problem/solution format to show how the product solved a problem.

### 6. The copy provides the information needed to convince the greatest number of qualified prospects to take the next step in the buying process.

The length and number of sales points to be included in the copy depends on what you're selling, who you're selling it to, and what the next step is in the buying process.

Here are some observations on ad length that come from flipping through a single issue of *Good Housekeeping* magazine:

• A full-page ad for Sophia perfume shows a color photo of the perfume bottle superimposed against a background of fireworks. The ad contains no body copy, just a headline and tag line.

SOPHIA IS DESIRE.

SOPHIA IS MYSTERY.

SOPHIA IS FANTASY.

SOPHIA BY COTY. WEAR IT WITH A PASSION.

Apparently, there is not a lot to say about perfume; it is sold on the mystique of what wearing perfume does to enhance your sex appeal.

• An ad for Caltrate 600, a calcium supplement, contains a diagram, a chart, more than 400 words of body copy, and a straightforward headline announcing, "New Caltrate 600 Helps Keep Bones Healthy." Apparently, there is a lot to say about health products. The ad also invites the reader to write in for a price-off coupon for the product and a "calcium counter."

• Many food ads contain recipes that center around the product being advertised. The food advertiser hopes the reader will like the recipe and, as a result, purchase the product every time he or she makes the dish.

• The ads for more expensive items—blenders, telephones, flooring, a kit for pregnancy tests, real estate—all invite the reader to write or phone for additional information. The advertiser knows there is more to say about these products than can be put in a magazine ad; brochures and salespeople will have to augment the efforts of the ad.

When you sit down to write your ad, ask yourself: "What do I want the reader to do? And what can I tell him that will get him to do it?"

### 7. *The copy is interesting to read.*

"You cannot bore people into buying your product," writes David Ogilvy in *Ogilvy on Advertising.* "You can only interest them in buying it."

People will only read your ad as long as it is interesting to them. They will not read copy that is boring, in content or in style.

As a writer and a reader, you know when writing is interesting to read and when it is dull. The style should be crisp, lively, and light. The copy should have rhythm and clarity.

But great style won't save an ad without substance. The copy must appeal to the reader's self-interest. It must contain benefits, or news, or it must solve the reader's problem. It cannot entertain for entertainment's sake; it must present compelling reasons why the product is desirable to the reader.

Here are a few things that add interest to advertisements:

- Copy that speaks directly to the reader's life, the reader's emotions, the reader's needs and desires
- Copy that tells a story
- Copy about people
- Copy written in a personal style, so that it sounds like a letter from a friend: warm, helpful, and sincere
- Testimonials from celebrities
- A free offer (of a gift, a pamphlet, a brochure, or a sample)
- Copy that contains important news
- Copy that addresses major issues: beauty, health, old age, parenting, marriage, home, security, family, careers, education, social issues
- Copy that answers important questions readers have in their minds
- Copy about a subject that interests the reader

Here are some things that make ads boring:

- Copy that centers on the manufacturer—that talks about the company, its philosophy, its success
- Copy that talks about how the product is made or how it works rather than what it can do for the reader
- Copy that tells readers things they already know
- Long-winded copy with big words, lengthy sentences, and large unbroken chunks of text
- Copy in which all sentences are the same length (varying sentence length adds snap to writing)
- Copy that gives product features instead of customer benefits
- Copy without a point of view—without a strong selling proposition or a cohesive sales pitch (such copy presents the facts without really showing the reader how these facts relate to his needs)
- Ads with cluttered layouts and poorly reproduced visuals look boring and turn the reader off

## 8. *The copy is believable.*

"Cynicism and suspicion abound today," says Amil Gargano, "much of it with good reason. That's why advertising won't work unless it is trusted, no matter how clever it might seem. And the way to be trusted is to be honest and sensitive to the people you want to reach."

The copywriter's task is not an easy one. In addition to getting attention, explaining the product, and being persuasive, you must overcome the reader's distrust and get her to believe you.

We've already discussed a number of techniques for building credibility: testimonials, demonstrations, research tests. But these are just techniques. The key to being believed is to tell the truth.

This is not as radical as it sounds. Contrary to the image of advertising executives as slick hucksters, most are honest, professional businesspeople who believe in the products they're selling. Most would not create advertising for a product they felt was harmful or inferior. And, although ethics plays a part, the real reason for this is a simple fact about advertising.

*Clever advertising can convince people to try a bad product once. But it can't convince them to buy a product they've already tried and didn't like.*

So you see, there's no percentage in writing ads that tell lies. Besides being unethical, it's unprofitable for the agency and the advertiser and gives all advertising a bad name.

Few practitioners engage in such unethical behavior. The majority believe that the product they are advertising can do you a lot of good. When you believe in your product, it's easy to write copy that is sincere, informative, and helpful. And when you are sincere, it comes across to the reader and they believe what you've written.

### 9. The ad asks for action.

The ad should ask the reader to take the next step in the buying process, whether that step is to send in an order, call a sales office, visit a store, try a sample, see a demonstration, or just believe the advertiser's message.

You are already familiar with coupons, toll-free numbers, and other devices used to urge the reader to respond to the ad. Barry Kingston, merchandising director of *Opportunity Magazine,* offers these tips on getting the best response to your ad:

- Use a street address instead of a post office box number. A street address gives the impression that your firm is large, stable, and well established.
- If most of the magazine's readers qualify for your offer, use a toll-free phone number to increase response. But if

you want to qualify your leads, use a regular company phone number.

- If the product can be ordered directly with a credit card, include a toll-free number.
- Use a company phone number for selling expensive items that involve inside salespeople.
- A coupon boosts response between 25 and 100 percent.
- Asking the reader to send in a letter reduces response but produces highly qualified leads (people with genuine interest in the product).

## DOES YOUR AD NEED A SLOGAN?

A slogan, also known as the tag line, is a phrase or sentence that appears beneath the company logo in an ad or series of ads. The slogan is used to sum up the central message of the ads, or to make a broad statement about the nature of the company.

Some well-known slogans:

WE'RE AMERICAN AIRLINES: DOING WHAT WE DO BEST

MAXWELL HOUSE: GOOD TO THE LAST DROP

LIKE A GOOD NEIGHBOR, STATE FARM IS THERE

NOTHING BEATS A GREAT PAIR OF L'EGGS

PRUDENTIAL: GET A PIECE OF THE ROCK

IF THEY COULD JUST STAY LITTLE TILL THEIR CARTER'S WEAR OUT

LONG DISTANCE: THE NEXT BEST THING TO BEING THERE

AMERICAN EXPRESS: DON'T LEAVE HOME WITHOUT IT

These slogans have built consumer awareness of brand-name products because they are pithy, memorable, and because they sum up the nature of the product or service. However, there are hundreds of slogans that have been used for a few months and then dropped from ads, never to be written or uttered again.

Should you use a slogan in your ad?

It depends on whether your product lends itself to this technique. In copywriting, the rule should be, "Form follows function." In other words, use a technique if it works and seems natural. But don't force-fit a copy technique in an ad where it doesn't belong.

Applying this rule to slogans, I'd say use a slogan if your product's key selling proposition or its nature can be summed up in a single, catchy statement. But if the essence of your product or business can't be captured in a one-liner, don't force it, or the result will be an artificial slogan that detracts from the ad and makes you, your ad agency, your employees, and your customers embarrassed and uncomfortable.

For example, let's say your company manufactures flypaper. The company president says, "Our slogan should be: The Leader in Quality Flypaper." But this slogan restricts you to a narrow product category. If you decide to expand and manufacture flyswatters, you'll have a hard time because people will think of you as a flypaper company only.

Then your ad agency says, "Let's think big. You're not just in flypaper; you're in 'pest control.' How about "Leaders in the Science of Pest Control" as a slogan?" But this is too general. Pest control can be anything from spraying termites to catching rats. And your company really doesn't plan to get involved in these areas.

So the danger with slogans is that some are too narrow and pigeonhole you in a specialty, while others are so broad-based that they lose any real meaning or applicability to your business.

Slogans work best when they are memorable and when they are repeated to the target audience numerous times over a prolonged period. For instance, 87 percent of consumers surveyed by Emergence, an Atlanta-based marketing consultancy, knew Allstate's slogan, which is nearly half a century old: "You're in

Good Hands with Allstate." But Wendy's scored zero after two years with "It's Better Here."

## MANUSCRIPT FORMAT FOR AD COPY

Unless you already work in advertising, you've never seen an ad in its manuscript form. You only see the finished product in a newspaper, magazine, or directory.

There is no "official" manuscript format for submitting ad copy to your client. Different agencies use slightly different formats. All of them are fine.

Some agencies and copywriters type their copy on special forms that have the word COPY printed on them along with the name of the agency or the writer and room to fill in other information (client, date, word length, publication in which the ad will appear).

This is fine, but unnecessary. I type my copy on plain white paper, and so do many other writers. No client has ever asked me to do otherwise.

Copy should be typed double-spaced, with generous margins. You want to leave enough room for reviewers to pencil in comments and changes.

My page format is to type double-space with four spaces between paragraphs (but only two spaces between a heading and the paragraph that follows). I do not indent at the beginning of paragraphs.

Today most of my copy is sent to clients via e-mail as attached Microsoft Word files. If your clients are PC literate, they can use the Word "Track Changes" feature to make their comments on your copy, eliminating the need to print it out and mark it up by hand.

All copywriters include labels in their copy that indicate whether the text the reviewer is reading is for a headline, subhead, body copy, caption, boxed material, or the description of a visual. Some writers type these descriptions in parentheses in the left margin. I type them in capital letters flush against the left margin, with a colon following the label but with no parentheses. This way, my manuscript looks very neat because everything is flush with the left margin.

A sample page of manuscript is shown here:

ThermoPal ad—page 1

HEADLINE:
How to Keep Your Iced Tea on Ice

VISUAL:
Tall glass of iced tea sitting next to an open ThermoPal thermos.

COPY:
Nothing quenches thirst like a cold iced tea on a hot summer's day.

But the tea in a can or a carton won't stay cool in summer heat. And an ordinary thermos won't fit in your briefcase or bag or lunch box.

Introducing ThermoPal, the pint-size thermos that makes sure your cool summer drinks stay cool . . . and is small enough to go where you go.

SUBHEAD:
A big gulp in a tiny bottle

COPY:
ThermoPal is tiny enough to fit in the slimmest briefcase or in a tightly packed backpack. But it's big enough to hold a frosty 8 ounces of tea, lemonade, or fruit juice. That's as much as you get in a tall, cool glass at home or from a machine.

But by carrying your lunchtime drink in ThermoPal, your refreshment costs a few pennies instead of the better part of a dollar, as it would from a vending machine or fast-food stand. So ThermoPal pays for itself in just a few weeks . . . and brings big savings over the long, hot summer.

We know you'll be delighted with ThermoPal for years to come. If not, just send the lid back in the mail for a full refund—no questions asked.

To order ThermoPal, clip and mail the reply coupon. But hurry—supplies are limited, and we usually sell out by the middle of Spring.

COUPON:

❑ *YES*, I want to keep cool. Please send me ___ ThermoPals at $8.95 each plus $1.00 each for shipping and handling. My check is enclosed. If not satisfied, I'll send back the top of the thermos for a full refund of my money.

Name _____

Address _____

City _____ State _____ Zip _____

Mail coupon to:        ThermoPal
                       Box XXX
                       Anytown, USA XXXXX

## A CHECKLIST OF ADVERTISING IDEAS

Copywriters don't sit down with an assignment and say "I want to do a testimonial ad" or "Let's make it a how-to ad." They first study the product, the audience, and the purpose of the advertisement. Then they use the technique that fits the assignment.

Still, it helps to be familiar with the various types of ads that have been successful over the years: how-to, testimonials, before-and-after, and others.

Below is a checklist of many of these categories. When you're stuck for an idea, a quick review of the list might give you inspiration—you might scan the list and say, "Hey, here's an approach that works with what I'm selling!" Turn to this checklist not as a crutch but as an aid in producing ideas:

- ❑ QUESTION AD—asks a question in the headline and answers it in the body copy.
- ❑ QUIZ AD—copy presents a quiz. Reader takes quiz. Her answers determine whether she is a prospect for the product or service being offered.
- ❑ NEWS AD—announces a new product or something new about an existing product.
- ❑ DIRECT AD—gives a straightforward presentation of the facts.
- ❑ INDIRECT AD—has an obscure headline designed to arouse curiosity and entice the reader to read the body copy.
- ❑ REWARD AD—promises a reward for reading the ad.
- ❑ COMMAND AD—commands the reader to take action.
- ❑ PRICE-AND-WHERE-TO-BUY AD—announces a sale. Describes the product, gives the price and discount, and tells where to buy it.
- ❑ REASON-WHY AD—presents reasons why you should buy the product.
- ❑ LETTER AD—an ad written in letter form.
- ❑ BEFORE-AND-AFTER—shows the improvements gained by using the product.
- ❑ TESTIMONIAL—a user of the product or a celebrity speaks out in favor of the product.
- ❑ CASE HISTORY—a detailed product success story.
- ❑ FREE INFORMATION AD—offers free brochure, pamphlet, or other information. Ad concentrates on getting the reader to send for free literature rather than on selling the product directly.

❏ STORY—tells a story involving people and the product.

❏ "NEW WAVE"—relies on far-out graphics to grab attention.

❏ READER IDENTIFICATION—headline is used to select the audience.

❏ INFORMATION AD—ad gives useful information relating to the use of the product in general rather than pushing the product directly.

❏ LOCATION AD—features the product used in an unusual location to highlight its versatility, usefulness, convenience, or ruggedness.

❏ FICTIONAL CHARACTERS—ad centers around a fictional character such as Mr. Whipple or the Green Giant.

❏ FICTIONAL PLACES—ad centers around a fictional place such as Marlboro Country.

❏ CARTOONS AND CARTOON STRIPS.

❏ ADVERTISER IN AD—the advertiser appears in the ad to speak about his own product.

❏ INVENT A WORD—the advertiser invents a word to describe his product or its application. (The term "athlete's foot" was invented by ad man Obie Winters to sell his client's product, a horse liniment that could also cure ringworm of the foot; Gerald Lambert popularized "halitosis" to sell Listerine.)

❏ COMPARATIVE ADVERTISING—shows how your product stacks up against the competition.

❏ CHALLENGE—challenges the reader to find a better product than yours.

❏ GUARANTEE AD—focuses on the guarantee, not the product.

❏ OFFER AD—focuses on the offer, the sale, and not the product.

❏ DEMONSTRATION—shows how the product works.

❏ PUN—headline attracts attention with clever wordplay. The pun is explained in the copy.

❏ CONTESTS AND SWEEPSTAKES.

❑ TIE-IN WITH CURRENT EVENTS—to add timeliness and urgency to the selling proposition.

## WRITING SMALL DISPLAY AND CLASSIFIED ADS

As a copywriter, you will mostly be writing full-page ads in magazines and newspapers. But occasionally you may be asked to write small display ads. So you should understand how these small ads work, which is differently than large ads.

Your classified ad should not ask directly for an order. It usually won't work. There is not enough copy in a classified ad to make the complete sale.

Classified advertising works best when you use a two-step direct-marketing technique. In step one, you run a small classified ad to generate an inquiry, which is a request for more information about your product. In step two, when people inquire, you send out an inquiry fulfillment kit, which is a sales package promoting your product.

The inquiry fulfillment kit usually consists of an outer envelope, sales letter, circular or brochure, order form, and reply envelope. A successful inquiry fulfillment kit should convert 10 to 15 percent of the ad inquiries to orders. Some inquiry fulfillment kits have achieved conversion rates as high as 20 to 30 percent or more.

The way to measure classified ad response is to count the inquiries and divide the cost of the ad by the number of inquiries to determine the cost per inquiry. For instance, if it costs you $100 to run a classified ad and you get 100 inquiries, your cost per inquiry is $1. A successful classified ad will generate inquiries at a cost of between $.50 and $2 per inquiry.

Sales appeals that work in classified mail-order advertising include promises that the customer will obtain love, money, health, popularity, success, leisure, security, self-confidence, better appearance, self-improvement, pride of accomplishment, prestige, pride of ownership, or comfort; will receive entertainment; will save time; will eliminate worry and fear; will satisfy curiosity, self-expression, or creativity; or will avoid work or risk.

Effective words and phrases to use in your classified ads include: *free, new, amazing, now, how to, easy, discover, method, plan, reveals, show, simple, startling, advanced, improved,* and *you.*

One of my most successful mail-order ads, which ran continuously for many years in *Writer's Digest*, reads as follows:

> **MAKE $85,000/YEAR** writing ads, brochures, promotional material for local/national client. Free details: CTC, 22 E. Quackenbush, Dept. WD, Dumont, NJ 07628.

Here are some other examples of how to write classified mail-order ads:

> **EXTRA CASH.** 12 ways to make money at home. Free details . . .

> **MAIL ORDER MILLIONAIRE** reveals moneymaking secrets. FREE 1-hour cassette . . .

> **SELL NEW BOOK by mail! 400% profit!** Free dealer information . . .

> **GROW** earthworms at home for profit . . .

> **CARNIVOROUS AND WOODLAND** terrarium plants. Send for FREE catalog.

> **ANCESTOR HUNTING?** Trace your family roots the easy way. Details free . . .

The measure of a successful classified ad is the cost per inquiry. Therefore, if you can get your message across in fewer words, you pay less for the ad and, as a result, lower your cost per inquiry.

Make your classifieds as short and pithy as possible. Here are some tips for reducing your word count:

• *Be concise.* Use the minimum number of words needed to communicate your idea. For example, instead of "Earn $500 a Day in Your Own Home-Based Business," write "Work at Home—$500/Day!"

• *Minimize your address.* You pay the publication for every word in your classified, including your address. Therefore, instead of "22 E. Quackenbush Avenue," I write "22 E. Quackenbush." The mail will still be delivered, and I will save one word. This can add up to significant savings for ads run frequently in multiple publications.

• *Use phrases and sentence fragments* rather than full sentences.

• *Remember your objective.* You are asking only for an inquiry, not for an order. You don't need a lot of copy, since all you are asking the reader to do is send for free information.

• *Use combination words, hyphenated words, and slash constructions.* For instance, instead of "GROW EARTH WORMS," which is three words, write "GROW EARTHWORMS," which counts as two words, saving you a word.

As stated earlier, the best way to generate a response is to ask for an inquiry rather than an order. This is done by putting a phrase such as "free details," "free information," "free catalog," or similar phrase, followed by a colon and your address (e.g., Free Details: Box 54, Canuga, TN 44566).

Should you charge for your information? Some advertisers

ask the prospect to pay for the information either by sending a small amount of money (25¢, 50¢, $1, and $2 are typical) or by sending a self-addressed envelope with the postage already on it.

The theory is that asking for postage or a nominal payment brings you a more qualified lead and therefore results in a higher percentage of leads converted to sales. My experience is that it doesn't pay to charge for your information kit, since doing so dramatically cuts down on the number of leads you will receive.

Whenever you offer information to generate an inquiry, I believe it's best to make it free. The exception might be if you are offering a very expensive and elaborate catalog, for which you charge $1 or $2 to cover your costs.

In your classified ads, put a key code in the address, so when you get inquiries, you can track which ad generated them. For instance, in my ad "MAKE $85,000/YEAR WRITING," the key code "WD" refers to *Writer's Digest* magazine. Since the ad runs every month, I don't bother adding a code number to track the month. If you wanted to do so, you could. For example, "Dept. WD-10" would mean *Writer's Digest* magazine, October issue (the tenth month of the year). Keep track of the key code on each inquiry, and record the information in a notebook or on your PC to measure ad response.

We have already discussed the two key measurements of two-step classified advertising: the cost per inquiry and the percentage of inquiries converted to orders. The bottom line is this: Did the sales the ad generated exceed the cost of the ad space? If they did, it was profitable. If they didn't, the ad isn't working, and a new ad should be tested.

Place your classified ads in publications that have mail-order classified ad sections. Contact the magazines that interest you and ask for their media kits, which include details on circulation, advertising rates, and readership, and a sample issue of the publication. Ask if the publisher will send several sample issues.

Look at the classified ad sections in the publications. Are the ads for products similar to yours? If so, that's a good sign. See if these ads repeat from issue to issue. The advertisers would not repeat them unless the ads were working. If this publication is working for their offers, it can work for yours, too.

Classified ad sections are divided by various headings. Place your ad under the appropriate heading. If you don't see an appropriate heading, call the magazine and ask if it will create one for you.

If you sell information by mail, avoid putting your classified under the heading "Books and Booklets." This will reduce orders. Instead, put the ad under a heading related to the subject matter. For example, if you are selling a book on how to make money cleaning chimneys, place the ad under "Business Opportunities."

You can test a classified ad by running it just one time in a publication. The problem is, most magazines, and even weekly newspapers, have long lead times—several weeks or more—for placing classified ads. If you place the ad to run one time only and the ad pulls well, you then must wait several weeks or months until you can get it in the publication again.

In a weekly newspaper or magazine, I test a classified ad by running it for one month—four consecutive issues. For a monthly publication, I test it for three months—three consecutive issues. If the first insertion is profitable, I will probably extend the insertion order for several months so the ad runs continuously with no interruption.

With a full-page ad, you usually get the greatest number of orders the first time the ad runs in the magazine. Response declines with each additional insertion; at the point where the ad is not going to be profitable in its next insertion, you pull it and try another ad.

The reason for this response pattern is that the first time the ad runs, it skims the cream of the prospects, getting orders from those most likely to buy. Those who buy from the first insertion of the ad will not buy when it runs again. Therefore, each time the ad runs it reaches a smaller and smaller audience of potential new buyers.

While response to full-page mail-order ads declines with each insertion, the response to a classified ad can remain steady for many insertions. Indeed, some mail-order operators (and I am one of them) have run the same classified ad monthly in the same magazine for years at a time, with no decline in response. Response sometimes increases during the first twelve months the ad is run, as people see the ad over and over again and eventually become curious enough to respond.

Some people who responded once, received your sales literature, and didn't buy, may respond several times, and get your literature several times, before they eventually break down and buy. Also, keep in mind that each issue reaches a number of new subscribers via subscriptions and newsstand circulation, so the total audience for a classified remains fairly constant.

# 7

# WRITING DIRECT MAIL

According to an article in *Forbes,* Dr. Roger Breslow, a New York state internist, kept and crated every piece of direct mail he received. Within a year, the crate tipped the scale at 502 pounds.

No doubt about it: Direct mail is more popular than ever before. According to the Direct Marketing Association, the amount of money spent on direct mail in 2004 was $21.21 billion, up from $11 billion in 1982.

Today, more than 50 billion pieces of direct mail pass through the post office each year. That averages out to about one piece of "junk mail" for every American every other mailing day.

There are a number of factors that account for direct mail's popularity as an advertising medium.

First, you can measure the results by counting how many order forms or reply cards come back. With print ads and broadcast commercials you usually don't know how effective your efforts have been. But direct-mail advertisers always know whether a mailing is profitable or not.

Second, direct mail can be targeted to select groups of

prospects through the careful selection of the proper mailing lists. The copy for each mailing can be tailored to the needs of the various groups of prospects you want to reach. And, you can send as few—or as many—mailing pieces as your budget allows. Which makes direct mail cost-effective for both big corporations and smaller advertisers alike.

Third, direct mail gives you great flexibility in your presentation. Print advertising is limited by the size of the page, broadcast by the length of the commercial. Direct-mail writers can use as many words and pictures as it takes to make the sale. (I recently received a direct-mail piece that featured a 16-page sales letter!) Your mailing can even include a sample of the product or a gift for the reader.

Because of these advantages, many advertisers use direct mail for a wide variety of applications:

- To sell products by mail
- To generate sales leads
- To answer product inquiries
- To distribute catalogs, newsletters, and other sales literature
- To motivate the sales force
- To keep in touch with former customers
- To get more business from current customers
- To follow up inquiries
- To tie in with other media such as telemarketing, print advertising, and broadcast (Publishers Clearing House, for example, runs TV commercials alerting consumers to look for the Clearing House sweepstakes offer in the mail)
- To invite prospects to attend seminars, conferences, hospitality suites, and trade show exhibits
- To renew subscriptions, memberships, service contracts, and insurance policies
- To get customers to come to the store

- To distribute information, news, product samples
- To conduct research surveys
- To build goodwill
- To announce a sale

## A PERSONAL MEDIUM

The main difference between direct mail and space advertising is that mail is a personal medium. A letter is a one-to-one communication from one human being to another. An ad appearing in a magazine will be seen by thousands or millions of other readers. But a letter is for your eyes only.

Now, it's true that most direct mail is mass-produced and distributed in bulk mailings to thousands of prospects. Still, the reader views mail as more personal than a magazine or newspaper. The trick is to take advantage of this—by creating direct mail that captures the best characteristics of personal mail.

Unlike an ad, a sales letter is signed. So the writer can use the first person—"I" writing to "you," the reader—to personalize the sale message.

The tone of the letter should also be personal. Successful direct-mail writers favor an informal, conversational style. They use contractions, colloquial language, and short, snappy sentences. Their letters brim with personality, enthusiasm, warmth, and sincerity.

Unlike print advertising, which is a new medium for the novice copywriter, direct mail should come easy; we all have experience in letter writing. But too many direct-mail letters sound like . . . well, like advertising. When you write direct mail, don't suppress your natural style. Let the words flow in your own voice. Write the direct-mail letter as if you were writing a letter to a friend.

Direct mail is almost always a response-oriented medium. It asks for the order (or at least for some type of action) *now*, not in a day or a week or a month from now. Direct-mail writers need to generate an immediate response from the reader. This is why most direct-mail packages include an order form, a reply envelope, and copy that tells you to "act now—don't delay—send in your order TODAY!"

As I mentioned, you have great flexibility in the elements you include in your mailing package. As the copywriter, you decide. Should the package contain a letter? A brochure? An order form? A reply card? A sample? A second letter? A second or third brochure?

The "classic" direct-mail package contains an outer envelope, a letter, a brochure, and a reply card. But knowledgeable direct-mail writers vary this format to suit their objectives. Of course, there's always the option of using a completely different format, such as a self-mailer or an invoice-stuffer.

The heart of the package is the sales letter. Most of the selling is done in the letter; the brochure is used to highlight sales points, illustrate the product, and provide technical information not appropriate to a letter. There's an old saying among direct-mail writers: "The letter sells; the brochure tells."

This chapter focuses on writing the sales letter. I'll also talk about envelopes and order forms. Brochures are touched on briefly here and covered in more detail in chapter 8.

## SALES LETTER MECHANICS

It's easy to begin an ad, because they all follow the same format: headline first, visual that illustrates the headline, and lead paragraph that expands on the headline.

But the writer has more options with the start of a sales letter. First, there's the choice of whether to personalize the letter with the individual recipient's name and address, or send out a form letter.

To personalize, you use a computer to generate customized letters for each person on the mailing list, and that's expensive. Personalized letters generally get a better response, as long as they look personally typed and sound personal in tone. Don't overdo it by repeating the person's name over and over in the letter ("so, MR. RAYMOND, we have reserved this special offer for you and the whole RAYMOND family . . ."). This technique sounds insincere; you wouldn't use the person's name that often if you were speaking face to face.

Also, avoid the old-fashioned "ink jet" printing systems that produce letters in which the name is obviously inserted into a form letter. The letter should look as if it were typed by hand; you can achieve this effect with a PC and laser printer.

In most assignments, economy will require that you use preprinted letters. Some advertisers print form letters and then type in each prospect's name and address (this is the "match and fill" technique). But match and fill is time-consuming, and mailing tests show that match-and-fill letters often don't pull any better than form letters with headlines running across the top.

There are exceptions. It pays to personalize sales letters going to existing customers, and also when writing to high-level executives. The bigger the corporation and the higher up the corporate ladder the recipient, the more likely personalization is to pay off.

Set the letter headline in large, bold typeface, such as 20-point Arial Black. You can place the headline above the salutation, and as an option, you can center the headline and put it in a box to call attention to it. Such a box is called a Johnson Box.

The body copy of the letter should be set in a typewriter

font, not in Times Roman or another PC font, because the direct-mail letter should look like a personal letter, not like an ad or brochure. I recommend Prestige Elite or New Courier for sales letter body copy.

In some letters, you may decide against a headline and simply start with the salutation: Dear Friend, Dear Reader, Dear Business Executive, Dear Friend of the Smithsonian Institute.

A salutation that identifies with the reader's special interest—Dear Farmer, Dear Lawyer, Dear Computer Enthusiast, Dear Future Millionaire—is always better than Dear Sir, Dear Madame, or Dear Friend.

Sometimes you will use a salutation only. Sometimes, a salutation and a headline. In some cases, a headline without a salutation may be more appropriate.

## 15 WAYS TO START YOUR SALES LETTER

The first sentence of your letter is the most important one. This sentence signals whether there is something of interest in your letter or whether it is worthless junk mail to be thrown away without a second glance. The lead must hook the reader's attention, but it must also entice him to read further.

Over the years, letter writers have found that there are certain types of openings that are more effective in direct mail than other types. Here are samples of 15 of those leads. When you're struggling with your first letters, turn to these examples for possible ideas on how to structure your own opening.

### 1. State the Offer

The offer consists of the product for sale, its price, the terms of the sale (including discounts), and the guarantee.

If your offer is particularly attractive, you may make the offer—and not the product or its benefits—the theme of the letter. Here's how the International Preview Society featured a free ten-day trial offer in a sales letter selling Beethoven CDs:

Yours FREE for 10 days—
the legendary music of Beethoven—
Nine Symphonies that epitomize the
beauty and harmony denied him in life.

Plus FREE Preview bonus.

Dear Music Lover,

Beethoven. The name alone calls to mind some of the greatest music of the ages . . .

The letter writer figured that the reader already appreciated Beethoven, so there was no need to sell her on Beethoven's symphonies. And it's hard to sell one set of classical recordings over another based on the orchestra or conductor or the quality of the performance. So, the copywriter concentrated on the offer—a free trial plus a free bonus CD—just for accepting the trial offer.

The headline was typed with an ordinary typewriter font and positioned where the reader's name and address would normally appear in a personal letter.

## 2. Highlight the Free Literature

Letters that seek to generate inquiries from potential customers usually offer the reader a free brochure, booklet, catalog, or other piece of sales literature. You can increase response by stressing the offer of free literature, and by centering the sales pitch on the benefits of the literature rather than those of the product or service.

Here's an example from a letter sent to me by The Mutual Life Insurance Company of New York:

Dear Friend:
We have reserved for you a free copy of Prentice-Hall's *TAX-SAVING STRATEGIES*, a helpful book for Corporate Executives and Professionals. It contains practical, timely, and useful ways for you to maximize the value of your deductions and save dollars.

## 3. Make an Announcement

If you have something new to announce—a special offer, a new product, a new club, a one-of-a-kind event—start your letter with this important news.

From the publishers of *Encyclopedia Britannica:*

Now . . . we've overcome the last reason
for not owning *The New Encyclopedia Britannica.*
Money.

Dear Friend:
If money were no object, would you own *Britannica 3*? Of course. Most people would.
   Well, now I'm happy to say that you can acquire *Britannica 3* for far less than you thought possible. You can do so . . . direct from the publisher . . . at a substantial Group Discount.

Another example, this one a letter from Calhoun's Collectors Society:

In the world of U.S. stamps, there is only one name older than that of the Federal Bureau of Engraving and Printing itself. The revered house of Scott—known since 1863 as the ultimate authority on American philately.
   Now, for the first time ever, Scott's stamp experts have selected the subjects to be commemorated in a limited philatelic edition that is unprecedented in collecting annals.

## 4. Tell a Story

Copy written in story format has great reader appeal. First, it creates empathy with the reader. By telling a story that relates to the reader's own situation, you build a bridge between the reader's needs and your sales pitch. Second, people are familiar with stories and enjoy reading them. The news they get from newspapers, magazines, and television is related to them in narrative form. Stories hold their interest and get them to read letters they might otherwise put aside.

A subscription letter for *INC.* magazine begins with the story of a man who quit his job to become an entrepreneur—a move many of us with corporate positions daydream of now and then:

Dear Executive,

Three years ago this month, a man I know—he was then a vice president of a big corporation in Illinois—walked into his boss's office and handed in his resignation.

Two weeks later, he started his own company.

The man had everything going for him. He was smart, he was energetic, he was dedicated, and he knew his particular field inside out.

Almost from the start, the new company caught on. It grew quickly, adding new customers, new employees, new equipment.

But then, about a year ago, the picture began to change. Orders were still coming in, but the company was stumbling. Things went steadily from bad to worse until . . .

A week ago Friday, that man—who had started out on his own with such high hopes just three years before—was forced to go out of business. His company closed its doors for good.

What happened? What went wrong? Could it have been avoided? How? . . .

This story holds our attention because it could happen to us someday. We want to know what went wrong and how *INC.* magazine can help us avoid the same mistakes.

## 5. Flatter the Reader

One reason many people take a negative view toward direct mail is that they know it isn't really personal. They know they are just one of thousands of people whose names the advertiser obtained from a mailing list.

But you can turn this fact to your advantage by using flattery. Tell the reader, "Yes, I got your name from a list. Yes, you're part of that group. But that group is special; the people in it have superior characteristics that set them apart from the crowd. And you're superior, too. That's why I'm writing to you."

There is flattery in the opening of a letter from the Maserati Import Company, a seller of luxury automobiles:

> Dear Mr. McCoy:
> One of a kind. Is that phrase a little trite?
>     I used to think so until I tried to find you.
>     Now I know what "one of a kind" really means.
>     The process of finding your name and address was the advertising equivalent of panning for gold. . . .

The letter goes on to offer the reader a free bottle of French champagne if he will test drive a Maserati luxury sedan.

## 6. Write to the Reader Peer-to-Peer

The logic here is that people in special-interest groups—and most direct mail is aimed at narrow groups of prospects—will be more receptive to a sales pitch from a peer than from an outsider.

So, a letter aimed at farmers should be signed by a farmer.

And it should be written in the plain, straightforward language of one farmer talking to another.

With this approach, the writer can achieve empathy with the reader by saying, "Look . . . I am like you. I know your problems. I've been through them myself. And I've found a solution. You can trust me."

In a subscription letter for *Writer's Digest*, the pitch is made by one writer talking to other writers:

> Dear Writer:
> I don't have the great American novel in me.
> I flunked Poetry 102 in college. My first, last, and only short story was rejected by 14 magazines. . . .

### 7. A Personal Message from the President

In direct mail, the owner or manager of a business can talk directly with his or her customers.

Customers like dealing with the person in charge. When the top person in your company signs the letter, it makes the reader feel important. And having the owner's signature on the advertising adds a bit more credibility to the message. (I've often heard people say of such mail, "Well, he wouldn't sign it if it wasn't true.")

FutureSoft begins a brochure on its Quickpro software package with a letter from the company president:

> Personal Message to Microcomputer Owners from Joseph W.
> Tamargo, President of FUTURE-SOFT . . .
> I want to tell you why I have chosen to send you an actual condensation of the Operating Instructions of our exciting and unique QUICKPRO, which writes programs for you.

Another example, this one from John L. Blair, president of the New Process Company, a mail-order clothing manufacturer:

Dear Mr. Bly:

A memo recently crossed my desk that said I would have to
RAISE MY PRICES—NOW—to offset our spiraling operating
costs!

But I said, "NO! NOT YET!"

I know that customers like you, Mr. Bly, expect the BEST
VALUE for their money when they shop at NPC. And that's
why I'm going to hold the line on higher prices just as long as
I possibly can! . . .

## 8. Use a Provocative Quote

The quote should contain news, a startling statistic or fact, or
say something outrageous. The quote must be like the lead of a
news story—it must raise a question or arouse curiosity to make
the reader want to read the body of the letter to find out more.

In a letter selling a new book on advertising, Prentice-Hall
began with a quotation taken directly from the book itself:

Advertising agencies and other consultants score something on
the order of a 9 on my Least-Needed scale of 1-to-10. . . .

This is what Lewis Kornfeld has to say, based on his extraordinary success as Radio Shack's master marketer for over 30
years.

## 9. Ask a Question

Question leads are effective when the answer to the question is
interesting or important to the reader, or when the question
arouses genuine curiosity.

Here are a few examples of letters that lead with a question:

Dear Friend,

What do you think when you see a letter that starts with "Dear
Friend" . . . a letter from someone you've never met?

WHAT DO JAPANESE MANAGERS HAVE THAT AMERICAN
MANAGERS SOMETIMES LACK?
How about workers with good attitudes?

Dear Mr. Blake:
Is freelance a dirty word to you? It really shouldn't be . . .

## 10. Make It Personal

The most personal direct-mail piece I ever received began as
follows:

Dear Friend,
As you may already know, we have been doing some work for
people who have the same last name as you do. Finally, after
months of work, THE AMAZING STORY OF THE BLYS IN
AMERICA is ready for print and you are in it!

This letter is highly personal for two reasons. First, my
name appears several times in the body of the letter. Second,
the product is designed especially for me, a Bly. (But the letter
is weakened by the stock opening "Dear Friend." A better salutation is the more personal "Dear Friend Bly.")

Personalized mail usually gets more attention than form
letters. So whenever possible, make it personal. Insert the
reader's name in the copy once or twice (if your budget allows
for computer letters). And, more important, make sure the
copy speaks to the needs, interests, and ego of the reader (as a
book called *The Amazing Story of the Blys in America* has
strong appeal to people named Bly).

## 11. Identify the Reader's Problem

If your product or service solves a problem, you can create a
strong sales letter by featuring the problem in the lead, then
telling how the product or service solves the problem.

There are two advantages to this technique. First, it selects a specific group of readers for your letter. (Only single people will respond to a letter that begins, "Are You Sick and Tired of Paying Extra Taxes Just Because You Aren't Married?")

Second, the format shows in a clear and direct manner how the product solves the reader's problem. When you start with the problem, the natural next step is to talk about the solution.

Manhattan dentist Dr. Brian E. Weiss used this technique in a letter inviting me in for an appointment:

> Dear Mr. Bly:
> You know how difficult it is to look your best if dental problems are causing discomfort and pain or if the appearance of your teeth needs improvement.
>
> Have you been putting off a dental checkup or consultation on an existing problem? This note may encourage you to take the important step to help yourself feel better by making a dental appointment. . . .

Politician Jim Thompson used the technique in a campaign letter aimed at voters in Chicago:

> Dear Mrs. Vanderbilt:
> If you can't afford higher taxes.
> If you're afraid to walk the streets at night.
> If you're sick and tired of corrupt government officials.
> If your children aren't getting the education they deserve.
> Then you don't need a Governor appointed by Chicago's City Hall. . . .

### 12. Stress a Benefit

A straightforward presentation of a benefit can outpull other techniques if the benefit is significant and has strong appeal to the reader.

A sales letter from Prentice-Hall offering a new book on advertising began with the headline, "Just published . . . HOW TO MAKE YOUR ADVERTISING MAKE MONEY. A clear, concise guide to effective advertising . . ." The headline is effective because it's safe to assume that all advertising professionals who receive the letter want to create more effective advertising.

To get results, a benefit-oriented headline must appeal to the reader's self-interest. As Cahners Publishing points out in their booklet, *How to Create and Produce Successful Direct Mail*, "Don't tell your prospect about your grass seed, tell him about his lawn."

### 13. Use Human Interest

People enjoy reading about other people, especially about people who have anxieties, fears, problems, and interests similar to their own.

Some of the strongest sales letters center around powerful, dramatic human interest stories. The readers get hooked because the events in the story relate somehow to their own lives. And the letter leaves more of an impression because it deals with human emotions, not just technical product features or abstract sales arguments.

The publisher of *Cardiac Alert* newsletter used an autobiographical approach to add human interest to a sales letter asking for subscriptions to his publication. The headline read:

When I was 16, my father died of a heart attack . . .

You can't help but be interested in the letter that follows.

### 14. Let the Reader in on Some Inside Information

When a consumer sees your ad in a magazine, he knows he is sharing your message with tens of thousands of other people.

But he has no way of knowing whether you've sent the sales letter he received to thousands of prospects, or just a select few.

Direct mail is an excellent medium for appealing to the reader's need to feel special, important, exclusive. And nothing is more exclusive than revealing some inside information on a sale or product that others don't know about.

Here's exclusive news from a cover letter mailed along with a reprint of a magazine ad:

> Here's a fresh-from-the-printer reprint of our latest *WALL STREET JOURNAL* ad . . .
>
> We'll be running the ad in June because we want potential customers to know more about our latest financial planning services.
>
> But, as someone we've done business with before, we consider YOU even more important than the "new business" out there.
>
> Which is why we're sending you our new ad months before it will break in the press.
>
> You see, we wanted you to be the first to know about our new services which can save you time and build your retirement nest egg.

The message is: We're telling you first because we think you're special.

And what reader of direct mail doesn't think he or she is special?

### 15. Sweepstakes

A sweepstakes can greatly increase the response to a direct-mail campaign. One sweepstakes mailing I received began:

> American Family Publishers Announces America's First By-Mail
> GUARANTEED   MULTIMILLION-DOLLAR   SWEEPSTAKES

OFFER: R BLY, A LOCAL NY RESIDENT, MAY HAVE ALREADY WON ONE MILLION DOLLARS.

There are three ways of structuring a sweepstakes:

YOU MAY WIN . . .

YOU MAY HAVE WON . . .

YOU HAVE WON . . .

The "you have won" sweepstakes generates the most entries because the consumer is guaranteed a prize. This sweepstakes is expensive to run because you must award the consolation prize to everyone who claims it.

The "you may have won" is the second most effective sweepstakes. Here the reader is told that the winning entry number has been preselected by computer—and that you just may hold that winning entry number in your hand.

These are 15 common ways of starting your sales letter. There are others. Read the direct mail you receive and keep a file of effective direct-mail leads and letters to use as a reference in your own work.

## SHOULD YOU USE AN ENVELOPE TEASER?

The outer envelope is the first thing the reader sees when receiving your mailing package. It is here the selling starts. If the outer envelope fails to entice the reader to open the letter, or worse, if it prompts him to throw the letter away, the brilliant copy of your sales letter will be wasted.

There are two basic approaches to outer envelopes. The first is to start your sales pitch right away with headlines and copy printed on the outer envelope. This copy, known as "teaser copy," is designed to entice the reader to open the envelope by arousing curiosity or promising a strong reward for reading the package.

The problem with this strategy is that teasers are labels that instantly identify the package as containing advertising matter. Large headlines and copy lines printed on an envelope shout at the reader, "This is advertising . . . junk mail . . . it's worthless . . . throw it away!"

My rule is: Use a teaser only if it contains an irresistible message that will compel the reader to open the envelope. But don't feel you must use a teaser; a weak teaser can actually reduce response versus a package with a plain envelope!

We know that people always open their personal mail before they open junk mail. We also know that many people throw away every "teaser" envelope they receive without a second glance.

Teasers are effective only when the message is compelling. For example, I'd have a hard time ignoring an envelope with the teaser, "Inside: The Secret to Living Longer and Feeling Better . . . Without Dieting or Special Exercise."

On the other hand, you'd probably save yourself the trouble of opening an envelope that began, "Sawyer Life Insurance Announces its 50th Year of Operation . . . Quality Service to the Community for Over Half a Century."

Teasers can take many forms. You can have a headline only. Or a headline plus copy.

You can use an envelope with a window so the teaser is copy that shows through the window.

You can mail the package in a clear plastic bag so the whole package shows through to tease the reader.

You can even print illustrations, graphics, and photos on the outer envelope.

However, most teasers seem to follow one of three basic formats:

1. THIS IS THE BEST WIDGET EVER MADE
2. THIS WIDGET MAY SAVE YOU UP TO $500
3. ENCLOSED IS YOUR FREE WIDGET

The third teaser works best because it promises a reward for opening the envelope. (The promise of a prize inside has sold millions of dollars' worth of Cracker Jacks and breakfast cereals.) Even though you know you hold advertising material in your hands, teaser #3 overcomes your resistance to junk mail by making you wonder what's inside.

Teaser #1 is the worst. It's pure boasting, and the reader's reaction to the smug claim will be to throw the mailing away.

Teaser #2, though not as effective as #3, is still an improvement over #1 because it makes the promise of a benefit. This promise says to the reader, "Yes, you hold junk mail in your hands. But it might be worth your while to open the envelope and see what we can do for you."

Often a blank envelope—one with no teaser—is more effective than one with a teaser. The idea behind the no-teaser approach is to make the direct-mail package resemble personal mail. When the reader sees the envelope, he's not sure whether the envelope contains personal mail or advertising material—and so he opens it, just to be sure. Once the mailer is opened, the battle is half won; if the letter contains a strong, compelling lead, you will hook the prospect and get him to read the body copy.

When using the no-teaser approach, take pains to make the letter look like personal mail. Use a plain white or off-white envelope. Don't let any brightly colored sales literature show through the window, if there is one. And don't embellish the envelope with a company logo; just have the return address set in plain type.

## THE LETTER SELLS, THE BROCHURE TELLS

Many direct-mail packages do an effective selling job with a letter and reply form only.

Every direct-mail package should contain a letter; flyers and brochures are optional. As the writer, you must decide whether a flyer is needed.

Here are some helpful suggestions:

Use a flyer when you are selling products that are colorful or visually impressive: subscriptions to colorful magazines, flowers, fruit, fine foods, coins, collectibles, sports equipment, consumer electronics.

Some products are most effectively sold through demonstration. But you usually can't demonstrate by mail. The next best thing is to take step-by-step photos of a demonstration and put them in a flyer to be included in the mailer.

Sometimes the offer is so strong that the writer decides to devote the letter solely to the benefits of the sale. The benefits of the product itself can then be covered in an accompanying flyer.

Use a flyer for transmitting technical data or product information that is too detailed to be explained or listed in the letter.

In writing direct mail to sell books, I list a detailed table of contents in a flyer separate from the letter. This way, the small percentage of readers interested in some esoteric topic can scan the contents to see if it is included. And if it is, the flyer will have tipped the odds in favor of a sale.

You are not limited to one flyer or one letter or one order form. You can include whatever you think it will take to make the sale.

## HOW TO INCREASE RESPONSE TO YOUR MAILINGS

In direct mail, response is the name of the game. Maintaining a dignified image or getting people to remember your message is not important. The only thing that counts is how many sales or inquiries your mailing generates. The more responses, the more successful the mailer.

Reaching the right audience with the right offer and the right copy is the key to successful direct mail. But a number of response-increasing techniques have little to do with copywriting skill or common sense. Here are a few that you can use:

- Always include a response mechanism. This can be a business reply card, reply envelope, order form, Web site URL, or toll-free 800-number.
- Use self-addressed, postage-paid envelopes and reply cards (known as business reply envelopes and business reply cards). They generate more response than cards or envelopes that require a postage stamp from the prospect.
- Order forms and reply cards with tear-off stubs or receipts generate more response than those without.
- The letter should be the first thing the reader sees when he opens the envelope. The package should have a natural flow from outer envelope to letter to flyer to reply card.
- Offer a premium: a gift to prospects who respond to the mailing. The premium should be something that they want, and it should relate to the product or the offer.
- Offer something of value in return for responding to the letter: a free brochure, booklet, catalog, demonstration, survey, estimate, consultation, or trial offer.
- Allow for a negative response. And turn it into a positive. The reply card for a letter promoting my freelance copywriting services gives the reader the option of checking off a box that reads, "Not interested right now. But try us

again in _____." Even if the reader doesn't need my services now, she can still respond to the mailing.

- Use physical objects in the mailing. An envelope that feels bulky almost always gets opened. These objects can include product samples, premiums, 3-D pop-ups, and other gimmicks. (In the last year or so I've received direct-mail packages that contained instant coffee, chili powder, a set of coasters, a calendar, pens, pencils, a flashlight, and a magnifying glass.) Although costly, mailings with objects enclosed can really stand out in a mailbox or in a basket full of flat envelopes containing regular letters and flyers.

- Put a time limit on the offer. Once the reader puts the letter aside, she probably won't come back to it, so you'll get the most response if you urge her to act now . . . by putting a time limit on the offer.

- You can put a real date limit on the offer ("Remember, Beethoven's Violin Concerto is yours to keep just for taking advantage of this offer within the next 10 days").

- You can hint that the offer won't last forever ("But hurry—supplies are limited").

- Or, you can add a sense of urgency to your call for action ("Remember—the time to buy insurance is before tragedy strikes. Not after").

- Make the outer envelope resemble an invoice, telegram, or other "official-looking" document. People almost always open such envelopes.

- Use a plain outer envelope with no copy, not even a return address. The mystery of such a mailing is irresistible.

- Use a P.S. in the letter to restate the offer or reemphasize a sales point; 80 percent of readers will read a P.S.

- Guarantee the offer. When you sell by mail, make a money-back guarantee good for 15, 30, 60, or even 90 days.

- When you are generating leads, tell the prospect that he's under no obligation and that no salesperson will call (unless he wants one to).
- Envelopes addressed with labels are as effective as envelopes individually typed with the recipient's address. Addressing envelopes by hand reduces response, perhaps because it looks amateurish.
- If your mailing list contains titles but not names, print a description of the person you're trying to reach on the outer envelope ("Attention Buyers of Electronic Components— Important Information Inside").
- A preprinted postage permit or postage-metered envelope outpulls an envelope with stamps.
- An order form printed in color, or designed as an elaborate certificate, or printed with a lot of information outpulls a clean, ordinary-looking order form.
- Letters with indented paragraphs, underlined words, and portions of the text set in a second color outpull plain letters.
- Letters with a lot of "bells and whistles"—arrows, fake handwritten notes in the margins, spot illustrations, highlighting—can increase response when mailed to low- and middle-class consumer audiences. Avoid these techniques when writing to business executives or upper-class consumers.
- A form letter with a headline is just as effective as a form letter with the recipient's name and address typed in by hand.
- A package with a separate letter and brochure does better than a combination letter/brochure.
- Repeat the offer on the reply card.
- Use action words in the first sentence of the reply card and restate the offer in the body copy. ("YES, I'd like to know

how I can cut my phone bill in half. Please send literature on your long-distance service. I understand I'm under no obligation and that no salesperson will call.")

• Avoid intimidating, legal-type wording. State your offer, terms, and guarantee in plain, simple English.

• Make it simple to respond to the mailing. This means having a simple offer and an easy-to-complete order form. And be sure to leave enough space on the form for the reader to fill in the required information (a surprising number of reply cards and coupons don't).

• Keep in mind the buyer's level of interest in your product so you don't oversell or undersell. (Prospects whose names were taken from the *PC Magazine* mailing list probably have a greater interest in video games than the subscribers of *Field and Stream.*)

Writing direct mail is the best education I can recommend for both novice and experienced copywriters alike. Within a few weeks of your mailing, you know whether your copy is successful or not. No other form of copywriting, except for online marketing, yields such immediate or such precise feedback on your work.

# 8

# WRITING BROCHURES, CATALOGS, AND OTHER SALES MATERIALS

Promotional literature has been around for a long time. According to *Ripley's Believe It or Not*, the first brochure was written by Hernán Cortés 465 years ago. It was circulated as a broadside to the people of Spain by Charles V, and it advertised a sale on turkeys.

Today, few businesses operate without some kind of printed sales literature to hand out to customers and prospects. Travel agents, supermarkets, department stores, industrial manufacturers, consultants, insurance agents, colleges, and dozens of other types of organizations depend on brochures, circulars, flyers, catalogs, and other printed advertising matter to help make the sale.

Advertisers need sales literature for two reasons. First, credibility—people expect a "real" company to have printed product literature. Anyone can spend $50 on letterhead and business cards and call themselves a corporation. But a brochure proves you are in business and shows you're more than a fly-by-night operation.

Second, the brochure is a time-saving device. People want printed information they can take home with them and study at their leisure. But it would take too much time to type individual letters of information to every prospect that asked about your product.

The solution is to collect your basic product information in a single, mass-produced brochure. The brochure gives prospects most of the information they need to know; the rest can be filled in by letter, phone, or a visit to the store.

Even PC-literate consumers, who can find out what they need to know about your product by going to your Web site, will frequently ask to receive sales literature. A brochure saves them the trouble of printing out your Web site and circulating those pages to other decision makers in their organization.

Brochures support advertising and direct-mail programs. They are also used as sales tools by salespeople and distributors. Brochures are a handy way of quickly communicating the essentials of your business to new customers, prospects, employees, and dealers.

Brochures are primarily a medium of information. They tell prospects what the product is and what it can do for them. Your brochure should also explain how the product works, why people should buy it, and how they can order.

But a good sales brochure does more than explain and inform. It also persuades. Remember, the brochure is a sales tool, not an instruction manual. Good brochure copy does more than list facts or product features; it translates these facts and features into customer benefits—reasons why the customer should buy the product.

## 11 TIPS ON WRITING BETTER SALES BROCHURES

Here are 11 tips on writing brochures that tell readers what they want to know and sell them on buying the product:

**1. Know where the brochure fits into the buying process.**
Unlike package goods you buy off a supermarket shelf (soap, shampoo, canned beans, cigarettes), products that require a brochure are seldom sold in a single step. Computers, cars, vacation trips, insurance, telephones, financial services, seminars, club memberships, real estate, and dozens of other products and services require several meetings or contacts between buyer and seller before the sale is closed.

For most of these products and services, a brochure comes in somewhere between initial contact and final sale. But where? Do you write the brochure for the uninformed buyer who shows initial interest in the product? Or is the brochure used to build credibility and answer questions as you get closer to closing the sale?

The answer is: It depends on the product, the market, and the advertiser's individual approach to making the sale. Some advertisers might even use a series of brochures to guide the buyer through the steps of the buying process.

For instance, I make my living as an advertising copywriter. I get sales leads from many sources: ads I run in advertising journals, direct mail, publicity from articles and speeches I give, word of mouth, and referral from other clients.

When a lead comes in, I chat with the caller to determine his level of interest. By asking a few questions over the phone, I can quickly determine whether the caller is a likely potential customer for my service.

Once I qualify the lead by phone, the next step is to send a comprehensive package of sales literature. It contains seven or eight separate pieces including a biography, client list, four-page sales letter, reprints of articles I've written, samples of my copy, a price list, and a form the prospect can use to order copy by mail. In short, it contains everything the prospect needs to know about my freelance copywriting services.

From this material, the prospect should be able to decide whether to hire me. There may be a follow-up call or a mailing of more samples of my work, but the basic literature package allows the client to order the service directly, by mail. No additional information or sales visits are required.

On the other hand, a friend of mine who is a management consultant mails very little information to prospects. He sends a brief cover note along with a slim booklet that presents his services in concise outline form.

The reason he sends incomplete information is that the next step in his sales sequence is a meeting with the prospect. If he sent a package as weighty as mine, there would be nothing left to follow up with. But by sending less, he whets the reader's appetite with key sales benefits of his service, while raising questions that can only be answered if the reader requests a face-to-face meeting with the consultant.

Keep in mind that we both have Web sites with extensive information about our backgrounds, qualifications, services, and clients. But many prospects who are willing to take the time to visit my Web site also say "send me some information in the mail."

Here are some of the ways brochures can fit into the buying process:

• *As leave-behinds.* A leave-behind is a brochure you leave behind after a meeting with a potential customer. The leave-behind brochure should summarize your sales pitch and contain a fairly complete description of the product and its benefits.

• *As point-of-sale literature.* Point-of-sale literature is displayed at the point of sale. A travel agent's office, for example, contains racks of brightly colored pamphlets on faraway places. The cover of the point-of-sale literature should have a catchy headline and visual that team up to make passersby stop, pick up, and keep the brochure.

• *To respond to inquiries.* An inquiry is a request for more information about your product. The person making the inquiry became interested in you through your advertising, publicity, or referral, and represents a "hot" sales lead— someone much more likely to buy than a prospect who has not contacted you.

The inquiry fulfillment package should contain enough information to answer the prospect's questions and convince him to take the next step in the buying process. The hot prospect has already expressed interest in your product, so don't hesitate to load your inquiry fulfillment package full of facts and sales points.

• *As direct mail.* As mentioned in chapter 7, brochures and flyers are used to add information to direct-mail packages. The sales letter does the selling; the brochure provides additional sales points, lists technical features, and contains photos and drawings of the product. In the interest of keeping mailing costs down, this type of brochure is usually slim (and is designed to fit in a standard mailing envelope).

• *As a sales support tool.* Many products—hospital supplies, office equipment, life insurance, industrial equipment—are sold by salespeople who visit prospects at their home or office. These salespeople use brochures as selling aids in their sales pitches (and also as leave-behinds). Such brochures have large pages, big illustrations, and bold headlines and subheads that lead the salesperson and prospect through the pitch. Sometimes, a standard product brochure is adapted for use as a sales aid and printed as separate panels in a three-ring binder or self-standing easel that sits on the prospect's desk.

Whatever your application—leave-behind, point-of-sale, inquiry fulfillment, direct mail, or sales support—let the advertiser's particular method of selling be your guide in writing and designing the brochure. The best brochures contain just the right amount of product information and sales pitch to lead the prospect from one step of the buying process to the next.

One additional tip on designing sales literature: Think about how the reader will use and file the brochure. A small pocket-size brochure may be ideal for direct mail or point-of-sale display, but it will be lost in a file folder or on a bookshelf of full-size literature (8½ by 11 inches, the kind your competition is probably publishing).

In the same way, a brochure of unconventional shape or size may stand out from the crowd but might be thrown away because it won't fit in a standard file cabinet. And a brochure aimed at purchasing agents will probably be punched for a three-hole binder, which means part of your copy will be punched out unless you leave margins for binding.

### 2. Know whether the brochure stands alone or is supported by other materials.

In some selling situations, the brochure stands alone. Aside from the salesperson, it is the only sales tool the company has.

Other firms use a brochure to supplement their promotional campaign, which may consist of print advertising, radio and TV commercials, direct mail, publicity, trade shows, and seminars.

Some companies have one product—and one brochure. Others use a series of brochures, each describing one product in their product line, or one segment of the total market they sell to.

The brochure writer must know whether his brochure stands alone or is supported by other material, because the existence of other material determines the content of his brochure.

For example, a company that has detailed product features and specifications on its Web site may elect to simply summarize the high points in the brochure, and include the Web site URL as a source of more detailed information.

Some duplication between different promotional pieces may be necessary, but avoid creating too many redundant sales brochures. For instance, I normally devote half a page of an eight-page product brochure to a description of the manufacturer and their capabilities and resources as a major corporation.

But, if the manufacturer already had a separate "corporate capabilities brochure," I wouldn't need to do that. Instead, we could mail both brochures—product and company—to prospects requesting more information.

Another example: A client asked me to write a sales brochure on an industrial mixer. He wanted to include detailed calculations on how to determine the energy consumption of the mixer.

Although some engineers might be curious as to how the calculation is done, such an elaborate mathematical treatment is wasted space in a selling piece. The solution was to talk about energy savings without showing the calculation in the sales brochure, and create a separate "technical information sheet" that showed the detailed calculation.

Find out the environment in which your brochure will be working. Is it a stand-alone brochure or part of a series? Is it supported by print ads, direct mail, publicity?

Has the advertiser also published an annual report, corporate capabilities brochure, catalog, or other general brochure describing the corporation? Are there article reprints, fact sheets, or other pieces of literature that can be mailed along with the main brochure?

Form should follow function. I was asked to write sales literature describing a system of modular software. For this modular product, I wrote a modular brochure. The main piece is a four-page folder. Copy giving the reader an overview of the system is printed on the left inside page; the right page is a pocket containing 16 sheets, each describing a different software module.

This approach allows salespeople to use the sheets as separate flyers for presentations and mailings. In addition, the brochure is easy to update. When a new modular program is added to the package, we just add a flyer to the brochure.

*3. Know your audience.*

We've already seen that a brochure must fit into the right step in the buying process. Your brochure must also fit the informational needs of your audience. Think about the readers and what they expect to get out of the brochure. Ask yourself, "How can I use the brochure to convince the reader to buy the product?"

Let's say you are writing a brochure selling alfalfa seeds to farmers. The farmer probably isn't interested in the history of alfalfa (or the history of your company). And he doesn't much care about alfalfa's biological structure or the chemical composition of the seed.

The farmer wants to know that your seeds are plump and healthy . . . that they're free of weeds . . . that they'll yield a good, healthy crop of alfalfa . . . and that the price is right.

How do you convince him? One way is to show the results. Put two photos of alfalfa fields on the cover of your brochure. The one on the left shows weed-infested, scrawny alfalfa. The one on the right shows a field of lush, healthy plants. Add a caption that tells him the field on the right was planted with your seeds, and how your seeds can increase crop yield 40 percent.

The brochure can go even further. Why not attach a sample bag of seed to the brochure and mail it to the farmer?

The brochure copy can begin, "Our alfalfa is clean, healthy, practically weed-free. But don't take our word for it. See for yourself."

Know your reader. Farmers don't want hype or a scientific treatise; they want straightforward talk that shows them how to run their farms more profitably. Scientists are most comfortable with charts, graphs, and tables of data, so include plenty of them in a brochure aimed at scientists.

Engineers are at home with diagrams and blueprints. Accountants understand tables of financial figures. Human resource managers will probably be interested in photos of people.

Also, the length of your copy depends not only on the amount of information you have, but on whether your customer is someone who will read a lot of copy. A brochure selling a new microfilm system to librarians can be long, because librarians like to read.

A brochure aimed at busy executives should probably be shorter, because most executives are pressed for time. A brochure offering a new cable TV service will probably contain mostly pictures, because people who watch a lot of TV would rather look at pictures than read.

### 4. Put a strong selling message on the front cover.

The first thing readers see when they pull your brochure out of an envelope or off a display rack is the cover. If the cover promises a strong benefit or reward for reading the copy, the reader will open the brochure and read it (or at least look at the pictures, captions, and headings).

If the selling message on the cover is weak, or worse, if there is no selling message on the cover, the reader has no motivation for opening the brochure. It is just junk mail, something to be thrown away.

A surprising number of brochure covers contain no headline or visual, just the product name and company logo. This is like running an ad without a headline: It wastes a valuable selling opportunity.

For instance, a brochure from the Prudential Insurance Company of America has the headline: "Now . . . you can enroll in this AARP Plan of Group Hospital Insurance—designed to help pay expenses your other insurance does not cover!" The cover is illustrated with a drawing of a retired couple enjoying a life of leisure.

This brochure cover is effective because it offers a strong, solid benefit, simply stated: "Designed to help pay expenses your other insurance does not cover!" What gimmick or clever cover design could do a better selling job than this promise? My only complaint with the headline is the use of the abbreviation "AARP." I didn't know what it meant and was annoyed that I had to search through the copy to find out.

Sometimes, the visual communicates the benefit more strongly than the headline. My favorite summer retreat is Montauk, Long Island, and no words can make me long for a weekend on the Island as much as a beautiful color photo of the waves rolling in and lapping against the soft sands of the shore. If you own a hotel on the Montauk beach, put such a photo on the cover, and I'll be sold!

Occasionally, a brochure writer attempts to lure the reader into the brochure with a gimmick that doesn't relate to the product. In front of me is a brochure whose cover features a drawing of a church and a diamond ring and the headline, "Forget about marriage . . . why not just 'get engaged.'"

This caught my eye years ago, when I was engaged. But when I opened the brochure, I was given a sales pitch on why it's better to rent cars instead of buying them. The brochure had nothing at all to do with engagement or marriage. I was more than disappointed: I felt misled. I'm sure other folks felt the same and doubt that this brochure sold many car rental contracts.

The traditional brochure cover contains a headline and graphic only, with no text; body copy begins inside. But you can get people to start reading your sales pitch by breaking this tradition and beginning your body copy on the front cover. The readers' eye will automatically go to the lead paragraph, and if it's strong enough, they'll be hooked.

### 5. Give complete information.

Give as much information as it takes to get the prospect to take the next step in the buying process.

The average brochure contains a lot of words. Certainly more than you read in most ads or hear in TV commercials.

But remember that the brochure is a medium of information. Ads, commercials, and direct mail may be an unwanted interruption in the reader's life. But the reader has asked for the brochure, and he is interested in the information it contains.

Don't be afraid to make the brochure as long as it has to be. Include all the necessary information—prices, product specifications, ordering information, guarantees, descriptions.

The reader who represents a serious potential customer will read every word of the copy as long as it is interesting and engaging. The minute you write boring copy, or copy that doesn't give useful information, you'll turn the reader off.

There is a ridiculous tendency among brochure designers to use a large amount of white space on the page and very little copy. I've seen 8½- by 11-inch brochures where each page had only one or two paragraphs in small type in the upper corner. The rest of the page was mostly blank and decorated by some graphic design: stripes, color patterns, lines, shapes.

This is a waste of space and printing costs. Your customer doesn't send for your brochure to look at fancy designs; she sends for it because she wants information. If you want proof that this myth is untrue, take a look at your daily newspaper: pages and pages of sold text and photos. No white space, no graphic "design elements." Just information that the reader wants and has paid for.

Of course, not every page in your brochure should be solid type to the edges. Margins and space between paragraphs help increase readability. Photos, illustrations, captions, and subheads break up the text and help tell the story. But to think your brochure should be largely blank space is folly. Don't be afraid to write and print all the words it takes to make your sales pitch. Give the reader complete information.

### 6. *Organize your selling points.*

People read brochures in much the same order they read paperback novels. They look at the cover first, maybe take a quick peek at the back cover, and thumb through the book once. Then, if it looks promising, they open to page one and start reading.

Your brochure, like a novel, should have a logical structure to it. A good brochure tells a story—a product story—with a beginning, a middle, and an end. The organization of a brochure is dictated both by the product story you want to tell and by the informational needs of the reader.

For example, my in-laws had a business in which they bought books from publishers and resold them to corporations. This is a rather unusual service, one the corporate librarian may not have thought about before, so my in-laws began their brochure with a summary of the service they offered and why corporate librarians would find it useful.

Next, they presented six major benefits of using the service. These benefits were listed in simple 1-2-3 fashion so the reader could quickly see how she could come out ahead by doing business with the book-buying service.

Finally, the brochure told the reader the technical details of how the service worked and gave instructions for placing orders.

Let the organization of your brochure be dictated by what your customer wants to know about your product. If you own a computer store, and you find that customers coming in off the street seem to ask the same questions over and over, you might write a booklet titled, "Six Important Questions to Ask Before You Buy a Computer." The booklet would present computer shopping tips in a simple question-and-answer format.

If your company designs and decorates offices, your brochure could be organized as a walking tour of the modern office. At each point of the tour, from the copier to the water cooler, the copy could point out how redesigning that section of the office can make the office a better place to work and improve productivity.

There are many ways to organize a brochure: alphabetical order, chronological order, by size of product, by importance of customer benefit, question and answer, list of customer benefits, by product line, by price, by application, by market, by steps in the ordering process. Choose the approach that best fits your product, your audience, and your sales pitch.

### 7. *Divide the brochure into short, easy-to-read sections.*

As you organize your brochure, devise a way to organize your material: an outline that breaks the topic into a number of sections and subsections.

You should keep this organizational scheme in the final copy. Write the brochure as a series of short sections and subsections, each with its own headline or subhead.

There are a number of benefits to this approach. First, the use of headings and subheads allows readers to get the message even if they only scan the brochure. Many people won't read all the copy, but a series of heads and subheads gives them the gist of the sales pitch at a glance.

Be sure to write headings and subheads that tell a story. Avoid headings that are just straight description or clever plays on words. Instead of "Hitachi plays it cool," write, "Hitachi chiller-heaters cut cooling costs in half."

Second, breaking the copy into short sections makes the brochure easier to read. People are intimidated and tired by long chunks of text; they prefer to read a short section of copy, stop, take a rest, and absorb the information before going on to the next section. (This is why novels are divided into chapters.)

Third, short sections make the brochure easier to write. You just follow your outline and put the information in your notes under the appropriate section. If you uncover new facts that don't fit anywhere in the outline, you can simply add a new section to the brochure. And, like your reader, you can rest after writing one section before you go on to the next.

When you write your brochure, think about how the sections will appear on the pages of the published brochure. For example, you might like the clean look and feel of having a six-page brochure with four sections (one on each page), a headline on the front cover, and the company logo and address on the back cover.

Some brochure writers design their brochures so that each page contains a complete section or two. Other writers claim that a good way of getting the reader to turn the page is to have the sections run off one page and continue on the next. Both techniques have their merits, and the choice is really a matter of taste. But you should be aware of how organization and layout work together.

If your brochure is folded or designed in an unusual format, make a mock-up out of scrap paper. Use the mock-up (called a "dummy") to show the layout and how the copy flows from page to page. Make sure that the reader will see the various sections of text in the same order you wrote them in the manuscript.

### 8. *Use hardworking visuals.*

Photos in brochures are not ornaments. They are included to help sell the product by showing what it looks like, how it works, and what it can do for the reader.

The best brochure photos demonstrate the product's usefulness by showing it in action. Putting people in these photos usually adds to the visual's appeal (people like looking at pictures of people).

Photos make the best visuals because they offer proof that a product exists and works. But artwork is also useful for many purposes.

A drawing can illustrate a product or process that is not easily photographed (such as the inner workings of an automobile engine).

A map can show where something is located.

A diagram can show how something works or how it is organized. An organizational diagram, for example, uses arrows and boxes to show how the divisions and branches of a company are organized.

A graph is used to tell how one quantity changes as another quantity changes. In a brochure on air-conditioning, a graph could show how your electric bill goes up as you lower the temperature setting on your air conditioner.

Pie charts show proportions and percentages (for example, the percentage of your company's annual income spent on research and development). Bar charts demonstrate comparisons among quantities (this year's sales versus last year's). And tables are a handy way of listing a body of data too large to include in the text of the brochure.

Use visuals when they can express or illustrate a concept

better than words can. If the visual doesn't improve on the written description, don't use it.

Popular brochure visuals include:

- Product photographs
- Pictures of the product photographed next to other objects to give a sense of the size of the product. (A brochure on semiconductors might show a photo of a microchip on a postage stamp to dramatically convey the smallness of the integrated circuit.)
- Photos of actual installations of the product
- Photos of the product in use
- Photos of the product being manufactured
- Tables of product specifications
- Tables summarizing product features and benefits
- Photos of items made with (or from) the product
- Photos of the company headquarters, manufacturing plant, or research laboratories
- Photos of the product packed and ready for shipping
- Photos of the product being tested by company scientists or inspected for quality control
- Photos of people who are enjoying the use of the product
- Photos of people who attest to the product's superiority
- Tables listing the various models and versions of the product
- Graphs presenting scientific proof of the product's performance (heat tests, ability to stand up under pressure, longevity of operation, etc.)
- Photos of available parts and accessories
- A series of photos demonstrating the product's performance or how to use it
- Diagrams explaining how the product works or how it is put together
- Sketches of planned product improvements, forthcoming new products, or planned applications

Always use visuals that illustrate your key selling points. In an automobile brochure that extols the benefits of rack-and-pinion steering, it would be helpful to have a diagram that shows how rack-and-pinion steering works. But if rack-and-pinion steering is not a selling point, there would be no reason to include a picture of it.

Label all visuals with captions. Studies show that brochure captions get twice the readership of body copy. Use captions to reinforce the body copy or make an additional sales point not covered in the copy.

Make captions interesting and informative. Instead of labeling a photo "Automatic wiring device," write "A tape-controlled, fully automatic wiring device (above left) makes approximately 1,000 wire-wrap connections an hour, significantly reducing manufacturing costs."

## 9. Find the next step in the buying process—and tell the reader to take it.

Do you want your reader to buy pasta from your gourmet shop? Enroll for membership in your health spa? Visit your factory? Or test-drive a new luxury sedan?

A brochure moves the customer from one step in the buying process to the next.

To do this successfully, the brochure must identify this next step and tell the reader to take it.

Typically, this "call for action" appears at the end of the brochure. The copy urges the reader to call or write for more information, or to take some other action. Make it easy for the reader to respond by using such devices as reply cards, self-addressed stamped envelopes, order forms, toll-free 800-numbers, and listings of local dealerships and distributors.

End the brochure with copy designed to generate an immediate response. Use action words and phrases: "Give us a call today." "For more information, write for our FREE catalog." "Please complete and mail the enclosed reply card." "Visit our store nearest you." "Order today—supplies limited."

Here's an effective closing from a brochure for an advertising agency:

### THE NEXT STEP

Now that you know something about us, we'd like to know a little bit more about you.

Send us your current ads, sales literature, and press releases for a free, no-obligation evaluation of your marketing communications program.

If you'd like to meet with us, give us a call. We'll be glad to show you some of the work we've done for our clients, and take a look at what we can do for you.

This closing is effective for three reasons: 1) it's personal; 2) it asks for specific action ("Send us your current ads," "Give us a call"); and 3) it offers the reader something for free ("a no-obligation evaluation of your marketing communications program").

Always ask for the order in your brochure. Or at least for action that will lead to an eventual sale.

### 10. Don't forget the obvious.

Sometimes you get so wrapped up in the creative aspects of copywriting that you forget to include basic information—phone numbers, directions, street addresses, store hours, zip codes, and guarantees.

When you write a brochure, don't forget the obvious. Often, seemingly minor details can mean the difference between a sale and a no-sale.

For instance, one company forgot to include its second telephone number in a direct-mail brochure. As a result, the phone was frequently busy when prospects called in to order the product, and many sales were lost.

When you're proofreading your brochure copy, be sure you've included the following items:

- Company logo, name, and address
- Phone and fax numbers
- Street address in addition to box number
- Directions ("located on the corner of Fifth and Main off I-95")
- Prices, store hours, branch locations
- List of distributors, dealers, or sales reps
- Instructions for placing orders by phone or mail
- Credit cards accepted
- Product guarantees and warranties
- Shipping and service information
- Trademarks, registration marks, disclaimers, and other legal information
- Form numbers, dates, codes, copyright lines
- Web site URL

Also, be sure to proofread for errors in spelling, punctuation, and grammar.

These details are important. For instance, mail-order firms know their sales can double when they add a toll-free number and "major credit cards accepted" to their brochures.

## 11. Make the brochure worth keeping.

When the customer receives your brochure, he can do one of three things:

1. Respond to it by placing an order or asking for more information.

2. File it for future reference.
3. Throw it away.

You want the first two things to happen. You want the customer to respond to your brochure. And you want her to save it for when she needs the product again in the future.

To get someone to save your brochure, you must write a brochure that is worth keeping. Brochures that are worth keeping are valuable because of the information they contain. This information may be directly related to the product. Or it may be service information of a general nature that is indirectly related to the product.

For example, a brochure for a resort hotel in Montauk might print a detailed map of the town on the back cover. Travelers will save the brochure because of the map.

The literature package I mail to potential clients for my freelance copywriting services includes a reprint of an article I wrote ("Ten Tips For Writing More Effective Industrial Copy"). The reprint includes my picture, name, address, and phone number. Even if prospects throw away the promotional part of my package, they are likely to keep the article because it contains information that may be useful to them in their work.

Most people don't have a good idea of how the stock market works. So if a broker published a booklet titled, "A Layperson's Introduction to the Stock Market . . . and How to Play It," people would be likely to save this booklet. Later, when they accumulate enough money to invest in stocks, they would find the brochure in their files and call the broker to have him handle their business.

So, if you want your brochure to keep selling for you, make your brochure worth keeping. Another example: A casino added value to its promotional brochure by printing the rules of blackjack on the back cover.

## HOW TO ORGANIZE YOUR BROCHURE COPY

This is an oversimplification, but basically, there are only three types of brochures:

1. Brochures about a product
2. Brochures about a service
3. Brochures about a company (known as "corporate" brochures or "capabilities" brochures)

The content and organization of every brochure is unique, because every selling situation and product, service, or company is unique. However, many brochures share common characteristics. Most brochures describing consulting services, for example, include a list of the consultant's clients.

Below are three outlines for "typical" product, service, and company brochures. These will give you a rough idea of what to include in the sales literature you write for your clients.

### For a Product Brochure

• Introduction—a capsule description of what the product is and why the reader of the brochure should be interested in it.

• Benefits—a list of reasons why the customer should buy the product.

• Features—highlights of important product features that set the product apart from the competition.

• "How it works"—a description of how the product works and what it can do. This section can include the results of any tests that demonstrate the product's superiority.

• Types of users (markets)—this section describes the special markets the product is designed for. A wastewater plant, for example, might be sold to municipalities, utilities, and industrial plants: three separate and distinct markets, each with its own special set of requirements. This section might also include an actual list of names of well-known people or organizations that use and endorse the product.

• Applications—descriptions of the various applications in which the product can be used.

• Product availability—lists of models, sizes, materials of construction, options, accessories, and all the variations in which you can order the product. This section can also include charts, graphs, formulas, or other guidelines to aid the reader in product selection.

• Pricing—information on what the product costs. Includes prices for accessories, various models and sizes, quantity discounts, and shipping and handling. Often printed on a separate sheet inserted into the brochure so the brochure does not become obsolete when prices change.

• Technical specifications—electrical requirements, power consumption, resistance to moisture, temperature range, operating conditions, cleaning methods, storage conditions, chemical properties, and other characteristics and limitations of the product.

• Questions and answers—answers to frequently asked questions about the product. Includes information not found in the other sections.

• Company description—a brief biography of the manufacturer, designed to show the reader that the product is backed by a solid, reputable organization that won't go out of business.

• Support—information on delivery, installation, training, maintenance, service, and guarantees.

• "The next step"—instructions on how to order the product (or on how to get more information on the product).

## For a Brochure Describing a Service

• Introduction—outlines the services offered, types of accounts handled, and reasons why the reader should be interested in the service.

• Services offered—detailed descriptions of the various services offered by the firm.

• Benefits—describes what readers will gain from the service and why they should engage the services of your firm instead of the competition.

• Methodology—outlines the service firm's method of doing business with clients.

• Client list—a list of well-known people or organizations who have used and endorse the firm's services.

• Testimonials—statements of endorsements from select clients. Testimonials are usually written in the client's own words, surrounded by quotation marks, and attributed to a specific person or organization.

• Fees and terms—describes the fees for each service and the terms and method of payment required. Also includes whatever guarantee the service firm makes to its clients.

• Biographical information—capsule biographies highlighting the credentials of the key employees of the service firm.

• "The next step"—instructions on what to do next if you are interested in hiring the firm or learning more about their services.

## For a Corporate Brochure

• The business or businesses the company is engaged in
• The corporate structure (parent company, divisions, departments, subsidiaries, branch offices)
• Corporate "philosophy"
• Company history

- Plants and branch offices
- Geographical coverage
- Major markets
- Distribution system
- Sales
- Ranking in its field relative to competition
- Extent of stock distribution
- Earnings and dividend records
- Number of employees
- Employee benefits
- Noteworthy employees
- Inventions
- Significant achievements (including industry "firsts")
- Research and development
- Quality-control practices
- Community relations (environmental programs, contributions to public welfare, charitable activities, support of the arts, etc.)
- Awards
- Policies
- Objectives, goals, plans for the future

The above outlines are suggestions only, not mandatory formats. Mold them to suit your needs; let your product, audience, and sales objectives be your primary guide to content and organization of the copy.

## CATALOGS

Catalogs are similar to brochures but with two important differences:

1. Brochures usually tell an in-depth story about a single product. Catalogs give short descriptions of many products.

Because each item is given limited space, descriptions must be terse. Catalog copy is often written in a clipped, telegram-like style, with sentence fragments that convey a great deal of information in the fewest possible words.

2. The brochure's mission is usually to provide enough information to take the reader to the next step in the buying process. Most catalogs are mail-order vehicles from which you can order the product directly; salespeople are rarely involved. (The exception is the industrial product catalog.) As a result, a great deal of the copywriter's time is spent designing an order form that is easy to use and encourages the reader to send in an order.

Catalog writing is a separate art from brochure writing. The basics are the same but the mechanics are different. Here are a few tips to help you write successful catalogs:

*Write Snappy Headlines*

Even if space requires that your catalog headlines be short, you can still add selling power to them. Don't be content to simply describe the product in the headline; add a snappy phrase, a strong benefit, a descriptive adjective that hints at the product's distinct qualities.

In its order-by-mail book catalogs, Boardroom Books turns mundane book titles into strong, hard-selling catalog headlines. Instead of "The Book of Tax Knowledge," they write, "3,147 Tax-Saving Ideas." For a book titled *Successful Tax Planning*, the catalog description reads, "Did your tax accountant ever tell you all this?" And a book on how to buy computers is advertised with the provocative headline, "What the computer salesmen don't tell you."

### Include a "Letter From the Manufacturer"

Many catalogs include a "personal" letter from the company president, either printed on letterhead and bound into the catalog or printed directly onto one of the pages in the front of the catalog, often the inside front cover.

In the letter, the president talks about the quality of the products in the catalog, the firm's commitment to serving its customers, and the manufacturer's guarantee of customer satisfaction. The letter may also be used as an introduction to the company's product line, or to call attention to a particular product or group of products that is especially noteworthy or attractively priced.

Here's a homey paragraph from a letter in an L.L. Bean catalog:

> "L.L." had a simple business philosophy: "Sell good merchandise at a reasonable profit, treat your customers like human beings and they'll always come back for more." We call this "L.L.'s" golden rule. Today, 72 years later, we still practice it.

You can't help but be won over by the good sense of this honorable business philosophy and the sincerity of its statement. Putting a letter in your catalog adds warmth and a human quality to an otherwise impersonal presentation of product facts, specifications, and prices.

### Give All the Key Product Facts

A catalog description must give the reader all the information needed to order the product. This includes sizes, colors, materials, prices, and styles. The copy should also give readers a concise but complete description of the product, so they can make a decision as to whether they want to buy it.

### Devote the Most Space to Your Best Sellers

Devote a full page or half page to your best-selling items and list them up front. Less popular items get a quarter page or less and appear toward the back of the catalog. Items that don't sell should be dropped altogether.

### Use Techniques That Stimulate Sales

These include toll-free phone numbers; credit card orders accepted; a gift to the customer for placing an order; two-for-one offers; arrows, stars, bursts, and other graphic devices used to highlight special discounts within the catalog; last-minute items added as a special insert sheet or printed on the order form; volume discount for large orders ("10% off when your order exceeds $25"); gift packaging available for merchandise ordered as gifts; special sale items featured on the order form.

### Make the Order Form Simple and Easy to Fill Out

Give the customer sufficient space for writing in his order. Print step-by-step instructions for ordering right on the form. Print the guarantee in large type and set it off with a border. Provide a business reply envelope in which the customer can enclose his check.

### Indicate Discounted Items in the Copy

One way of doing this is to write, "25% Off! Was $11.95—Now $8.95." Another is to cross out the old price and write in the new price-$11.95 "$8.95."

## OTHER TYPES OF SALES LITERATURE

Brochures and catalogs account for most of the sales literature published in the world. Still, there are a few other types of sales literature you may be asked to write.

### Annual Reports

Annual reports are summaries of the company's performance for the past year. They combine the company information found in "capabilities brochures" with financial data on the company's sales, profits, revenues, and dividends. Annual reports are usually lavish affairs, printed on glossy stock and featuring expensive four-color photography, sophisticated graphics, and stylish copy.

### Flyers

Flyers are sales literature printed on one or two sides of an unfolded 8½- by 11-inch piece of paper. Visuals, if used, are limited to simple line drawings. Flyers are used as handouts at conventions and trade shows or as bulletins posted around the neighborhood. Many small businesses find flyers an inexpensive way of reaching new customers.

### Broadsides

Broadsides are flyers folded for mailing. Companies that maintain mailing lists of customers often send monthly broadsides announcing sales, new products, or other news of interest to their customers.

### Invoice Stuffers

Invoice stuffers are small pieces of promotional literature designed to fit in #10 envelopes. They are mailed to customers along with the monthly bill or statement and used to announce a sale or solicit mail-order sales of a special item.

The advantage of using invoice stuffers is that they get a "free ride" in the mail because they're sent with routine correspondence rather than in separate mailings.

## Circulars

Circulars are printed advertising sheets that are mailed, inserted in packages or newspapers, or distributed by hand. They are usually four to eight pages long, printed in color, and contain price-off coupons for products sold in local retail outlets.

## Pamphlets

Also called booklets, pamphlets are similar to brochures, except they usually contain useful information of a general nature while brochures describe the features and benefits of specific products and services.

## White Papers

A white paper is a promotional piece in the guise of an informational article or report. Just as many infomercials convey the look and feel of an informative, unbiased TV program rather than a paid commercial, a white paper attempts to convince readers that they are being educated—about the issue or problem your product addresses (e.g., computer security, improving customer service, managing your sales force, saving for retirement), rather than being sold on a specific product.

The white paper serves the same sales purpose as a brochure—to sell or help sell a product or service—but it reads and looks like an article or other important piece of authoritative, objective information.

Unlike a sales brochure, a white paper must contain useful "how-to" information that helps the reader solve a problem, or make or justify a key business decision (e.g., whether to lease or buy a new warehouse).

But make no mistake, both the brochure and the white paper have the same ultimate objective: to sell or help sell a company's product or service.

Where white papers and brochures differ is their approach to making the sale: Brochures contain a straightforward presentation of product features and benefits, while white papers take more of a "soft-sell" approach.

# 9

## WRITING PUBLIC RELATIONS MATERIALS

"Do you also write press releases?"

Although public relations is a different discipline than advertising, they overlap, and almost every copywriter is asked to write press releases or other public relations materials at some point.

To the copywriter trained in hard-sell persuasive writing, the soft-sell touch of PR writing takes some getting used to.

Advertising reaches readers directly and makes a blatant, undisguised pitch to part them from their money. Press releases are sent to editors, not advertising departments, in the hopes that editors will publish them in their magazines or papers.

Once you send out a release, you have no control over when it will appear, in what form it will appear, or even whether it will appear. The editor can publish the release as is, rewrite it or cut it as he or she pleases, use it as the basis for a different story, or ignore it altogether. The editor has total control, and, unlike the publication's advertising department, has no interest in helping you promote your firm.

The editor's only concern is publishing a magazine or paper filled with news and information of interest to his readers. If your press release contains such news or information, the editor is likely to use it. If the release is just a warmed-over ad, the editor will recognize it as such and trash it.

Companies new to public relations ask me, "Do editors really use press releases?" The answer is that they do. The *Columbia Journalism Review* surveyed an issue of the *Wall Street Journal* to find out how many of the stories were generated by press releases. The survey revealed that 111 stories on the inside pages were taken from press releases, either word for word or paraphrased. In only 30 percent of these stories did reporters put in additional facts not contained in the original release.

There are no figures on how many press releases are generated each year, but my guess is that it runs into the hundreds of thousands—maybe even the millions.

One reason why press releases are so popular is that they are inexpensive. To print a one-page release and mail it to a hundred editors costs less than $50.

If an editor picks up your release and runs it as a short article in the magazine, your firm receives the space free. Running an ad of the same size could cost hundreds or even thousands of dollars.

What's more, publicity is more credible than paid advertising. The public has a built-in skepticism for advertising but is trained to believe almost everything they read in the paper or hear on TV. They do not realize that most of the news they read and hear is generated by press releases— releases sent out by the same firms that run ads and commercials.

But there is no guarantee that a press release will be picked up by the media or, once picked up, will generate much interest or new business. Some releases are ignored; others generate spectacular results. When Leisure Time Ice, a trade association of ice manufacturers, sent out a press kit claiming that packaged ice is clearer and purer than homemade ice, the head of the association was interviewed by at least 25 editors and appeared on 15 radio and TV talk shows.

The *Wall Street Journal, New York Times, Los Angeles Times*, United Press International, and Associated Press all ran feature stories on Leisure Time Ice. The association's membership increased by 10 percent. And sales of manufactured ice went up. More and more firms are using publicity to promote their products and services.

Even professionals who traditionally look down upon public relations—doctors, lawyers, architects, engineers, management consultants—are now writing releases, placing stories, and appearing on radio and TV talk shows: a survey of 523 members of the American Bar Association revealed that 20 percent of these lawyers use publicity to promote their practices.

## WHAT IS A PRESS RELEASE?

A press release is a printed news story prepared by an organization and distributed to the media for the purpose of publicizing the organization's products, services, or activities.

Here's a sample of an effective release typed in the proper press-release format:

FROM: Kirsch Communications, 226 Seventh Street, Garden
     City, NY 11530
For more information please call: Len Kirsch, 516-555-4055

FOR: Pinwheel Systems, 404 Park Avenue South, New York,
     NY 10016
Contact: John N. Schaedler, President, 212-555-5140

FOR IMMEDIATE RELEASE

## INTRODUCTORY KIT FOR NEW "RUFF-PROOFS" COLOR COMPS OFFERED BY PINWHEEL SYSTEMS

A special Introductory Kit of watercolor dyes and other supplies which can be used with its new "Ruff-Proofs" do-it-yourself coloring system has been developed by Pinwheel Systems, New York, it was announced today by John N. Schaedler, president of the company.

Ruff-Proofs are latent-image prints made from black and white artwork. They can be transformed into multicolor art for layout and design comps, packaging, flip charts and other graphics, Schaedler said, merely by applying watercolor dyes or markers. (Patents are pending on the process.)

The prints are delivered in sets of four to give the artist an opportunity to experiment with different colors and explore varying color combinations. They are available from franchised Pinwheel Studios.

The Introductory Kit has a retail value of $45, Schaedler said, and is being offered to artists and designers for $20 with the purchase of Ruff-Proofs. It contains a complete set of coloring materials:

• A 36-bottle assortment of Dr. P. H. Martin's Synchromatic Transparent Watercolor Dyes, with a swatch card of actual color chips.

• A 30-cup palette for mixing colors, squeeze-bottle dispensers for water and cleanup solution, plus absorbent tissues and cotton swabs used in the coloring process.

More information about the kits and the Ruff-Proofs process is available from John Schaedler at Pinwheel Systems, 404 Park Avenue South, New York, NY, telephone 212-555-5140.

Len Kirsch, author of the above release, gives these 12 tips on press-release format and content.

1. What you say is more important than using fancy printed PR letterheads or layouts. Clarity and accuracy are critical.

2. When an outside public relations firm writes the release for you, its name and your own should appear as the sources for the release. If you wrote the release yourself, you become the source for more information. Either way, be sure to include names and phone numbers so the editor can get more information if needed.

3. The release can be dated with a release date or with the phrase "For Immediate Release." Date the release one day in advance of the actual mailing to make it timely.

4. Leave as much space as possible between the release date and the headline (to give the editor room to write instructions for page layout).

5. The headline should sum up your story. Maximum length: two to three lines. This tells a busy editor, at a glance, if the story is worth considering.

6. The lead contains the "who, what, when, where, why, and how." If the editor chops everything else, at least you've gotten the guts of your story across.

7. Include a person to be credited if there's something worth quoting or if you make any claims. Editors don't want to take the position they are claiming something—they'd rather hang it on you. The personal credits often get deleted, but it's wise to put them in where needed.

8. The body of the story picks up the additional facts. Lay off the superlatives and complimentary adjectives. "We're dealing with news space, not advertising where you can say anything you want as long as it isn't indecent, immoral, or fattening," says Len.

9. Length: Shoot for a single page, no more than two pages. Beyond that, reading becomes a burden for the editor. If you go to a second page, put the word *more* at the bottom of page 1 to let the editor know there is more to the story (in case the pages get separated). Put an abbreviated version of the headline (one or two words) and the page number in the upper left-hand corner of the second page.

10. When the reader might need it, include the name, address, and phone number of someone to contact for more information (this usually appears in the last paragraph of your story). Also indicate the end of the story by writing "—END—," "###," or "—30—" after the last line of the text.

11. If you use photos, type up a photo caption on a separate piece of paper and attach it to the back of the photo with transparent tape. Be sure to include your sources, contacts, and release date on the caption sheet.

12. Keep the release simple, straightforward, newsy. If you need only two paragraphs, don't write ten. Excess verbiage turns editors off.

### YES, BUT IS IT NEWS?

Editors look for press releases containing news. Like a good ad, the headline of the press release must instantly transmit the news to the reader.

Editors are flooded with press releases and don't have time to wade through your release and dig for the real story: Pamela Clark, formerly with *Popular Computing*, once said her staff received 2,000 press releases a month. Your release must telegraph the news in the first five seconds of reading.

But what makes for a news story? It depends on your industry and your audience. *Forbes* and *Fortune* would not consider publication of your new ball-bearing catalog to be news. But the editors of *Machine Design, Design News,* and other trade magazines whose readers use ball bearings might very well run a short news release on the catalog and a picture of its cover.

One thing that is not news is advertising and promotion. Editors will not publish descriptive stories about your product, service, or organization unless the story tells them something new, or provides service information useful to the publication's readers.

A press release with the headline, "Ajax Dry Cleaners Provides Top-Quality Cleaning at Reasonable Prices" will probably not generate any coverage. But if Ajax sent out a release titled "Ajax Dry Cleaners Offers Expert Advice on How to Remove Tough Stains," the editor of your local paper's home section might reprint the advice as a how-to article. Ajax gets publicity by being listed as the source of the expert advice. (And Ajax can also use reprints of the article as flyers or direct mail.)

Here is a list of possible topics for news releases about your company. They all hold interest because they contain either news or useful information, or both. You can write a press release about:

- A new product
- An old product with a new name or package
- A product improvement
- A new version or model of an old product
- An old product available in new materials, colors, or sizes
- A new application of an old product
- New accessories available for an old product
- The publication of new or revised sales literature— brochures, catalogs, data sheets, surveys, reports, reprints, booklets
- A speech or presentation given by an executive
- An expert opinion on any subject

- A controversial issue
- New employees
- Promotions within the firm
- Awards and honors won by your organization or its employees
- Original discoveries or innovations (such as patents)
- New stores, branch offices, headquarters, facilities
- New sales reps, distributors, agents
- Major contracts awarded to your firm
- Joint ventures
- Management reorganization
- Major achievements, such as number of products sold, increase in sales, quarterly earnings, safety record
- Unusual people, products, ways of doing business
- Case histories of successful applications, installations, projects
- Tips and hints ("how-to" advice)
- Change of company name, slogan, or logo
- Opening of a new business
- Special events such as a sale, party, open house, plant tour, contest, or sweepstakes
- Charitable acts or other community relations

The only type of press release that does not need to contain news is the "background release," or "backgrounder." Backgrounders present a brief (three to five pages) overview of your company. They are not mailed alone but are included with other releases when editors want background information on your company.

Even though the backgrounder is not, strictly speaking, a news story, you should try to put something new, or at least some little-known fact or startling piece of information in the backgrounders you write. This will grab an editor's interest more strongly than a bland summary of your organizational chart.

Another special type of press release is the "fact sheet." Fact sheets contain detailed information, usually in list form, too lengthy to be included in the body of the main release.

A press release announcing the opening of a new gourmet food store might be mailed with a fact sheet listing recipes for three or four of the store's specialties. A fact sheet for a consulting firm could contain a list of clients or brief biographies of the firm's principals.

Often copywiters are faced with a client who wants publicity and asks us to write a press release, but has nothing new to report. In such instances, a creative publicist or copywriter can "manufacture" a hook or angle strong enough to gain the media's attention.

For instance, when Jericho Communications, a New York City PR firm, was looking for a way to gain publicity for their client Domino's Pizza, someone said, "When we work late at night, we order pizza. Maybe the White House does the same thing. Can we see whether pizza deliveries to the White House increase when there is a national emergency?"

Sure enough, they did. And Jericho created the "Pizza Meter," publicizing the fact that you could judge the state of the nation by the volume of pizza delivery to the White House. The tactic was successful, garnering major media coverage for the pizza maker.

When gigapets were the rage, my seven-year-old son dropped his into the toilet, and was upset that it "died" (the water shorted out the electronics). To make him feel better, we buried the gigapet in our backyard and held a mock funeral, which gave me an idea for some PR.

I sent out the press release below, and within a week, a major New Jersey newspaper did a large feature article on our "gigapet cemetery" (please don't send for the booklet, which I lost track of long ago):

FROM: Microchip Gardens, 174 Holland Avenue, New
       Milford, NJ 07646

CONTACT: Bob Bly, phone 201-385-1220

*For immediate release*

## MICROCHIP GARDENS, WORLD'S FIRST "GIGAPET CEMETERY," OPENS IN NORTHERN NJ

When 7-year-old Alex Bly's gigapet died after he dropped it in the toilet, he couldn't find a place to bury it. So his father, NJ-based entrepreneur Bob Bly, created Microchip Gardens—the world's first gigapet cemetery—in the family's suburban backyard.

Now if your child's gigapet dies and can't be revived, instead of unceremoniously tossing it in the trash, you can give it a proper burial in a beautiful, tree-lined resting place.

For fees starting at $5, based on plot location and method of interment (burial, mausoleum, cremation), Bly will give your dearly departed gigapet an eternal resting place in Microchip Gardens, complete with funeral service and burial certificate.

"Even gigapets don't last forever," said Bly. "There are pet cemeteries for dogs and cats; now gigapets have one, too."

To help owners get the most pleasure from gigapet ownership, Bly—author of 35 published books including *The "I Hate Kathie Lee Gifford" Book* (Kensington) and *The Ultimate Unauthorized Star Trek Quiz Book* (HarperCollins)—has written an informative new booklet, "Raising Your Gigapet."

The booklet covers such topics as purchasing your first gigapet; taking the pet home; care and feeding; and play and discipline. Gigapet burial rituals and the origins of Microchip Gardens are also covered.

To get your copy of "Raising Your Gigapet," which includes complete information on the Microchip Gardens gigapet cemetery, send $4 to: CTC, 22 E. Quackenbush Avenue, Dumont, NJ 07628.

## QUESTIONS AND ANSWERS ABOUT PRESS RELEASES

Here are some questions I'm frequently asked by companies who are just getting into public relations:

**Q:** *What's the best length for a press release?*
**A:** For a new product release, one to two pages. If you have a lot to tell, three pages is acceptable. But certainly no longer than that.

   Case histories and backgrounders usually run longer; three to five pages is average. If it takes more than five pages to tell your story, make it a feature article, not a press release.

**Q:** *Should I print the release on my stationery or on a special PR letterhead? Or can I just use regular paper?*
**A:** Some companies design special forms for their news releases. But this doesn't increase the release's chance of being published. You are better off printing on plain white paper.

   Some novices print their releases on purple, pink, or other brightly colored paper, hoping this will make the release stand out from the crowd. It has the opposite effect; editors are turned off by this gimmicky approach to serious news gathering.

**Q:** *Is there one "right" format for typing the release?*
**A:** Formats vary, and there's no "official" format you must follow. Just make sure your release is typed double-spaced, neatly, and with no misspellings or typos. The

format in Len Kirsch's release for Ruff-Proofs is a good one to follow (see p. 205).

**Q:** *Should I enclose a letter with the release?*
**A:** No. It's not necessary. The editor is accustomed to receiving releases and knows what to do with yours. If you feel a need to explain the content of your release, you haven't done a good job writing the story.

**Q:** *Is it better if the release comes from a PR firm or straight from the company?*
**A:** What counts is not who wrote the release, but whether the release contains interesting news clearly presented. Some people have a theory that editors are wary of dealing with public relations people and prefer to go straight to the source. I know a few editors who feel this way. But the majority don't.

**Q:** *How do I reproduce the release?*
**A:** Offset printing is best and doesn't cost very much. Photocopies are acceptable if they are crisp, sharp, and free of smudges or streaks. Or, you can run off copies on your laser printer.

**Q:** *Do I need to send a photo out with my release?*
**A:** It's helpful but not mandatory. An interesting photo of a product, person, plant, process, or package will heighten the editor's interest. Remember, most magazines and papers publish pictures as well as words.

Photos should be glossy, black-and-white, and 8 by 10 inches. Color is better, but expensive. To save money, take both color and black-and-white; then mail out the black-and-white and write "color photos available upon request" at the end of the release. This way, you'll be sending costly color prints only to those magazines that ask for them.

Type a caption on a piece of paper and tape it to the back of the photo. Do not write or type a caption directly on the photo; doing so will make an impression that can ruin the photo.

**Q:** *What's the best way to distribute a press release?*
**A:** The basic methods are mail, e-mail, and fax. You are always safe mailing a press release to an editor. Never send a press release or any other copy as an attached e-mail file to an editor who does not know you and is not expecting it; the editor will delete it without opening for fear of catching a computer virus. When in doubt, call editors prior to sending your release and ask how they prefer to receive materials.

## WRITING A FEATURE ARTICLE

Copywriters also get called upon to "ghostwrite" full-length feature stories for trade and business publications.

Take a look at a bunch of trade journals. They contain many articles written by outside contributors: scientists, engineers, managers, and other professionals employed by companies.

These contributors write not for pay (most trade journals pay a small honorarium or nothing at all) but to promote their own careers as well as the companies they work for. Many companies have a regular scheduled program of placing feature articles in magazines. And they hire professional writers to ghostwrite these articles.

Although each article is different, there are four basic types of articles that magazines publish:

## 1. Case Histories

A case history article is a product "success story." It tells the story of how a product, service, or system was helpful to a specific customer.

"Case history reporting derives its effectiveness from the principle that what works for one customer might work for others," explains Jim Hayes, a writer-photographer specializing in case histories. "Case histories are effective, too, because they're credible. They deal in specifics rather than in claims or generalities. Finally, case histories are an inherently story-telling approach to selling."

Here's how a typical case history article gets started: A telephone manufacturer installs a new office phone system in a sales office. The office manager finds that the new system has increased the productivity of the sales force 25 percent and cut phone bills in half.

When the telephone manufacturer gets wind of this, he asks the office manager if he can write up this success story and place it with an appropriate trade journal. If the office manager agrees, the telephone manufacturer hires a writer.

The writer interviews the office manager at the sales firm and writes the story. After it is approved, it is submitted to the magazine and published. The byline may be that of the manufacturer, the office manager, or the writer. It depends on the nature of the article.

## 2. How-to Articles

These provide useful information that helps the reader do something better ("How to Choose the Right Computer for Your Small Business," "Seven Ways to Cut Energy Costs," "A Guide to Ball-Bearing Selection"). How-to articles are also known as "tutorials," perhaps because they tutor the reader in a new skill or area of knowledge.

The how-to article does not discuss your product directly (your company shouldn't even be mentioned, except in the byline). Instead, it promotes you indirectly by establishing your firm's reputation as a leader in the field. Readers tend to clip and save how-to articles. So, although your article may not generate immediate business, people will keep it for years and call on you when the need arises.

### 3. *Issue Articles*

In issue articles, industry experts speak out on some topical, controversial, or technical issue of the day. These articles help strengthen your company's image as a leader in its field. Example: "Should Internet Users be Prosecuted for Illegal Downloading of Movies, Music, and Other Copyrighted Materials?"

### 4. *News*

News articles are usually prepared by staff editors and reporters, not outsiders. Occasionally, though, a corporation with big news to report—a merger, an acquisition, a revolutionary new invention—will work with a reporter to develop a feature story. The reporter gets a scoop, while the company gets good press.

### QUERY LETTERS

The first step in getting a feature story published in a magazine is to get an editor interested in the article topic. This means first suggesting the topic to the editor, either in a phone conversation or by letter.

Some editors will listen to your pitch over the phone. Most want to see the idea written up in a short proposal known as a "query letter." This is a one- or two-page outline, in letter form, of the article you propose to write.

The query letter explains what the article is about, what

your "angle" is, why the magazine's readers will be interested in the article, and what makes you qualified to write it. The letter is also a demonstration of your writing style. Boring query letters rarely result in an article assignment, because the editor assumes your article will be as boring as your letter.

Here is a sample of a query that got me an assignment to write an article for *Amtrak Express*:

Mr. James A. Frank, Editor

AMTRAK EXPRESS
34 East 51st Street
New York, NY 10022

Dear Mr. Frank:
Is this letter a waste of paper?
    Yes—if it fails to get the desired result.
    In business, most letters and memos are written to generate a specific response—close a sale, set up a meeting, get a job interview, make a contact. Many of these letters fail to do their job.
    Part of the problem is that business executives and support staff don't know how to write persuasively. The solution is a formula first discovered by advertising copywriters—a formula called AIDA. AIDA stands for Attention, Interest, Desire, Action.
    First, the letter gets attention . . . with a hard-hitting lead paragraph that goes straight to the point, or offers an element of intrigue.
    Then, the letter hooks the reader's interest. The hook is often a clear statement of the reader's problems, her needs, her desires. If you are writing to a customer who received damaged goods, state the problem. And then promise a solution.
    Next, create desire. You are offering something—a service, a

product, an agreement, a contract, a compromise, a consultation. Tell the reader the benefit he'll receive from your offering. Create a demand for your product.

Finally, call for action. Ask for the order, the signature, the check, the assignment.

I'd like to give you a 1,500-word article on "How to Write Letters That Get Results." The piece will illustrate the AIDA formula with a variety of actual letters and memos from insurance companies, banks, manufacturers, and other organizations.

This letter, too, was written to get a specific result—an article assignment from the editor of *Amtrak Express*.

Did it succeed?

Regards,
Bob Bly

P.S. By way of introduction, I'm an advertising consultant and the author of five books including *Technical Writing: Structure, Standards, and Style* (McGraw-Hill).

Editors usually respond to query letters within a month or so. (If a month goes by and you haven't heard, follow up with another letter or a phone call.)

A positive response to a query is, "Your proposed article idea interests us. Send a manuscript." This means the editor wants to see the article. It doesn't mean a promise to publish it. The editor won't make that decision until after reading it. A positive response to a query letter is no guarantee that your article will be printed.

If the editor turns down your proposal, you can send your query letter to other publications. Few article ideas are restricted to one magazine only. Most are appropriate to at least half a dozen publications or more.

## HOW TO WRITE A SPEECH

Business executives don't always express themselves by writing articles. Sometimes they make speeches. And, as with article writing, executives often hire ghostwriters to write their speeches for them.

When I got my first speech-writing assignment, I was paralyzed with fear because I had no idea how long—in minutes or words—a speech should be.

Now I do. The average speaker speaks at a rate of 100 words a minute. It follows that a 20-minute speech should be 2,000 words long (about eight double-spaced, typewritten pages).

The best length of time for a speech is 20 minutes. Less seems insubstantial. More can get boring. No speech, no matter how important, should last more than an hour.

Every speech should have a clear-minded purpose. Most speeches are given to entertain, to teach, to persuade, or to inspire.

Speeches are effective at getting across ideas, opinions, and emotions. They are less effective at transmitting a large body of facts (print is the appropriate medium for that).

Here are some additional tips for writing speeches that accomplish their goals without boring the audience to tears:

### 1. Find Out What the Speaker Wants to Say

Few writing assignments are as personal or as idiosyncratic as writing someone else's speech. You'll avoid headaches if you take the time to know the speaker's requirements before you sit down to write.

"You have to ask the right questions of your client to prepare a speech that he'll deliver as if he really means it," writes freelancer Nancy Edmonds Hanson. "Sometimes a lengthy discussion of the topic is necessary before the client himself clarifies his position on it. Your job is to probe, to ask him to carry his own thoughts a little further until he's worked the topic through in his own mind."

Interviews with the client reveal the basic thrust of the speech and provide most of the facts. Information gaps can be filled in through library research or by browsing through the client's private files on the subject.

## 2. *Know Your Audience*

Learn as much as you can about the group you'll be speaking to. This will help you tailor your talk to their specific interests. For example, a speech on podcasting should be geared toward the professional interests of the audience. Engineers are interested in the technology: how it works. Advertising executives want to know more about podcasting as a marketing medium.

## 3. *Write a Strong Opening*

The first sentence uttered by the speaker is like the headline of an advertisement or the lead paragraph of a direct-mail piece. An engaging opening grabs attention and gets the audience enthusiastic about your topic. A bland opening is a turnoff. A sample speech introduction:

> Today, I would like to share with you some of my innermost thoughts and memories, which have been locked away deep in my heart for the longest time. It has been seven years since the passing of my husband, Joseph. This is the first time many of these memories and thoughts will see the light of day. I have agreed to speak with you today in order to impress upon you the importance of Sephardic Bikur Holim (SBH) and what it meant to my children. My story starts with something we all know, yet very rarely face, and that is how vulnerable we all really are.
>
> Joseph was a wonderful husband, a caring father and a successful businessman. He had such a passion for helping others,

and he took the plight of the unfortunate very personally. He was instrumental in making SBH the organization that it is today, and it was always his dream to become a social worker. To, me it seemed like a natural progression for Joseph to trade in his business career for college life.

## 4. Then, There's Humor

Speechwriters are always uncertain when it comes to using humor. They know that humor can quickly warm an audience to the speaker. But a joke that bombs can ruin the whole talk.

My advice is to pepper the speech with little tidbits of warm, gentle, good-natured humor. Not big gags, old jokes, or nightclub-comic routines. Just a few well-chosen, humorous comments that make the speaker seem a bit more human.

Never lead off with a prepared joke. Chances are, it will fall flat because the audience isn't expecting it. Worse, people will think you are there to clown and have nothing important to say.

## 5. Don't Try to Cover Too Much

Remember, a 20-minute speech has only 2,000 words—just eight pages of double-spaced manuscript. Add to this the fact that the spoken word is not as compact as written English and you'll see that there's only so much information you can put in your talk.

Don't try to cover your whole subject. Just break off a little piece of it and tell your story with warmth, wit, humor, and authority. Delete trivial information and limit your talk to the important key points.

For example, "Your Career" is too broad a topic for a speech. "How to Break Into the Advertising Business" is a more manageable subject for an after-dinner talk.

## 6. Write in Conversational Tone

Speeches are to be heard, not read. A speech is one person talking, and it should sound like talking, not like an academic thesis or a corporate memorandum.

Write in a conversational tone. That means short words. Short sentences. Plenty of contractions. Even a colloquial expression every now and then.

The best test of a speech is to read it aloud. If it doesn't sound natural, rewrite it until it does.

Use bullets, headings, and numbers to divide the speech into sections. The speaker can catch her breath during the pauses between sections.

If the copy can't be broken up this way, then indicate places where the speaker can pause between paragraphs. These stops give nervous speakers a chance to slow down.

## 7. Keep It Simple

A speech is not the appropriate medium for delivering complex ideas and sophisticated theories.

For one thing, a speech is limited in the amount of information it can contain. For another, the listener can't stop to ponder a point or go back to information presented earlier (as he can when reading an article, ad, or brochure).

Ideally, your speech should be centered around one main point or theme. If a fact or observation doesn't tie in with this point, throw it out.

Give the listener easy-to-grasp tidbits of information and advice. Don't try to get the audience to follow a rigorous mathematical proof, a complex argument, or a complicated process. They won't.

## 8. *What About Visuals?*

When I worked in the corporate world in the 1970s, slides were the rage. No speaker would think of giving a presentation without a carousel full of brightly colored slides to back him up. Today, PowerPoint presentations run on a laptop and projected onto an LCD monitor have replaced photographic slides.

In some cases, visuals can be useful. If you want to introduce the new corporate logo, you must show a slide or a chart; words alone can't adequately describe a graphic concept. But visuals often seem to hinder speakers. Instead of acting relaxed and giving the talk at a natural pace, speakers have to match their pace with that of the PowerPoint presentation.

Worse, in most 20-minute speeches, only two or three graphics are really needed to communicate. So the rest of the PowerPoint is filled with "word slides." The word slides use bulleted phrases, called "talking points," that highlight key phrases from the speech and are for the most part unnecessary.

Another problem with visual aids is that they put the speaker completely at the mercy of mechanical devices: laptops with a hard drive crash; slides that get stuck in their trays; film projectors with bulbs that burn out; overhead transparencies that smudge in sweaty palms; unsteady flip-chart easels that collapse at the slightest touch. These mechanical disasters can ruin a speech. And they are not uncommon.

## 9. *Handouts*

Do not distribute your handouts until after the speech is over. If you distribute them beforehand, the audience will read the handouts and ignore the speaker. A typed or typeset copy of your speech, cleanly reprinted on good-quality white paper, is the best handout you can give. If you don't have time to prepare copies of the speech, then distribute reprints of articles you've written on the same topic as the one covered in your talk.

### 10. Pick a Catchy Title for Your Speech

When you speak, you'll lead off with the first sentence, not the title. But the title will be used in mailings, flyers, and other promotions aimed at attracting an audience for your talk. "The name of your speech can make the difference between an empty house and an attentive crowd," notes Ron Huff, executive creative director of Foote, Cone & Belding, New York.

"Effective Management of Overseas Trade Show Exhibits" is a boring title. "How to Set Up a Booth at a Japanese Electronics Show—And Live to Tell About It" is much more enticing.

## WRITING PROMOTIONAL NEWSLETTERS

Many organizations publish newsletters that they distribute free to customers, clients, prospects, employees, journal editors, and decision makers in their industries.

The stories in these newsletters are similar in tone and content to the press releases and feature stories I've discussed. They are designed to promote, either directly or indirectly, the organization and its activities, services, or products.

The newsletter has less credibility than a story appearing in a trade magazine because readers know it is self-published by the firm. On the other hand, a company can use the newsletter to say whatever it wants without fear of being censored, rewritten, or misquoted by an editor.

Newsletters do not tend to generate leads or sales. Rather, they build your image and reputation with a select group of prospects (those who receive the newsletter) over a period of time. For this reason, the newsletter is usually the first item to be cut when a company's advertising program goes over budget.

Many clients start out with ambitious plans to publish the newsletter on a regular basis—every quarter, every other month, every month. But when production costs run over budget for the new corporate brochure or product catalog, the ad manager will make up the difference by skipping an issue or two of his newsletter.

Companies try to lure freelancers and agencies to do their newsletters for a low price with the logic, "It's not as key as advertising or direct mail so we can't afford to spend a lot. But we'll make up the difference with volume, since it's a steady thing."

Writers and agencies should approach newsletters with caution. Often a promised assignment of six newsletters turns into two.

The typical print promotional newsletter is four pages long. Text is set in two or three columns, and there is little or no white space. There are three or four major feature stories (about 1,000 words each), a few short items (two to three paragraphs), and a number of photos with captions.

Most of the stories are not written especially for the newsletter but come from other sources: press releases, condensed feature articles, speeches, case histories, sales literature, ad campaigns. In this way, the newsletter gives additional exposure to messages you're communicating in other media.

For instance, a bank published a newsletter called "As a Matter of Fact: A Consumer Newsletter With Money Facts for You." It was available from a rack display at local branches and filled with helpful information on personal finance. Articles included "The Mortgage Maze," "The 10% Factor . . . The Facts Behind Withholding Taxes On Interest," "Recovering from the Recession," and "The Pathway to Investing."

The relationship between a bank and its customers is based on trust. By providing investment counseling at no cost through their newsletter, the bank was helping to cement that relationship.

A supermarket, The Food Emporium, published a four-page newsletter on food, available at the checkout counter. It contained tips on nutrition, exercise, food shopping, and cooking. Each issue also featured a number of recipes.

By helping me exercise and eat right, Food Emporium gained my goodwill. By giving me recipes, they got me to come into their store to buy more food.

## A CHECKLIST OF NEWSLETTER STORY IDEAS

The above examples give you an idea of the types of stories published in promotional newsletters. The checklist below can serve as a source of ideas for putting together your own newsletter:

- ❏ News
- ❏ Explanatory articles ("how it works")
- ❏ Product stories
- ❏ Case histories
- ❏ Background information
- ❏ How to solve a problem
- ❏ Technical tips for using the product
- ❏ General how-to information and advice
- ❏ Dos and don'ts; checklists
- ❏ Industry updates
- ❏ Employee news
- ❏ Employee profiles
- ❏ Community relations news
- ❏ Financial news
- ❏ Roundup of recent sales activities
- ❏ Interviews and profiles
- ❏ Letters column

❑ Announcements or write-ups of conferences, seminars,
  trade shows, meetings
❑ Photos with captions
❑ Product selection guides

Today, many companies are distributing their promotional
newsletters online, either in addition to or as a replacement
for a printed customer newsletter. For specific guidelines on
writing and publishing online newsletters, see chapter 11.

# 10 🪶

# WRITING COMMERCIALS AND
# MULTIMEDIA PRESENTATIONS

Writing television commercials is the most prestigious assignment in all of advertising. To a copywriter, getting a chance to write a commercial for a major prime-time advertiser is like a minor league baseball player getting to pitch for the Yankees.

As a writer who has spent 95 percent of his career writing print advertising, I acknowledge this fact with a sigh. Personally, I believe print advertising has far more selling power than TV and that there is no greater challenge than writing a print ad that brings back checks, orders, or people to the store.

However, I recognize that you are eager to find out how to write good television as well as print. And so I have combined my limited TV experience with the thinking of colleagues, consultants, and other experts to come up with advice you may find useful.

Today, more commercials are competing for our attention than ever before. The challenge is to make your commercial stand out from the rest and attract the consumer's attention. But advertisers are unsure as to how to do this.

One school believes the "creative" approach is the solution to TV's clutter. Dramatic stories, fast-paced action, surreal fantasy landscapes, animation, computer graphics, the "New wave" look, and other techniques are used to give commercials distinct graphic appeal—often, in my opinion, at the expense of the sales pitch. These commercials stand out, but they don't sell, because they tend to ignore the product and its appeal to the consumer.

A second school embraces old-fashioned values. They believe that simple commercials, with honest and straightforward presentations of the product and its benefits, are what convince consumers to write checks and open wallets. One example is the early MCI commercials using Burt Lancaster and Joan Rivers to deliver the pitch. No fancy computer graphics, no blue jeans turning into rocket ships—just good old-fashioned selling that works.

Many advertising experts are rising to defend the straightforward approach to TV commercials. Faith Popcorn, president of BrainReserve Advertising in New York, predicts that we're moving into an age of product intelligence, in which consumers will demand real information, "real sell."

Today's commercials don't fill this need. According to one study, 85 percent of those surveyed said commercials are funny or clever. But 68 percent of these people said commercials don't give them any facts but just create an image.

Not everyone in advertising believes commercials should be informative. Once, on the old Phil Donahue show, advertising executive Anne Tolstoi Wallach was asked why advertisers didn't make commercials that are plain, blunt, and honest, with no frills.

Wallach replied that information alone is not remembered. She pointed out that teenagers have been exposed to a continuous stream of anti-drug information, yet drug use is on the rise. "We don't take things in through information," said Wallach. "We take things in emotionally and in many other ways even we are not sure [of]." (Later in the broadcast,

Donahue remarked, "Style and form get more attention than substance.")

As an example, Wallach pointed to the Calvin Klein jeans commercials featuring Brooke Shields. She said the commercials were successful because of "one gorgeous girl and the world's greatest photographer."

It's true that certain ads and commercials achieve dramatic results by breaking the rules. But these successes are unpredictable. Only by knowing and using what works do copywriters achieve consistently high sales results.

And I disagree with the statement that people don't take things in through information. Browse the shelves of your local bookstore; you'll find that "how-to" and straight informational-type books dominate the publishing industry. What's more, the authors of these books don't resort to trickery, grandstanding, or gimmicks—they tell their story through a straightforward presentation of the facts. They know that the real customer for their book is someone who wants and needs the information it contains.

And so it is with products. The serious prospect is an information seeker; she wants to be well informed before she spends her hard-earned dollars. Too many commercials waste their effort pitching to the nonprospect, someone who is unlikely to turn into a paying customer.

Advertisers emulate the showmanship and production values of Hollywood feature films in their efforts to get these nonprospects to watch their commercials. They forget that the goal is not to get people to watch, but to get people to buy or to prefer one brand to another. Long ago, David Ogilvy and other advertising pioneers proved there is no correlation between a person liking a commercial and being sold by it.

There are numerous examples of factual commercials outselling entertaining ones. Malcolm D. MacDougall, who produced commercials for Ronald Reagan's 1980 presidential campaign, tells how the campaign was built entirely on direct, factual, tough commercials that worked. According to Mac-Dougall, research showed that hard-hitting, informative commercials were far more effective in selling Reagan for president than a soft-sell image commercial they had run early in the campaign.

"I have wondered often if 'creativity' doesn't sometimes get in the way of believability," *Advertising Age* columnist Sid Bernstein wrote in a column on TV commercials. "I have a feeling that what we really need is more simplicity. More simple, honest selling. More dignity, more clarity. Less confusion . . . less emphasis on sensational entertainment and more emphasis on making a sensible buy."

Some advertisers hope to make their campaigns stand out by spending large sums of money to produce lavish, dazzling commercials. But a big budget is no guarantee of success, nor does a small budget doom you to failure. TV's longest-running commercial, the one offering the record set of "150 Music Masterpieces" by mail, was made in 1968 for $5,000. To date, it has sold $25 million worth of albums.

## THE 12 TYPES OF COMMERCIALS

I've always thought writing fiction was an original act, one that didn't fit into a formula.

But in a class on screen writing, the instructor surprised us by saying, "I know you think what you've written is very special. But people who write and produce films have documented just thirty-six dramatic situations. All screenplays can be put in one of these categories." She listed some of the categories as revolution, madness, crimes of love, ambition, remorse, disaster, and adultery.

Although TV commercials seemingly offer infinite variety,

there are fewer TV commercial formats than there are screen-play situations. Twelve of these are described below.

## 1. Demonstrations

Demonstrations show how a product works. If you are selling a food processor, you show how quickly and easily it slices, dices, blends, and mixes.

Demonstrations are effective for comparing two products. On the left of the screen, you show how sticky and dull most car waxes are. On the right, you show how easily your wax goes on, how brightly it shines, and how it repels water like a duck.

Demonstrations can be quite dramatic. A commercial for HTH pool chlorinator showed a woman sitting by a pool as the voice-over told how crystal clear HTH makes pool water. Suddenly, the woman shoots up through the water. We find out she was actually in the pool and that the commercial was shot underwater, dramatically demonstrating the clarity of water treated with HTH.

Demonstrations are powerful sales boosters. Mail-order advertisers know that the best way to motivate a viewer to pick up the phone and order a product is with a straightforward demonstration commercial.

## 2. Testimonials

Testimonials are used to add credibility to a claim. People more readily believe praise for a product when it comes from a customer or a third party rather than the manufacturer.

Some of the most effective testimonials are those featuring real people who use and like the product. Real people are more believable than paid actors or "staged" interviews. To get genuine testimonials from real product users, commercial producers use hidden cameras to film reactions to product use and answers to questions.

Many advertisers pay celebrities to endorse their products, reasoning that celebrities draw attention and that people hang on their every word.

The jury is still out on celebrity advertising. Steve Wynn had great success promoting his casino with celebrity spokesman Frank Sinatra. Many other celebrity commercials—for example, Glenn Ford for Avis—have been failures.

Commercial makers do agree that a celebrity must be right for the product. Britney Spears can generate excitement for Pepsi, but is less appropriate for investment banking commercials.

### 3. Stand-up Presenter

In this type of commercial, an actor stands before the camera and delivers a straightforward sales pitch on the virtues of the product.

The stand-up presenter, also known as a "talking head" or "pitchman," can be especially effective when the sales pitch you have is so strong that it doesn't need to be gussied up. MCI used stand-up presenter Burt Lancaster to deliver one single, powerful sales fact: that MCI long distance reaches all the places AT&T does but costs at least 30 percent less.

### 4. Slice-of-Life

The slice-of-life is a miniature play centering around two or more people and a story involving the product. In one toothpaste commercial, a little boy in pajamas is teary-eyed. He is sad because Mom scolded him for not brushing his teeth. Dad explains that Mom is not mad but concerned for his health: Brushing will give him a mouth full of pearly white, cavity-free teeth. The little boy smiles and laughs; Mom loves him after all.

My condensed description makes the spot sound trite, and many copywriters do indeed look down upon this type of commercial as hackneyed. But remember, there is no relationship between people liking a commercial and being sold by it. Slice-of-life may be a cliché but it is still an effective sales technique.

### 5. Lifestyle Advertising

A lifestyle commercial focuses on the user and how the product fits into his lifestyle. Miller Beer dedicates each of a series of commercials to blue-collar workers in different trades; the commercials are celebrations of the working man and woman and how a good cold Miller rewards them for their labor. The commercials do not center on price, methods of brewing, ingredients, taste, or other ways in which Miller differs from competing brands.

Another example of lifestyle advertising is the commercial for Grey Poupon mustard. We see that Grey Poupon is the mustard of the rich; they all carry it in the refrigerators in the back of their limos. Grey Poupon is positioned as an upper-class mustard.

### 6. Animation

Animation—cartoons—is effective in selling to children. But animation generally fails to sell to adults. Today a popular technique is to combine live action with computer animation, such as the Captain Crunch commercials where kid actors interact with Captain Crunch and other animated figures.

### 7. Jingles

A jingle is an advertising slogan set to music. Famous jingles of the past include McDonald's "You Deserve a Break Today," Pepsi's "Catch That Pepsi Spirit," and Diet Coke's "You're Gonna Drink It Just for the Taste of It." The best jingles implant slogans in people's minds by setting the slogans to catchy, memorable tunes that people just can't stop humming or singing.

### 8. Visual as Hero

Some advertisers treat commercial making as filmmaking, not as selling. They produce mini-feature films with color and visual quality that surpasses most television shows and motion pictures. An example of this was the auto commercial for the "Turbo Z." The action takes place in a steamy, dark "city of the future" reminiscent of the science-fiction film *Blade Runner*.

Unusual graphic treatments can glue viewers to the set. But do these far-out entertainments sell products? I haven't read any articles or case studies that say they do.

### 9. Humor

Funny commercials are in. Witness the popularity of Wendy's "Where's the beef?" and the fast-talking spots for Federal Express. We know for a fact that people like funny commercials. Whether they are sold by them is another story.

Very few copywriters are able to write humorous copy. And when a funny commercial falls flat, it becomes a sales disaster. Unless you are 99.9 percent sure that you are funny (and that your audience will think so, too), avoid the funny commercial. What is funny to one viewer is foolish to another.

### 10. Continuing Characters

The use of a continuing character—a fictional person who appears in a series of commercials and print ads—is extremely effective in building recognition of a brand. Successful fictional characters include Mr. Whipple, the Jolly Green Giant, Aunt Bluebell, Mr. Goodwrench, and the Pillsbury Doughboy. If you create a fictional character that captures the public's fancy, use him continuously and heavily until research or sales show that your customers are tiring of him.

## 11. Reason-Why Copy

Reason-why copy lists the reasons why people should buy the product. A commercial for Hebrew National Franks showed people eating and enjoying hot dogs while the voice-over narration listed the reasons why people like to eat the franks. Reason-why commercials can be effective, although reason-why copy seems to work better in print than on the air.

## 12. Emotion

Commercials that use nostalgia, charm, or sentimentality to tug at your heartstrings (and your wallet) can be both memorable and persuasive. In one of AT&T's famous "Reach Out and Touch Someone" commercials, a mother sheds tears of joy because her son calls long distance just to say he loves her. I remember being moved and thinking how nice it would be to call relatives I hadn't spoken to in a long time. The commercial worked—at least for me.

Like humor, genuine emotional copy is hard to write. If you can do it, more power to you. Most copywriters have a better shot sticking to demonstrations, pitchmen, testimonials, and other "straight-sell" formats.

## TIPS ON WRITING TV SPOTS

Here are some tips on writing TV commercials that are arresting, memorable, and persuasive:

• TV is primarily a medium of pictures, not words. Be sure your pictures deliver a selling message. If you can't figure out what is being sold when the sound is turned off, the commercial is a flop.
• However, sight and sound must work together. Words should explain what the pictures are showing.

• Viewers can take in a limited amount of sight and sound in 30 or 60 seconds. So, if your sales pitch requires a barrage of words, keep the pictures simple. On the other hand, if you use complex graphics, keep the words to a minimum. Viewers can't handle a dazzling visual display and fast-talking announcer at the same time.

• Think about your customer—the guy or gal in front of the television. Is your commercial interesting and important enough to stop your customer from getting up and going to the refrigerator or the bathroom?

• Think and plan your commercial within existing budgetary limitations. Special effects, jingles, actors, animation, computer graphics, and shooting on location make the cost of commercials skyrocket. Only the stand-up presenter and straightforward, in-the-studio product demonstration are relatively inexpensive to produce.

• Make sure the lead of your commercial is a real grabber. The first 4 seconds of a commercial are like the headline of a print ad; they decide whether the viewer will sit through your presentation or fix a snack. Open with something irresistible: snappy music, an arresting visual, a dramatic situation, a real-life problem.

• If you are selling a product that can be purchased off the supermarket shelf, show the label. Use close-ups to draw attention to the package. People will buy the product later if they remember the package from your commercial.

• Use motion. Film, unlike slide shows, is a medium of motion. Show cars driving, maple syrup pouring, airplanes flying, popcorn popping, club soda fizzing. Avoid stagnant commercials. Keep it moving.

• Also, don't forget that television offers sound as well as pictures. Let the viewer hear the car engine roaring, the pancakes frying, the airplane whooshing, the popcorn popping, the club soda fizzing, the ice cubes plopping into a cold, tall drink. Many people find the sound of sizzling bacon more appetizing than the look. (Smell may be even more appetizing, but television with smell is not yet a reality. Nor do I know of any manufacturers who are developing such a device.)

• Use "supers." These are titles, in white type, superimposed over the picture. The super reinforces a sales point made in the commercial or makes an additional point not covered in the spoken narration. If you are selling vitamins by mail, put up a super that says, "NOT AVAILABLE IN STORES." People will not buy from a mail-order commercial if they think they can get the product in a store.

• Repeat the product name and the main selling point at least twice. There are two reasons why you should do this. First, repetition aids the viewer in remembering the product. Second, many viewers may not have been paying attention during the beginning of your commercial, so you want to make sure they know who you are and what you are selling.

• Avoid hackneyed situations that bore viewers. Make your commercial fresh, memorable, a little bit different. Burger King's commercials with Emmanuel Lewis were essentially stand-up presenter spots. But they were made memorable by the use of Lewis, then a cute, short, twelve-year-old boy who could pass for five.

• Don't neglect the product. Show people eating it, wearing it, riding it, using it, enjoying it. Demonstrate the product. Have people talk about how good the product is. Apply proven techniques of print advertising to television, and you will be delighted with the results.

• If you want viewers to call or write in to order a product or request more information, announce this at the beginning of the commercial ("Get paper and pencil ready to take advantage of this special TV offer . . ."). Few people keep a notepad handy while they watch TV.

• If you use a celebrity (either on camera or voice-over), identify the celebrity with a voice-over introduction or super-imposed title ("Bill Cosby for Jell-O Pudding"). A large number of people will not recognize celebrities unless you identify them. And they will not be impressed or swayed by the celebrity unless they know who he is.

• In local retail commercials, give the address and clear directions to the store. If you have many locations, urge view-ers to consult their phone books for the location nearest to them.

• The four basic commercial lengths are 10, 30, 60, and 120 seconds. Ten-second commercials are usually "ID" or identifi-cation spots. ID spots just drive home a product name and support the campaign's 30- or 60-second spots. However, some advertisers, such as C&C Cola, save money by delivering their entire pitch in 10-second spots. Commercials that build prefer-ence for a brand-name product are either 30 or 60 seconds long. Mail-order advertisers use 120-second campaigns because they need to deliver more complete information to convince people to respond.

• Ninety words is about the most you can cram into a 60-second commercial. Many contain much less.

• Because time is limited, a commercial should stick to one main thought or sales point: flame-broiling beats frying; Midas installs more mufflers than anyone else; Sprint costs less than AT&T; Apple makes nice, friendly, easy-to-use computers. Only in brochures, print ads, and direct mail do you have the space you need to cover all the facts. TV is more limiting.

## TYPING THE SCRIPT

The manuscript format for TV commercials is simple: Video (pictures) are typed on the left, audio (words and sound effects) are typed on the right.

What's important is writing a good commercial. Don't worry about the technical terms. You'll learn them when you need to, but they are not essential. All that counts is that your commercial is arresting, memorable, and persuasive.

Here are just a few of the basic terms to help get you started:

ANNCR—Announcer. The narrator of the commercial.

CU—Close-up. An extremely tight shot in which a single object, such as a package label, dominates the screen.

LS—Long shot. A shot of a distant subject.

MS—Medium shot. A shot of the subject in the foreground, showing a substantial amount of the scenery.

SFX—Sound effects. Background sound other than human voice or musical instruments.

TS—Tight shot. A shot leaving little or no space around the subject.

VO—Voice-over. The voice of an off-camera narrator.

The commercial below is typed in proper commercial manuscript format. It's also a good example of straightforward copy packed with product benefits.

Writer: Amy Bly
Product: Galantine Chicken (30 seconds)

| VIDEO: | AUDIO: |
|---|---|
| 1. MS to CU: Golden brown Galantine chicken on platter. | 1. ANNCR: (VO): You're looking at a plump, juicy Galantine chicken. But this is no ordinary chicken. Because we've taken out the bones. |
| 2. MS: Man slicing chicken. One-quarter to one-third of meat is already sliced on platter. | 2. You can slice right through it . . . |
| 3. CU: Array of chicken dishes on buffet table. | 3. Prepare any number of delicious chicken dishes, from chicken scampi to chicken salad, quickly and easily, without having to cut around bones. |
| 4. MS: Smiling family eating chicken. | 4. A Galantine chicken costs more than an ordinary chicken. |
| 5. CU: Fully sliced chicken on platter. | 5. But then there's no waste. You get one hundred percent meat. |
| 6. CU: Packaged chicken, showing Galantine name and logo. | 6. So if you have a bone to pick with ordinary chicken, try Galantine instead. At your butcher's and at fine grocers everywhere. |

There are a number of things I like about this commercial:

1. It's simple—easy to take in—and inexpensive to produce.
2. The visuals show the product, a demonstration of the product (easy slicing of boneless chicken), people enjoying the product, and the package—all in 30 seconds.

3. The narration tells us the unique selling feature of the chicken (no bones), the benefits of this feature (slice right through it, no waste, quick and easy), and shows what you can do with the product (prepare any number of dishes).

4. The ending ("if you have a bone to pick with ordinary chicken") is a clever play on words that leaves a smile on your face. And it tells you where you can buy the product.

Here's another effective 30-second spot from the same writer (Amy Bly, my wife):

Writer: Amy Bly
Product: YOURS beer for women (30 seconds)

| VIDEO: | AUDIO: |
| --- | --- |
| 1. MS: Well-dressed couple sitting in fancy restaurant. Man reaches for bottle of beer on table. Woman slaps his hand away playfully. | 1. WOMAN: Hey, that's YOURS! |
| 2. MS: Man's face. He looks over at her, puzzled, grinning. | 2. MAN: If it's mine, why can't I have it? |
| 3. TS: Woman's finger pointing at label on bottle. | 3. WOMAN: Because YOURS is the beer that's made for women only. |
| 4. MS: Woman pouring beer. | 4. SFX: Beer being poured into glass. ANNCR: YOURS is bubbly, light, and has fewer calories than ordinary beer. |

| | |
|---|---|
| 5. MS: Woman finishes pouring beer and picks up glass. | 5. ANNCR: And, it comes in convenient ten-ounce bottles that pour one perfect glass of beer . . . enough to quench your thirst without filling you up. |
| 6. MS: Man reaching for glass of beer. | 6. MAN: Why can't I have YOURS? |
| 7. MS: Woman pulls glass away, smiling. | 7. WOMAN: 'Cause it's mine . . . |
| 8. TS: Bottle of YOURS against black background. | 8. ANNCR: (VO): YOURS . . . the first beer for women only. |

This is basically a lifestyle commercial combined with a presentation of product benefits. YOURS is a beer for women who eat in fancy restaurants, dress well, and have attractive, personable dinner companions. You can picture Sarah Jessica Parker and Dylan McDermott playing the upscale duo.

Other things I like about the script:

1. It is fun, humorous, and playful. But all the playfulness is relevant to the product!
2. The product has a strong position: "The first beer for women only."
3. The commercial highlights product features that would appeal to women: light, few calories, small servings per bottle.
4. The name is repeated five times and the label shown twice.

## HOW TO WRITE RADIO COMMERCIALS

Radio is different from TV and print. And the difference is: no pictures.

The radio copywriter works with words and sounds. Words and sounds must create a picture of the product in the reader's mind.

A radio commercial for "Aunt Lucy's Luscious Blueberry Pie" can't show the family eating and enjoying the pie. So you must use sound to paint the picture of the pie being sliced, of a fork cutting into crust, of chewing, of people "mmm"-ing in delight and praising their hostess.

Suppose the blueberry pies are sold in local supermarkets in a distinctive blue foil wrapper. You can't show the package on radio. You must have the announcer say, "Look for the homemade pie in the blue foil wrapper at your local supermarket and bake shop."

A mini-industry has developed around independent radio production houses that write and produce radio commercials for ad agencies and their clients. Many ad agency writers and creative directors look down their noses at radio (perhaps because the money involved is insignificant compared with television) and are happy to pass on radio commercials to outsiders.

There are trends and stars in radio advertising. For years, Stan Freberg was the rage with humorous radio commercials for Chung King and others. Then, Dick Orkin and Bert Berdis were the reigning kings. Then John Cleese of Monty Python fame became a hit with his spots for Callard & Bowser candies and Kronenbourg beer. Now Jerry Seinfeld stars in American Express ads.

In an article published in *Writer's Digest*, copywriter David Campiti offered these tips to radio novices.

• Lock onto a salesperson's "keys." This is "inside information" a company's salespeople get from talking with customers.

• Feedback from customers can reveal key selling points. For instance, a copywriter interviewed farmers to find out why his radio commercial was not selling rat poison by mail. He discovered that farmers with rat problems were embarrassed about it and didn't want the postman or neighbors to see them receive rat poison packages in the mail. The copywriter added a line to the commercial about how the poison was mailed in a plain brown wrapper, and sales soared.

• Talk about benefits. Tell the audience what the client's goods will do for them.

• Be concise. Use short sentences.

• Repeat key information. Minimum: list store names twice; addresses once toward the end, or twice if confusing. Include phone numbers at least twice, more in a 60-second commercial.

• Know what you're writing about. Research the product.

• Know what resources are available to the producers of radio commercials. Learn to use production facilities. Know the extent of their music and sound effects libraries, the quality and capability of recording equipment, and the abilities of actors who will read your copy over the air.

Here are two radio commercials I like and the reasons why. First, a 60-second spot from the Masonry Institute of St. Louis:

MAN: Uh, today we're speaking with the Three Little Pigs, is that . . . ?

PIGS: Yes: That's right. You got it, buddy.

MAN: Yeah, well, tell me, ever since you guys opted to build with brick, have you had any further difficulties with uh . . .

PIG #1: Big, bad, and breathless?

MAN: Right.

PIG #2: No, he never comes around anymore.

MAN: That's good.

PIG #3: He knows better than to try and blow this pad down, boy!

MAN: Yes, well, besides solving your security problems, there must have been other reasons for your choosing brick.

PIG #1: Listen, when you're spending eighty big ones on a house these days you want something that'll last, right guys?

PIG #2: Oh yeah.

PIG #3: You said it.

MAN: Well, brick certainly does that, all right.

PIG #1: With little or no maintenance.

MAN: Right.

PIG #2: Not only keeps the wolf from the door but withstands fire, hail . . .

PIG #3: Aluminum-siding salesmen.

MAN: Yes, well, I notice you also have a solid brick fireplace as well.

PIG #1: Yes, we do.

MAN: Very attractive.

PIG #2: We think it adds a nice little touch.

PIG #3: Especially when the girls come over.

MAN: Safe too, I'll bet.

PIG #1: It is. They aren't. (Man and Pigs laugh.)

MAN: Is there anything else we should know about building with brick?

PIG #1: If there is, don't ask us.

MAN: Oh?

PIG #2: Ask the folks at the Masonry Institute.

MAN: The Masonry Institute?

PIG #3: They'll be happy to send you complete information.

MAN: On brick.

PIG #1: No, on paper.

MAN: What?!

PIG #1: They couldn't get a brick in the envelope . . .

(Music)

ANNCR: If you'd like to know more about building with brick, call the Masonry Institute of St. Louis at 550-5888. That's 550-5888.

The commercial caught and kept my attention because it is both fast-paced and genuinely funny. The banter between the three pigs and the interviewer keeps things lively. Yet, this clever little dialogue manages to pack a great deal of product information into 60 seconds. We learn that:

1. Brick stands up to the environment—hail, wind, storms.
2. Brick lasts a long time and requires little or no maintenance.
3. It is fireproof.

4. If your house is made of brick you won't need aluminum siding.
5. You can use brick to build a safe, attractive fireplace.
6. The Masonry Institute will send free information on building with brick to anyone who asks for it.

The second radio spot that caught my ear is this 60-second commercial for the California Milk Advisory Board. The commercial was produced and performed by Dick Orkin and Bert Berdis:

MILK EXECUTIVE: Hello.

SIDNEY: California Milk Advisory Board?

EXECUTIVE: Yes.

SIDNEY: May I make a small suggestion about your jingle?

EXECUTIVE: "Any time is the right time for milk"?

SIDNEY: Yes, it's real catchy, but maybe you ought to change it to, "Any time is the right time for milk except at a bullfight."

EXECUTIVE (laughs): Sounded almost like you said, "Any time is the right time for milk except at a bullfight."

SIDNEY: That's what I said.

EXECUTIVE: What . . . ?

SIDNEY: Allow me to introduce myself. I'm Sidney Feltzer, freelance matador.

EXECUTIVE: Uh-huh.

SIDNEY: I love your milk.

EXECUTIVE: Uh-huh.

SIDNEY: Drink it all the time. It's cold and refreshing . . .

EXECUTIVE: Go on, Sidney.

SIDNEY: But trying to drink milk with one hand and wave my cape with the other is just so . . .

EXECUTIVE: Sidney, you didn't try to, uh . . . ?

SIDNEY: Just today I went through six cartons.

EXECUTIVE: Of milk?

SIDNEY: Pants.

EXECUTIVE: Pants?

SIDNEY: See, when you turn and run, the bull is right there . . .

EXECUTIVE: Sidney, why not have your milk afterward?

SIDNEY: In the hospital?

EXECUTIVE: No, no, I meant after you exercise, milk is terrific, or with snacks, or just sitting down watching television.

SIDNEY: Oh, I can't do that.

EXECUTIVE: Watch television?

SIDNEY: No, sit.

EXECUTIVE: Oh.

SIDNEY: See, when you turn and run, the bull is right there.

EXECUTIVE: I see, I get it all right, Sidney.

JINGLE: Yeah! Any time at all . . . is the time for milk!

SIDNEY: Except during a bullfight.

EXECUTIVE: Hang it up, Sidney.

SIDNEY: My cape?

EXECUTIVE: The phone.

SIDNEY: Oh, right. (Music fades.)

ANNCR: This phone call brought to you by the California Milk Advisory Board.

Again, a fast-paced, humorous commercial with a persuasive message. Note the use of very short (one- and two-word) sentences to set the pace.

## NONBROADCAST AV

Radio and TV commercials are the most visible part of the copywriter's work, because we hear them every day. But each year, there are thousands of scripts written and produced that we never get to hear or see.

This area of copywriting is known as *nonbroadcast audiovisual (AV)*. These are audiovisual presentations created by a company and used to reach select, small audiences. Instead of being aired over radio or TV, these presentations are shown at meetings, trade shows, seminars, presentations, and in one-on-one sales pitches where the salesperson is sitting down with a customer.

Many different media are available for nonbroadcast AV. These include:

- PowerPoint
- CD-ROM
- Single-projector slide show
- Dual-projector slide show
- Videotape
- DVD

- Multimedia (combination video and slides with multiple projectors)
- Macromedia Flash
- Videotext
- Software

And these presentations are used in many different applications:

- Employee communications
- Trade show exhibits
- Seminars and conferences
- Recruitment
- Community relations
- Public relations
- Sales support
- Advertising inquiry fulfillment (tapes or films sent to select prospects who respond to your ads)
- Presentations to top management
- Training
- Product introduction
- Product demonstration
- Case histories
- Meetings
- Sales aids for company salespeople and sales reps
- Point-of-purchase display in retail locations
- Executive summaries of annual reports, sales presentations, and other printed literature
- To record historic events

The script format for slide shows and films is the same as for TV commercials: visuals on the left, audio on the right.

But nonbroadcast AV is not limited to 30 or 60 seconds. You can make it as long or as short as you like. Eight to ten minutes is the best length for a slide show or film. Twenty minutes is the maximum. Beyond that, your audience will begin to fade.

Nonbroadcast AV is much less expensive to produce than TV commercials. A one-minute commercial could cost $40,000 or more. A ten-minute nonbroadcast videotape can be produced for $5,000 or less.

John Baldoni, a freelance scriptwriter, offers these tips for writing nonbroadcast AV:

- Write words for the ear, not for the eye. A script is not simply words on a page, but words that are spoken aloud.
- The spoken words should be precise, coherent, and full of vivid images.
- Be crystal clear. The listener doesn't have the luxury of referring back to the text. Your writing must be readily understood the first time it is heard.
- Research. Find out all you can about the topic, the product, the purpose, the audience.
- The script should repeat the key selling points several times.
- The beginning is critical and must "hook" the audience, locking their attention.
- Be lively, catching, precise. Use active verbs, colorful words and phrases.
- Spoon-feed the audience. Don't assault them with fact after fact. Be selective about the facts you choose. An AV presentation doesn't tell the whole story but should leave the viewer hungry for more information.
- Use words to paint pictures that complement the actual visuals on the screen.
- Be as concise and direct as possible. Avoid complicated sentences.

## WRITING FLASH PRESENTATIONS

A relatively new medium for audiovisual presentations is Macromedia Flash, which enables animation on Web sites.

Once thought of strictly as a software tool for creating mostly ornamental animated Web presentations, Flash has evolved into a sophisticated application for developing Web sites. The Web components being produced with Flash today use media not to just entertain, but to add value to the user's interaction with the Internet. Flash makes transactions easier, more intuitive, and more efficient.

With the versatility to incorporate database-driven applications, animation, graphics, video, and audio, Flash can be used to create whatever kind of application interface or user experience you desire, with very few limitations.

The two main advantages of designing Web sites using Flash are: (1) a more contemporary, cutting-edge, graphically sophisticated user experience, and (2) increased usability through reduced latency and more efficient transaction processing. Translation: The pictures move smoothly on the screen without jerkiness or delays.

For instance, a Fortune 100 life insurance company wanted to give its sales force better tools for selling IRAs to their clients. Using Flash, the company built an online IRA calculator. With this new tool, its insurance agents and brokers can quickly and easily create a compelling, customized IRA plan to present to clients.

This online tool not only calculates investment contributions and savings growth; it also incorporates graphics (such as bar and pie charts) to enhance the presentation visually. The plan can be sent to a printer to produce a colorful, professional-looking printed document for the client.

The agent or broker can save all the IRA plans to a database for various clients. These IRA plans can be modified at any time, printed and mailed to the client, or e-mailed to the client as a PDF file.

Flash scripts are similar in style and format to TV commercials. Here is a sample Flash script for a Lucent Technologies Web site on fiber-optic cable:

| *VISUAL:* | *AUDIO:* |
| --- | --- |
| Title—"Metro Networks with AllWave Fiber"; against a background of white clouds in a blue sky. | Building metro networks . . . with high-capacity AllWave fiber from Lucent Technologies. |
| Camera zooms through clouds and we see a busy city from the sky; as the narration progresses, we get closer to the buildings. | There's no application more demanding then a metropolitan area network, or "MAN." The simple reason? The greater density of users in highly populated areas. |
| Map of United States. | How much denser is the user base in metro areas than the U.S. average? The entire United States has a population of around 260 million in an area of almost 4 million square miles. |
| Green dots appear on the USA map symbolizing a moderate density of users in the network. | That's a population density of around 65 people per square mile. |
| X ray of the city shown earlier—outlines of the buildings are in green. | Urban networks serve many more users. For instance, Manhattan, one of the largest cities, has over 7 million people in a 309-square-mile area. |

## WRITING FOR POWERPOINT

It's an insidious trend: Conference sponsors and meeting planners insisting that speakers create their presentations using a specific software product, namely PowerPoint.

Why is mandating use of PowerPoint by your speakers bad? For several reasons.

First, dictating a format and its software takes the focus away from where it should be—on the content, message, and audience—and puts it on the technology. It's like telling a writer, "I don't care how good the piece is as long as it's in Word 7."

Second, it encourages a conformity that can rob speakers and presentations of their individuality. Tell me you haven't thought more than once that all PowerPoint presentations look alike after awhile.

Third, it's boring. So many bad presentations have been prepared with PowerPoint that I believe the very use of the medium can be a signal to some audience members that says, "Prepare to be bored."

Fourth, it renders many speakers ineffective or at least less effective. When the speaker is focusing on his clicker, keyboard, or computer screen, he is not focusing on—or interacting with—his audience, a key requisite for a successful talk.

Fifth, it locks the speaker into the prepared slides, reducing spontaneity, ad-libbing, and the valuable ability to adjust the presentation in response to audience reaction and interest—another requisite for a successful talk.

Sixth, it can literally put the audience to sleep. What's the first step in preparing an audience to view a PowerPoint presentation? To dim the lights—an action proven to induce drowsiness in humans.

What should be done? Here are my suggestions for creating such an environment in the computer age:

• *Don't require PowerPoint.* If the speaker wants to use PowerPoint, fine. If she doesn't, also fine. Never force a speaker to use a format or medium she doesn't like or is uncomfortable with. It will compromise her performance and effectiveness significantly.

• *Don't require visuals at all.* Does this surprise you? The fact is, many subjects—telephone skills, for instance—do not lend themselves to charts, graphics, tables, and other PowerPoint-type visuals. If you force every speaker to use visuals—even with subjects that don't require it—you'll get that dreaded beast: a PowerPoint presentation created just because someone said the presenter had to have one. You've seen these: full of word slides and bullet lists that contribute nothing to communication.

• *Check out your speakers in advance.* See them live or watch their videos. Talk to clients who have hired them. Convince yourself that they're pros. Then leave them alone and let them do their job. Don't hire a trained surgeon, then tell him what surgical instrument to use on your brain during the operation.

• *Avoid the uniformity trap.* PowerPoint presentations suffer from sameness, which is the first cousin of dullness. Audiences crave freshness and difference.

• *Avoid the handout trap.* A key advantage of PowerPoint is the ability to easily turn slides into hard-copy handouts. The trouble is, most of these slide printouts, removed from the speech itself, are cryptic when viewed in isolation if not totally meaningless. If the world could communicate effectively with just diagrams and bullets, sentences would never have been invented.

Okay. Let's say you are putting together a presentation and PowerPoint is required. What can you do to make it more effective?

First, don't have the projector on all the time. Use Power-Point selectively, not throughout the entire presentation.

When there's a valuable picture to show, show it. When you're through with it, turn off the projector and turn the lights back on. The brightness rouses the audience out of their darkness-induced stupor. In a darkened room, it's too easy to close your eyes and nod off a bit.

Second, use visuals only when they communicate more effectively than words. If you are talking about quality, having the word *Quality* onscreen adds little to your point. On the other hand, if you want to explain what an aardvark looks like, there are no words that can do it as effectively as simply showing a picture.

Third, don't overcrowd your slides. Have no more than one major visual per slide, and keep it simple; avoid, for example, process diagrams with too many lines and connections. If the slide is text, limit it to five or six bullets of no more than 5 to 8 words each.

Fourth, consider adding other media as supplements or even alternatives to PowerPoint. When I taught telephone selling, the sound of a ringing telephone and a prop—a toy telephone—engaged the trainees in a way computer slides could not.

Fifth, design your presentation so that, if there is a problem with the computer equipment, you can go on without it. There's nothing more embarrassing than watching a speaker fall apart because he can't find the right slide. Use visuals as an enhancement, not a crutch.

Am I a dinosaur or a curmudgeon, to rail against Power-Point in this manner? Perhaps. I don't own a laptop computer, wireless phone, pager, or PDA.

But one thing I have learned in twenty years of teaching and giving presentations: The best presenters have conversations with their audiences. If you believe you need to have a computer running to have an effective conversation, maybe that's a premise you want to rethink.

Graphic design consultant Roger C. Parker offers the following tips for preparing your PowerPoint presentations:

- Keep visuals simple. Avoid decorative clip art. These often project a cartoon-like image. Add graphics only when they support your arguments.
- Use keywords, not sentences. Visuals should provide a framework, not a script, for your presentation. Limiting text to keywords permits you to use a large, easy-to-read type size.
- Avoid complex backgrounds. When in doubt, choose black type against a white background.
- Personalize your visuals. Add your logo to each visual, along with the presentation title and date.

# 11

# WRITING FOR THE WEB

Ten years ago, 100 percent of my copywriting was print and zero percent was on the Internet. Today, 50 percent of my copywriting is print and 50 percent is online.

The conclusion? A working copywriter today is going to be doing a lot of writing for the Internet. Some of your assignments will focus on driving traffic to an existing Web site. Others will focus on creating Web copy, either adding pages to existing sites or creating brand-new sites.

## WHAT'S WORKING IN ONLINE MARKETING TODAY

Here is one online marketing methodology that has been proven effective for many different types of businesses: Online marketing works best when you e-mail to people who already know you.

Therefore, successful online marketers build their "house file" or "e-list" (lists of prospects and their e-mail addresses) using the process outlined below, and then sell to those people via e-mail marketing. This is called the "Organic Model" or "Agora Model."

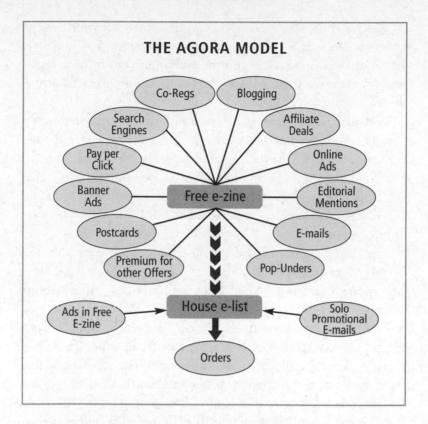

**THE AGORA MODEL**

First, the marketer builds a Web site that positions his company as an expert resource in a specific niche or industry. This is the client's "base of operations" for his online marketing campaign.

This Web site should include a home page, an "About the Company" page, and a page with brief descriptions of the client's products and services (each product or service description can link to a longer document giving more details on the item).

You should also have an "Articles Page" where you post articles you have written on your area of specialty, and where visitors can read and download these articles for free.

Write a short special report or white paper on your area of expertise, and make this available to people who visit your site. They can download it free, but in exchange, they have to register and give you their e-mail address (and any other information you want to capture).

Consider also offering a monthly online newsletter, or "e-zine." People who visit your site can subscribe free if they register and give you their e-mail address. You may want to give the visitor the option of checking a box that reads: "I give you and other companies you select permission to send me e-mail about products, services, news, and offers that may be of interest to me."

The more "content" (useful information) on your site, the better. More people will be attracted to your site, and they will spend more time on it. They will also tell others about your site.

The model is to drive traffic to your site where you get them to sign up for either your free report or free e-zine. Once they register, you have their e-mail address and can now market to them via e-mail as often as you like at no extra cost.

The bulk of your online leads, sales, and profits will come from repeat e-mail marketing to this "house e-list" of prospects. Therefore your goal is to build a large e-list of qualified prospects as quickly and inexpensively as you can.

There are a number of online marketing options that can drive traffic to your site. These include: free publicity, e-mail marketing, banner advertising, co-registrations, affiliate marketing, search engine optimization, direct mail, and e-zine advertising.

The key to success is to try a lot of different tactics in small and inexpensive tests, throw out the ones that don't work, and do more of the ones that are effective.

## COMMON ONLINE COPYWRITING ASSIGNMENTS

There is often confusion as to what the particular "deliverables" are in online copywriting, what the terms mean, and how much copy is involved.

For instance, what exactly do we mean by a "microsite"? How long is it? When should you use it?

Here are the most common online copywriting assignments I write for my clients, and the definition and scope of each:

• A *microsite*, also known as a *long-copy landing page*, is a Web site designed to sell a product—such as a newsletter, e-book, or conference—directly. Copy length is equivalent to a 4- to 8-page sales letter.

• A *short-copy landing page* is a simple landing page for a product or offer. Often used for white papers, software demos, and other inquiry fulfillment. Copy length is about the same as a magazine ad, with headline, a few paragraphs of descriptive product copy, and an online order form.

• A *transaction page* is similar to a short-copy landing page, but with even less descriptive product copy. It is basically an online form the visitor can use to either order the product or request more information.

• A *long-copy e-mail* is designed to sell a product directly by driving the recipient to a short-copy landing page or transaction page. Number of words is roughly the same as a 2- or 3-page sales letter. (E-mails are covered in the next chapter.)

• A *teaser e-mail* is a short e-mail designed to drive the readers to a microsite or long-copy landing page where they can order the product. It's the online equivalent of a ½- to 2-page sales letter.

• A *lead-generation e-mail* is similar to the teaser e-mail, but the purpose is to drive readers to a landing page or transaction page where they can request a free white paper or other information.

• An *online e-mail conversion series* is a series of follow-up e-mail messages, sent via autoresponder, designed to convert an inquiry into a sale.

• An *online ad* is typically a 100-word classified ad to run in an e-zine and drive readers to a microsite or landing page. A *banner ad* is an HTML ad on a Web site.

• A *pop-under* is a window that appears on a Web site when the visitor takes a certain action (typically trying to leave the site without ordering). It makes a special offer. Usually free, in exchange for the visitor giving his e-mail address.

## WRITING A CATALOG WEB SITE

A *catalog Web site* sells many different items, and is the online equivalent of a catalog. Catalog Web sites have the following characteristics:

• A large, searchable database of product photos and descriptions.
• A shopping cart that enables you to buy products online.

The most famous example of a catalog Web site is Amazon.com, which originally sold books only and has branched into numerous other products including videos, music, tools, and electronics.

Another example of a successful catalog Web site is www.bluenile.com, an online marketer of jewelry. It's a great example of how to set up an attractive Web site that sells merchandise online.

When you click on www.bluenile.com, you are immediately

served a pop-up window with an irresistible offer: In return for entering your e-mail address, sex, age, zip code, and marital status, you are entered into a sweepstakes to win a diamond with an appraised value of $5,000.

There is a checkbox where you can opt in to receive offers and announcements by e-mail, but this is already checked off. So you'd have to uncheck it to get off their list.

The home page is cleanly and clearly laid out; in fact, it's almost a little too stark. One could argue a jewelry site should be more elegant in design. But I don't: The jewelry shopper is well served here.

At the top is a banner with the Blue Nile logo and the tag line, "Education, Guidance, Diamonds, and Fine Jewelry." It does an adequate job of positioning the site, but it doesn't engage in a powerful way.

Copy under and to the right of the banner positions the site more effectively: "As the largest online retailer of certified diamonds and fine jewelry, we offer outstanding quality, selection, and value." They make no mention of saving money or time by buying online versus going to a local jeweler.

From there, the home page has pictures of jewelry and product descriptions that are hyperlinked to pages showing and describing those products. Simple and basic, but sensible; I wouldn't do it any other way.

There are also three additional value-added links on the home page:

1. "How to Choose a Diamond Ring" is a useful, informative guide to purchasing a diamond ring.
2. "Build Your Own Diamond Ring" lets you customize and then order a ring online with the stone and setting you select.
3. "Diamonds" searches for diamonds based on cut, color, clarity, carat weight, and price.

The mission of the Web site—to help the consumer shop for and buy a diamond or other jewelry online—is crystal clear. The entire site is designed to make the transaction as easy and painless as possible.

Most of the hyperlinks on the home page go to specific products, so you can see what stones and jewelry are available. These pages are augmented by a useful but not overwhelming choice of helpful hints on buying diamonds, product searches, and interactive jewelry design.

The major personalization feature is "Build Your Own Diamond Ring," which allows the consumer to mix and match stones and settings to personal preference, rather than buy a ring "off the shelf." There's not much other personalization, nor is it needed. The Web site allows you to enter your e-mail address to receive reminders of major holidays, but it does not allow you to enter other reminder dates, such as your anniversary or your mother's birthday.

It's fun and easy to shop for jewelry on Blue Nile. You can easily find what you are looking for, the shopping cart works well, and there are always links that let you drill down for more product detail and consumer information, whether it's a close-up photograph of a ring or a schematic diagram showing how a certain setting holds the stone in place. All told, Blue Nile is a case in point that functional, useful copy and design can help create an accessible and successful Web site.

## WRITING A WEB SITE USING THE WATERFRONT MODEL

The catalog Web site is a standard model of e-commerce proven to be profitable. Another is the "Waterfront Model."

Waterfront Media has developed a series of profitable Web sites, one of which is Denise Austin's fitness and health site, www.deniseaustin.com. All of these sites are based around what I call the "Waterfront Model," a business model for e-commerce that Waterfront has pioneered and per-fected. Let's look at the model, using Austin's site as the example.

In the Waterfront Model, the home page is what I call "tabloid-style": lots of interesting tips, items, and factoids. But prominent on the page is a section with an offer—in Austin's case, "Get your complete online fitness plan!"—with a large START HERE button.

The primary goal of the site is to get you to click on START HERE. When you do, you are offered some sort of an evaluation of your problem—as well as a plan or solution—in return for filling in the online questionnaire.

This is naturally a health and fitness evaluation, since Austin is a fitness guru. The evaluation centers on weight loss, although it touches on other topics, such as exercise. You click through a few screens, answering simple questions and giving some personal information, like how much you weigh now and your target weight.

After completing the assessment, you are offered the solution, which is typically customized (or seemingly customized) content delivered online. This is not a free offer, but the first step in converting you into a customer.

Since this is the "front-end" (first) sale, cost is typically low: just a few dollars a week or month. Once you buy, you get e-mails offering you add-on products, both Austin's and related items.

The beauty of the Waterfront Model and all Web sites built using it, is that the action to be taken is loud and clear: Click on the button labeled START HERE! And the core of the Water-front Model is innovative use of an interactive self-assessment questionnaire. The visitor must complete the questionnaire before she is offered the fitness plan, which she has to pay for. This creates the perception that the site is delivering personal-ized advice, not boilerplate content.

Not only does the site invite you to fill out a personal questionnaire, it won't offer you any sort of fitness plan until you do. In this way, the site actually *forces* you to personalize the content, which makes the advice seem more genuine. After all, how can you help me improve my health without asking personal questions (as www.deniseaustin.com does) about my health, exercise, diet, height, weight, etc.?

The most prominent involvement devices in Austin's site are several free online newsletters addressing various areas of health and fitness. There is also an "Ask Denise" page where you can post questions and have Denise answer them for you. To make the site even more interactive, I could see adding some forums or discussion groups where visitors can get information and support on relevant topics including weight loss, diet, exercise, and cardiac fitness.

The site is sensibly organized into quadrants and sections. A horizontal bar at the top of the home page gives us clearly labeled, one-click hyperlink access to the major site sections.

In the upper right quadrant of the home page, we have the cornerstone of the Waterfront Model, START HERE. There's no mistaking that the site wants you to do this, by (a) offering a fitness plan and (b) promising a number of bulleted benefits (e.g., "shed 1–2 inches from your waist").

In the upper left quadrant, you gain access to "Ask Denise," a Q&A section where Denise Austin answers your fitness and exercise questions.

In the lower left quadrant, you get a mix of free content: success stories, news ("What's doing with Denise?"), and daily tips.

In the lower right quadrant, you are given a window where you can buy some of Denise's new videos and related fitness products online.

The primary graphics are various images of toned, fit, slim, attractive Denise Austin in exercise clothes, clearly communicating that (a) the site offers help with fitness and exercise, and

(b) the methods used obviously achieve the results desired (at least for Denise).

Copy on the site indicates that it is aimed at women (for instance, it talks about reducing your dress size). If men were an equal target, I could see using more photographs of Denise and other fitness competitors in slightly more revealing exercise outfits. Not only does sex sell, but such outfits clearly show the tone and fitness achieved.

Another example of a Web site built around the Waterfront Model is www.ediets.com, a diet, nutrition, and fitness site. On February 2004, when I first clicked onto the www.ediets.com home page, the main graphic featured a picture of Victoria Principal with some article titles, and it seemed to deliberately resemble the front cover of a women's magazine—in particular, *Ladies' Home Journal*.

So right away, as a male, I could not relate to the home page. Maybe eDicts is mainly targeting women. But half of the 100 million or so males in America are overweight, too.

The home page is, again, "tabloid style"—lots of interesting little items to choose from. Unfortunately, with a tabloid-style home page, there's no single point of focus, and no unifying positioning copy to tie it all together or define the brand of the site.

Although the large magazine cover graphic catches the eye, I was drawn to an interactive box that said "Lose 20 Pounds by March 25."

You enter your height, weight, and age—and then click through a series of screens asking you more questions, so that eDiets can design a customized weight-loss plan for you, for which they charge $11.96 a month. Along the way, you are offered a number of free e-zine subscriptions and information on advertised products, which makes it a little bit confusing and overwhelming.

The request for $11.96 a month at the end of the process came as a surprise; I somehow thought everything would be free. The reason it surprised me was that there is no "sell" copy preceding the questioning process.

So being asked for money came as a bit of a shock. And I didn't buy. That's just my personal reaction; I have no idea what the actual conversion rate is.

Interestingly, when I went to the diet-plan questionnaire to run through it again, I was immediately served a page that said, "Welcome back, Bob. We've saved all your information. Click here to view it now. Click here for a special offer for return visitors!"

When I clicked on the special offer for return visitors, however, it was the same $11.96 a month I had been offered earlier. I didn't see what was special or different about it.

## WRITING A LONG-COPY LANDING PAGE

Depending on who's counting, there are at least 160 paid-subscription financial newsletters published in North America. The most popular focus on stock recommendations, but there are others covering everything from options and futures to precious metals and mutual funds.

There are also a few large—and numerous small—Web-based investment advisory services, many of which sell stock and mutual fund recommendations in a variety of online and offline formats.

Online, virtually all of these newsletters are sold with long-copy landing pages. A long-copy landing page is a Web site dedicated to selling a single product: the newsletter. Also known as a microsite, the long-copy Web site is the equivalent of a long sales letter (4 to 8 pages) posted on the Web.

Some marketers present their microsites in segments or pages. After reading one page of the letter, you must click to read the next page. The danger is that every time you ask readers to click to the next page without buying, some drop off.

Most marketers today run their landing pages as one (or at the most two) long continuous pages, so the prospect can read by scrolling rather than clicking.

Among these financial newsletter editors, Louis Rukeyser is perhaps the one most familiar to the general public—largely because of his TV show. He publishes two newsletters: *Louis Rukeyser's Wall Street* and *Louis Rukeyser's Mutual Funds*, the latter, as its name indicates, focused solely on mutual funds. Let's take a look at this online promotion as an example of how to write a successful long-copy landing page.

The landing page carries Mr. Rukeyser's byline directly under the headline. That's a good strategy for two reasons. First, it creates the impression that you are reading an article rather than a promotion. And second, it gets Mr. Rukeyser's famous name right up front, where it should be.

Promoting the famous Rukeyser brand is also accomplished by placing the newsletter masthead above the headline (remember, Rukeyser's name is prominent in the newsletter title) along with Mr. Rukeyser's photo and signature—these images provide graphic reinforcement of the brand.

The headline itself, "Here's how to put the best fund managers in the country to work for you," is a sensible statement and promise. But it could be much more powerful.

Part of the problem is that it's not specific. What does "best" mean? Are these the fund managers with the best performance today? This year? The past five years? The past ten years?

Also, what's the benefit of putting the best fund managers in the country to work for me? If it's to help me outperform the broad market, show me, right in the headline, how they did it—for instance, "How the top 10 fund managers helped my readers turn $100,000 into $398,450 in just 10 years."

The lead is specific and engaging, telling you how you would have turned $10,000 into $194,943 within twenty years by investing in a fund with a great manager, but would have turned $10,000 into $836 by investing in a fund with a lousy manager.

The rest of this long-copy landing page is similarly strong. It does a great job of explaining the "big idea" or system behind the newsletter, which is to increase mutual fund profits by finding the best-performing fund managers and revealing their favorite stock picks. (The reader can either buy those funds or the individual stocks.)

When discussing track record, the copy focuses not on the newsletter's performance but on the track records of the fund managers Rukeyser profiles, which are indeed impressive.

The one flaw is that there's not enough promise, early in the copy, of future benefit. I know these fund managers have done great, but they've already been covered in the newsletter. If I subscribe today, what will I learn that will help me make more money today and tomorrow?

The easiest way to remedy this is to create a premium with the best current stock or mutual fund picks, and offer that early in the copy—perhaps even in the lead.

The various links throughout the Rukeyser landing page promise a "100% risk-free trial" to the newsletter when you click on the link. Clicking brings you to a simple, easy-to-follow order page where you can sign up for that trial.

The one flaw—and it's a big one—is that the offer of a "100% risk-free trial" is not repeated or explained on the order page. (It is explained in the closing text of the right-hand column, but if you click on a link before that and go to the order page, you won't see it.)

The primary order option is to click on a link and go to the order page where you can subscribe online. Other contact information—an address, toll-free phone number, fax number, and e-mail for customer service—appear at the end of both the landing page and the order page.

You get two free special reports when you sign up for one

year, and four free reports when you subscribe for two years, and this is clearly indicated on the landing page and the order page.

You also get a nice discount off the regular rate. This is made clear on the landing page, but not on the order page, which only gives the price—but does not indicate that it's a discount off the regular rate.

When I clicked away from the Rukeyser site, I was not served a pop-up window offering me a bribe (e.g., a free e-newsletter or special report) in exchange for my e-mail address. This is a huge tactical error for any landing page.

Why? Because if you get the visitor's e-mail address before he leaves without ordering, you can serve him a series of follow-up e-mails via autoresponder attempting to convert him to a trial subscription. And, you've added another valuable name to your house e-list. Without his e-mail address, you have lost the opportunity for follow up, significantly reducing your conversion rate.

Several standard devices have been used to make this long-copy newsletter promotion work on the Web. One is the use of a two-column format, with a column running along the right margin used to get additional sales points across. The other is the placement of links to the order page early and periodically throughout the long copy, rather than waiting to the end to give the link.

Some experts say that placing a link to the order page too early in the copy can depress response. Reason: People click through to the order page before they are sold, and then click away without ordering.

On the other hand, some experts say that placing links to the order page early and often throughout long-copy landing pages increases the conversion rate, and that's been my personal experience in most instances. So this is something you may want to test.

## MORE TIPS ON WRITING WEB SITE COPY

Since putting up my Web site, www.bly.com, in April 1998, I've received a ton of unsolicited e-mails, faxes, and phone calls—from casual Internet surfers as well as Web professionals—with all sorts of advice on how to make my Web site better. Unfortunately, more than 90 percent of their suggestions are almost totally off the mark—and would be a complete waste of my time and money.

Why is this the case? It's not that site visitors don't have valid opinions on graphics or content, or that Web professionals don't have good ideas. They do.

The problem is, all the advice is given with no thought to the business objective of my site, and whether the enhancement would further this goal. For example, a Web consultant called and said, "You're not getting nearly as much traffic as you should. I can help you get much more." He would advise me, he promised, on how to help my Web site get more hits than the New York Yankees. I politely explained I had absolutely no desire to increase hits to my Web site, and was not interested in what he was selling.

Frankly, he was baffled. Maybe you are, too. "Who doesn't want more hits on their Web site?" you might be thinking. The answer: plenty of folks. Before you can meaningfully enhance a Web site, you need to understand the business of the person or company sponsoring that site, as well as the business objectives they want the site to achieve.

In the case of www.bly.com, I'm a freelance writer specializing in direct marketing. I serve a higher-end clientele—major direct marketers, Fortune 500 companies, and substantial technology firms—and charge accordingly.

This makes me different from many entrepreneurs who have Web sites—in two important ways.

First, 99.99 percent of people cruising the Internet are not my prospects. I'm highly selective, and I don't work with small firms, start-ups, mom-and-pop operations, home-based businesses, and wannabe entrepreneurs—precisely the mass market that's cruising the Internet looking for free marketing information and advice.

Second, with more business than we can handle, our office (I have two assistants) can't waste time responding to low-level leads. Handling inquiries from casual Internet surfers takes time and effort, and we need to devote those to the needs of our many ongoing clients.

Then why do I have a Web site? That's the key relevant question, and it's one almost no one who seeks to advise me asks.

My Web site exists primarily for instant inquiry fulfillment to qualified prospects.

What does that mean? Before the Internet, when a serious prospect called, we'd send him an information package describing my services. That meant a lot of priority mail and overnight courier bills. And even with overnight shipping, the prospect often waited up to 24 hours to get his hands on the material.

Having a Web site eliminates that cost and wait. When prospects want a package, we can send it, but first we ask, "Do you have access to the Web?" If they do, we send them to www.bly.com where they can instantly get all the information they need to make a decision about using my services.

What should that information be? In his book *Roger C. Parker's Guide to Web Content and Design*, my friend Roger Parker says that content on your Web site should consist of two components:

1. Information your prospects need to know in order to buy from you
2. Information you know that will convince prospects to buy from you

My Web site covers both these areas. The "need to know" stuff includes:

- An overview of my services (our home page)
- An online portfolio of my copywriting samples
- Pages on each major service (copywriting, consulting, copy critiquing)
- My credentials (on an "About Bob Bly" page)
- Client testimonials

The stuff that helps convince prospects that I'm the person they should hire to write their copy includes:

- Descriptions of the marketing books I've written
- Samples of how-to articles I've written on marketing
- A list of recommended vendors that shows I have the connections to help potential clients get whatever they need done

As you see, my Web site is totally oriented toward the needs of my potential clients, and hardly at all to the casual Web surfer. But does this mean I don't want you to visit www.bly.com? Not at all.

On the contrary, I invite you to stop by. You may enjoy reading and downloading the free articles I've posted (click on Articles). And I'd be pleased and happy if you clicked on Books and bought any of my books (though you would not be buying them directly from me—our publication page links to Amazon.com, from which we get a 15 percent commission on every book they sell through our site).

And what if you're a small entrepreneur and need professional marketing help? Just click on Vendors. You'll find a list of folks who can help you with everything from Web design to mailing lists. But do me a favor. When you call them, tell them

Bob Bly sent you. They're busy, too, and it helps if they know you're a qualified referral.

## SEO COPYWRITING

The growing popularity of the Internet as a marketing tool has given rise to a new discipline: *SEO (search engine optimization) copywriting*.

When writing copy for the Web, you have to consider not only how the reader will react to the copy, but also whether the words you use in your copy will attract search engines to your site and increase your rankings within these search engines and directories.

An article in a marketing magazine advised repeating keywords on your site as often as possible, and in multiple places, so search engine "spiders" can find them. But my friend and fellow copywriter Nick Usborne says that this advice is not only wrong, but actually harmful.

"This is the worst possible advice you can give to anyone about optimizing their site for the search engines," says Nick. It's an element of what is referred to as "keyword stuffing" and is either ignored by the search engine algorithms or, in bad cases, your page and site will be penalized. Worse still, it results in pages that read very strangely to human visitors.

"Using keywords too often on a page and in the meta-tags is worse than not using them at all. The frequency of keywords on a page has nothing to do with whether a spider will find the page. And if a spider finds the page, it doesn't need a keyword repeated frequently in order to find it."

Since I am not an SEO expert, I asked a number of consultants in this area—and others more knowledgeable than I—to comment on the topic of keyword usage on Web sites.

"I think stuffing keywords on a Web page is taking the focus off where it needs to be to be successful in any business," says

Sean Woodruff. "That focus should be trained squarely on the customer. Stuffing keywords is a gimmick that is focused on tricking the search engines."

"Yes, search engines are important," says marketing consultant Susan Getgood, "but it is far more important to have a good Web site that sells effectively. We should focus on writing good copy that effectively communicates the offer.

"I expect that keywords appear an appropriate amount in good selling copy versus some artificial stuffing exercise which doesn't fool the search engines and likely damages your overall communications effort.

"Remember, people do land on your Web site from other sources—advertising, direct mail, and so on—not just from search engines. It is silly to try to optimize for one source, if in doing so you end up with a suboptimal Web site for all the others."

"I often furrowed my brow at suggestions of altering copy to optimize search engine results," says marketing consultant Bruce DeBoer. "It wasn't so much that I knew my way was better, but rather that I couldn't imagine altering otherwise great copy to satisfy a search engine."

Writer Apryl Parcher advises, "When writing Web sites, it is more important to put keywords in meta-tags and descriptions that are only seen by spiders and not seen by the average person reading your page, and also to give your pages titles in HTML that truly reflect the page's contents.

"While it is true that words are picked up on your home page for the search engine description—unless the text block is made into an image—it's usually the first twenty words or so. So make sure that text is what you want people to see when they pick you up on Google. However, you can go all out in putting appropriate search keywords in your description tags without stuffing your actual copy with them."

"Never stuff a Web page with keywords; it's awful advice,"

says Paul Woodhouse, who markets metals online. "You make sure they're in your title and your meta data. Place them carefully in the beginning, middle, and end of your spiel—and in the H1, H2 tags if necessary."

Internet marketing expert Rich Scheffren offers the following tips for raising the search engine rankings of your Web pages:

1. Feature preferably just one—and at most two—unique keywords per page.
2. The title tag should start with your keyword.
3. The first sentence of the first paragraph should start with your keyword.
4. Mention your keyword three times in the next three sentences.
5. Out of every 100 words of text on the page, between three and eleven of those words should be the keyword—a "keyword density" of between 3 and 11 percent.

"It's not about 'stuffing' copy with keywords," says Richard Leader. "It's about making sure the keywords are in there. Some years back, I ran an online training company. Our course outlines were quite clearly course outlines to a human reader—but not to a spider. We realized we didn't once use the phrase 'HTML training course,' for example.

"So we added it in a few times—and yeah, it looked a bit clunky. But with just a couple of mentions (for example, 'In this HTML training course, you will learn . . .'), we increased our search engine traffic—and our conversions. So, my advice is not to stuff but to 'strategically place.'"

"Placing keywords within your site is certainly an important part of getting search engines to notice you," says communications consultant Joel Heffner. "However, my current favorite way to appeal to search engines is to ping entries that I make to my blogs. Search engines appear to love to run to see what's been added to a blog. If you create a link to a specific page, the search engine will take note of that page as well."

Here are some additional ideas for driving traffic to your Web site:

### 1. Google

The world's largest search engine, Google facilitates 250 million Web searches per day for its users. As an advertiser, you can buy preference in Google's search engine, based on keyword, on a cost-per-click basis.

It could cost you as little as a dime a click or more than a dollar a click, depending on the popularity of the keyword you want to buy. If the cost of the keyword is 30 cents per click, and 100 people click on your site that day as a result of a Google search on the keyword you bought, Google charges you $30. Google lets you put a limit on how much you spend per day, so the cost can fit any budget.

### 2. Overture

Another search engine that lets you buy preferential rating on key words, Overture reaches over 80 percent of active Internet users by displaying your business in search results on leading sites like Yahoo!, MSN, and Alta Vista.

How do you determine what you can afford to pay? Say your product costs $100 and out of every 100 clicks on your site, you get one sale, for a total of $100. You can afford to pay $1 per hit if breaking even on the initial sale is your goal.

### 3. Affiliate Marketing

Find Web sites that cater to the same market you do. Arrange for them to feature your products on their site and in their e-mails. Online ads, e-mail blurbs, and Web pages talking about your product link to your site where the user can purchase the product under discussion. The affiliate receives a percentage of the sale ranging from 15 to 50 percent. To recruit affiliates or make money being an affiliate for other marketers, visit www.affiliatesdirectory.com.

Amazon.com runs one of the largest affiliate programs, enabling you to feature books on your site that are related to your topic and of interest to your audience; when users click on the book page, they are automatically linked to www.amazon.com where they can buy the book online. It's a service for your visitors, and you earn a small commission on each sale.

### 4. Co-Registration

In co-registration marketing, the user who visits a Web site is served a pop-up window containing a number of special offers; most frequently these are subscriptions to free e-zines. By arranging to have your e-zine or another offer featured in these co-registration pop-ups, you can capture many new names for your online database at a relatively low cost compared with traditional e-mail marketing.

There are a number of companies that can find such co-registration deals for you. One of these is VentureDirect Online, www.venturedirect.com. Another is E-Tactics, www.e-tactics.com.

### 5. Banner Ads

Banner ads have seen a resurgence thanks to the increasing sophistication and popularity of Macromedia Flash; in an attempt to recapture the attention of the overloaded Internet user, animation and effects in banners have become more sophisticated and dynamic. Banner ads can work but should be tested conservatively and cautiously, and don't get your hopes of a breakthrough up too high. Banner ads usually supplement other traffic generation methods, and are only occasionally a primary source of unique visits. Exceptions? Of course.

### 6. E-mail Marketing

Sending solo promotional e-mails to a rented list of opt-in names is an expensive way to acquire new names. Say you rent a list of 1,000 e-mail names for $200, get a 2 percent click-through, and 10 percent of those sign-up for your e-zine. Your acquisition cost to acquire those two new subscribers is a whopping $100 per name. Business-to-consumer marketers have a better chance of success with careful testing of e-mail marketing, since consumer lists are more reasonably priced than business-to-business names.

### 7. Online Ads

While sending a solo e-mail to a company's e-list can run $100 to $400 per thousand names, a less expensive option is to run a small online ad in their e-zine. Cost can be as little as $20 to $40 per thousand names. The e-zine publisher specifies the format and length of your ad, which are typically 100 words of text with one URL link. The higher up (earlier) your ad appears in the e-zine, the higher the response.

### 8. Viral Marketing

At its simplest, viral marketing entails adding a line to your outgoing e-mail marketing messages that says, "Please feel free to forward this e-mail to your friends so they can enjoy this special offer." To work, the e-mail you want the recipient to forward must contain a special offer, either a free offer (typically free content) or a discount on merchandise. According to Bryan Heathman of 24/7 Media, 81 percent of viral e-mail recipients will pass the e-mail on to at least one other person.

## WRITING A BLOG

Blogging, which in its most basic form is journaling online—although it has farther-reaching ramifications—has gained national prominence in 2004.

According to *BusinessWeek,* blogging has undergone "explosive growth." In 2004, Merriam-Webster announced that *blog* was the most frequently requested word in dictionary searches. Technorati reports that there are 5 million blogs on the Internet, with more coming online daily. One out of ten Internet users reads blogs regularly.

There is growing evidence that blogging can be a useful adjunct to your online marketing. At GM, vice chairman Bob Lutz, who is in charge of product development, began a blog about GM cars. "Once readers realized it really was him and not an advertising ploy, they quickly warmed to the idea that he was talking candidly about GM and its competition," notes Jack Bowen, GM's general director of CRM (Customer Relationship Management). Seventy percent of auto buyers now go to the Web site for information, reports MIT professor of management Glen Urban.

One thing we know for sure is that blogging is an effective tool for increasing Web traffic. Search engines like content, and when you blog, you're posting lots of new content to your Web site on a regular basis. Adding an active blog to your Web site will almost surely boost your search engine rankings. Selling products in volume directly from a blog may be a while off, and won't become widespread until the first smart marketer figures out how to do it, after which others will notice and copy his model.

But blogging has more immediate value to businesses in two other areas: relationship management with prospects and customers and public relations.

Prior to the Internet, the only way most customers could get involved with the businesses they bought from was through one-on-one interactions with the sales staff. The Internet offers customers other ways to get involved with the company, such as sending e-mails to the management and posting messages on bulletin boards. On these boards, customers openly talk about what they like and don't like about a company and its product.

The blog essentially combines e-mails and a bulletin board for chatting in a single electronic vehicle. Customers can instantly publish their opinions about the company (or anything else) on a blog. Once posted, these opinions can launch a threaded discussion.

For me, the real value of my blog is editorial: more specifically, research for writing articles. When I have an idea for an article, instead of writing the entire article, I write a few paragraphs—a "teaser" summarizing the key idea—and post it to my blog. If no one comments, it may indicate that my readers are not interested in this topic.

On the other hand, if I get a heavier than normal volume of posts in response, I know my readers are excited by the subject. I can go ahead and write a complete article with greater confidence that they will read it.

Even more useful, I can go back to my own blog and read the threaded discussion my text has sparked. This use of blogs as an online research tool gives an added dimension to the article, because I can easily incorporate comments from readers who felt passionate enough about the topic to blog, rather than having to call them up to extract a quote from them.

So, let's say you want to test the waters with a blog for your business. Here are a few suggestions:

• Your blog should stand on its own with its own unique URL; for instance, Bob Bly's blog is at www.bly.com/blog. But readers should also be able to link to the blog by clicking a button on your publication's main Web site.

• Unlike articles and white papers, which are traditionally one-way communications (you write it, your subscribers read it), blogs are a two-way online medium, a means of starting a lively conversation about an interesting topic. I find an effective blogging technique is to make a strong statement and ask the reader for a response (I often end my posts with the question, "What do you think?"). Another blogging technique that stimulates conversation is to withhold your opinion but ask readers for theirs.

• If you are discussing an article you have already published, be sure to put a reference to the original article in your blog post. Hyperlink that reference to the actual article online, if it's available.

• Put a link from your blog back to your Web site's home page, and consider having one that goes to the order page for your paid publication.

• Unlike your company e-zine, the blog should be the work of a single author whose voice becomes familiar to the readership over time. Obvious choices include your editor in chief or managing editor, although a popular columnist could also be tapped to write either your main blog or a secondary blog.

• One way to build blog readership is to arrange mutual hyperlinks with other blogs talking about your topic or reaching your audience. Don't be a snob and link only with blogs from big companies. Blogging is a meritocracy, and snubbing amateur blogs, some of which can be very influential, is a mistake.

# 12

# WRITING E-MAIL MARKETING

There are two basic types of e-mails you will be writing as a copywriter. The first is the "solo e-mail." This is an e-mail promoting a single product or offer sent to a distribution list. The second is the "e-zine." This is an online newsletter, written and distributed for marketing purposes. A typical strategy is to build an e-list of prospects by offering a free subscription to your online newsletter. Then, once you own those names, you can send them both e-zines—which can contain ads for your products—and solo e-mails promoting your products.

## 15 TIPS FOR WRITING EFFECTIVE E-MAIL MARKETING CAMPAIGNS

The copy in your e-mail plays a big role in whether your e-marketing message gets opened and read, or trashed without a second glance. Here are 15 proven techniques for maximizing the number of e-mail recipients who open your e-mail and click through to your Web site or other response mechanism:

  1. At the beginning of the e-mail, put a "FROM" line and a "SUBJECT" line. The SUBJECT line should be constructed

like a short, attention-grabbing, curiosity-arousing outer envelope teaser, compelling recipients to read further—without being so blatantly promotional it turns them off. Example: "Come on back to Idea Forum!"

2. The e-mail FROM line identifies you as the sender if you're e-mailing to your house file. If you're e-mailing to a rented list, the FROM line might identify the list owner as the sender. This is especially effective with opt-in lists where the list owner (e.g., a Web site) has a good relationship with its users.

3. Some e-marketers think the FROM line is trivial and unimportant; others think it's critical. Internet copywriter Ivan Levison says, "I often use the word 'Team' in the FROM line. It makes it sound as if there's a group of bright, energetic, enthusiastic people standing behind the product."

For instance, if you are sending an e-mail to a rented list of computer people to promote a new software product, your SUBJECT and FROM lines might read as follows: "FROM: The Adobe PageMill Team/SUBJECT: Adobe PageMill 3.0 limited-time offer!"

Here are e-mail FROM line options:

| *From:* | *When to use:* |
| --- | --- |
| List Owner | • List owner requires it<br>• Community of interest<br>• E-zine<br>• Popular quality site<br>• Frequent visitors |
| Your Company | • Well-known company or brand<br>• Market leader<br>• Recipients may think they are your customers (e.g., Microsoft) |

| You | • Personal message |
| | • Your company is not well-known to recipients |
| Team (e.g., The Adobe Team) | • Collaborative effort |

4. Despite the fact that the word *free* is a proven, powerful response booster in traditional direct marketing, and that the Internet culture has a bias in favor of free offers rather than paid offers, some e-marketers avoid "FREE" in the subject line.

The reason is the "spam filter" software some Internet users have installed to screen their e-mail. These filters eliminate incoming e-mail, and many identify any message with "FREE" in the subject line as promotional.

According to a study by Return Path, an e-mail management firm, 22 percent of e-mail marketing messages were blocked by top Internet Service Providers (ISPs) in 2004. However, my experience is that, despite spam filters, "FREE" typically lifts response.

5. Lead off the message copy with a killer headline or lead-in sentence. You need to get a terrific benefit right up front. Pretend you're writing envelope teaser copy or are writing a headline for a sales letter. Example:

From: Doug Casey's International Speculator

Subject: 6 shocking financial forecasts for 2005

Dear [NAME],
What's in store for the U.S. economy in 2005?
   A new special report from Doug Casey, best-selling author of "Crisis Investing," warns of 6 new economic threats to unfold in 2005. Click here for a free copy: [URL]
   "I personally expect this to be the wildest bull market

of any sort I have ever seen," says Doug Casey, "and with
a looming economic crisis, the big returns are now
being made in gold, silver, and other natural resource
stocks."

Among Doug's observations and predictions . . .

6. In the first paragraph, deliver a mini-version of your
complete message. State the offer and provide an immediate
response mechanism, such as the option of clicking on a link
connected to a Web page. This appeals to Internet prospects
with short attention spans.

7. After the first paragraph, present expanded copy that
covers the features, benefits, proof, and other information
the buyer needs to make a decision. This appeals to the
prospect who needs more details than a short paragraph can
provide.

8. The offer and response mechanism should be repeated
in the close of the e-mail, as in a traditional direct mail letter.
But they should almost always appear at the very beginning,
too. That way, busy Internet users who don't have time to read
each e-mail and give it only a second or two get the whole
story.

9. John Wright, of the Internet marketing services firm
MediaSynergy, says that if you put multiple response links
within your e-mail message, 95 percent of click-through
responses will come from the first two. Therefore, you should
probably limit the number of click-through links in your
e-mail to three. An exception might be an e-newsletter or
e-zine broken into five or six short items, where each item
addresses a different subject and therefore has its own link.

10. Use wide margins. You don't want to have weird wraps
or breaks. Limit yourself to about 55 to 60 characters per line.
If you think a line is going to be too long, insert a character
return. Internet copywriter Joe Vitale sets his margins at 20

and 80, keeping sentence length to 60 characters and ensuring the whole line gets displayed on the screen without odd text breaks.

11. Take it easy on the all-caps. You can use WORDS IN ALL CAPS but do so carefully. They can be a little hard to read—and in the world of e-mail, all caps give the impression that you're shouting.

12. In general, short is better. This is not the case in classic mail-order selling where as a general principle, "the more you tell, the more you sell." E-mail is a unique environment. Readers are quickly sorting through a bunch of messages and aren't disposed to stick with you for a long time.

13. Regardless of length, get the important points across quickly. If you want to give a lot of product information, add it lower down in your e-mail message. You might also consider an attachment, such as a Word document, PDF file, or HTML page. People who need more information can always scroll down or click for it. The key benefits and deal should be communicated in the first screen, or very soon afterward.

14. The tone should be helpful, friendly, informative, and educational, not promotional or hard-sell. "Information is the gold in cyberspace," says Vitale. Trying to sell readers with a traditional hyped-up sales letter won't work. People online want information and lots of it. You'll have to add solid material to your puffed-up sales letter to make it work online.

Refrain from saying your service is "the best" or that you offer "quality." Those are empty, meaningless phrases. Be specific. How are you the best? What exactly do you mean by quality? And who says it besides you? And even though information is the gold, readers don't want to be bored. They seek, like all of us, excitement. Give it to them.

15. Include an opt-out statement that prevents flaming from recipients who feel they have been spammed. State that your intention is to respect their privacy, and make it easy for

them to prevent further promotional e-mails from being sent to them. All they have to do is click on Reply and type "UNSUBSCRIBE" or "REMOVE" in the subject line. Example: "We respect your online time and privacy, and pledge not to abuse this medium. If you prefer not to receive further e-mails from us of this type, please reply to this e-mail and type 'Remove' in the subject line."

## GETTING PAST THE ISPS AND SPAM FILTERS

Everyone seems to agree that e-mail marketing is one of the most effective and powerful forms of Internet marketing today. After all, it is quick to deploy, provides immediate measurable results, and delivers a high return on investment.

But there is a downside. Successful e-mail marketing requires experience, expertise, and knowledge of the constantly changing e-mail filtering, spam-eradicating, firewall-building software industry. It has been said that more than one out of five e-mails have problems with delivery—which significantly erode response rates and program effectiveness.

It's not enough to build a list of interested customers or clients, send them informative, engaging e-mails once a week or once a month, and market products or services to them in the process. You've got to know how to get the messages *delivered*, and then *read* by the recipient. In other words, creating wonderful e-mail messages is only *part* of the process—the messages are absolutely worthless to you if never received by list members.

As a result of corporate and ISP filters, blacklists, and constant e-mail address flux, permission-based marketers face obstacles in their attempt to deliver solicited, confirmed-consent messages to the inboxes of customers and subscribers with whom they've established relationships.

*Deliverability* is key. With e-mail, it's simply the ability to complete delivery of a message to a recipient's inbox. We're not talking about readability—those factors that increase the open/read rate—but the process of getting the message into the inbox of the intended recipient.

Simply put, what can you do to ensure receipt of your messages? Let's agree on one thing: Delivery *begins* when a recipient grants permission to receive your messages. If your e-mail marketing strategy is based on this premise, delivery challenges are significantly minimized. With permission, the customer or recipient can provide recourse if an ISP, spam filter, or blacklist blocks your messages.

A number of factors hinder or prevent solicited e-mail delivery:

• *ISP-blocked incoming mail.* The most common version of ISP blocking. Many ISPs, especially large ones, maintain internal blacklists of IP addresses that are denied any incoming connections. Frequent customer complaints about traffic from particular sources are the most common cause of this kind of blocking. ISPs tend to block IP ranges without any notification, as they routinely handle complaints about hundreds of thousands of individual e-mail sources.

• *ISP-blocked outgoing mail.* Your ISP blocks outgoing traffic to another ISP. This is rare, as most ISPs block incoming traffic, but it has been known to happen.

• *Distributed content filters.* Several anti-spam companies help ISPs and corporate Internet users cope with the influx of unsolicited e-mail. These blocking systems employ complex content analysis processes that scan message content and create message "signatures" that are disseminated among the filtering company's client base.

• *Public list.* Publicly accessible blacklists and whitelists, maintained by volunteers, are often used by smaller ISPs and companies without dedicated e-mail administrators. Listing criteria can be reliable or nearly arbitrary, depending on the list owner's preferences. Administrators select the lists that most closely match their company's policy.

• *ISP content filters.* Similar to distributed content filters, ISPs often employ content filters created internally or adapted from others. Content filters scan for a variety of red flags and they can even learn new patterns in spam e-mail, such as inserting periods in words that would normally trigger a block.

• *User content filters.* Almost every e-mail client provides junk mail filters. These vary widely in complexity. Microsoft Outlook's filter searches for offensive keywords and key phrases, whereas more robust filters can be configured to run from a user's desktop.

• *User lists.* Recent upgrades to e-mail applications, including AOL, MSN, Yahoo!, and Outlook, allow users to compile their own blacklists and whitelists of individual and domain addresses. There are also "challenge/response systems" which extend this process by requiring non-whitelisted senders to respond with a code or other confirmation before their messages are delivered.

• *Message bounces.* A "soft" bounce is a temporary failure where the e-mail wasn't delivered but may be retried in the future. It could be because the mailbox was full, or the receiving mail server didn't respond to the delivery attempt. A "hard" bounce means the message is permanently undeliverable. Maybe the address is invalid, or a remote server is blocking your server.

Naturally, you want to minimize the number of "hard" bounce backs, those permanently fatal messages that mean loss of contact and "no sale." There are a number of ways to ensure greater delivery rates. The first requires cooperation from the recipients, as you want them to add your e-mail address to their "accepted" messages list.

## HOW TO GET INTO THE RECIPIENT'S ADDRESS BOOK OR WHITELIST

Getting your "FROM" address added to your recipient's address book or personal *whitelist*—a list of approved sources from which the user will accept e-mail messages—is, more and more, a crucial step in getting your e-mails into the inbox, rather than into the spam, or worse yet, the trash folder. More and more people, both business and consumer e-mail users, are adopting the use of spam filters, or upgrading their e-mail programs to include some form of spam filtering/whitelist feature.

You need to remind people to take the step of adding your FROM address to their address book/whitelist. Consider adding a single sentence at the top of your e-mail. Here are three examples of effective reminder statements:

> To ensure our e-mail is delivered to your inbox, please add the e-mail address delightfulmessages@ourcompany.com to your Address Book or junk filter settings.

> To ensure regular delivery of our e-mails, please add us (youwantthis@thiscompany.net) to your Address Book. Thank you!

> To guarantee delivery of this newsletter, please add ournewsletters@mycompany.com to your e-mail Address Book.

You may wish to go so far as to explain to your recipients how to set their junk filter settings in a special section of an e-mail message, or devote an entire mailing to this issue. Review the process for the major e-mail applications and Internet Service Providers, and write up a step-by-step instructional e-mail message. I've had a number of clients offer phone customer support assistance to any reader who may need a "walk-through"!

## TRIGGERING SPAM FILTERS

The means which the various ISP and e-mail server programs use to identify unwanted or inappropriate e-mail messages change fairly often and it is necessary to be aware of new implementations. But some important essentials can be reviewed.

Be careful with terms and characters used in your promotional e-mail campaigns. Microsoft's Outlook Express junk e-mail filter will send your e-mails straight to the "Deleted Items" folder if it finds things such as "for free," "cards accepted," or "order today" in your e-mails. However, the list is under constant revision, and you should regularly update your in-house list of unwelcome words. Visit this URL to view a current list of words and terms that Outlook will filter: http://office.microsoft.com/assistance/9798.newfilters.aspx.

Among the various filters AOL applies to incoming mail, one in particular (while easily avoided) will *completely block* your AOL message delivery if triggered. This new filter is an HTML validator that scans incoming messages for HTML syntax and formatting errors. If invalid HTML is detected, the message will be rejected.

The error itself does not need to be a glaring omission to trigger this filter. Any syntax inaccuracy may be sufficient. Ending a link tag, for example, with "<a/>" instead of the correct "</a>" will cause your message to be rejected. This filter was presumably employed to combat a favorite spammer tactic of inserting nonsense HTML code to foil standard content filters.

Establish procedures for proofing e-mail campaigns. Your proofing checklist should include HTML validation. Popular HTML editing software already offers effective validation tools and will highlight any errors on the fly, as your message is being created.

For a complete reference specification of HTML formatting, visit the World Wide Web Consortium documentation pages (http://www.w3.org/MarkUp/). Also, you can use the HTML validator in your e-mail application or a third-party validator such as the W3C Markup Validation Service (http://validator.w3.org/).

Here are 10 ways to help increase the likelihood your e-mail messages will be accepted by the receiving ISP and avoid future deliverability problems.

1. **Create a reverse DNS.** Make sure your outgoing mailing IPs (Internet protocol) have valid RDNS (reverse domain name system) entries set up. This ensures that when a receiving e-mail server checks who owns the IP trying to connect to it, you'll come up as the result, passing one of the many basic checks ISPs do to deter spammers.

2. **Set up an SPF.** A Sender Policy Framework (SPF) is an additional step to verify an e-mail sender's identity. The protocol is fairly easy to set up; your network administrator should be able to do it in less than five minutes. SPF adds another layer of authentication to your outgoing e-mail and protects against "phishing" attacks on your brand. You should know that some ISPs, such as AOL, *require* SPF to be implemented to be considered for their whitelists.

3. **Make only one connection.** When connecting to an e-mail server, send only one message per connection. Some systems still try to shovel as many messages through one connection as possible, which can be likened to throwing 500 e-mail addresses into the "BCC" field. ISPs frown on this technique, as spammers who want to get as many messages in before being blocked typically use this approach.

4. **Limit sending rate.** Though the ideal send volume depends on the list's nature, a good rule is to limit your transmission to 100,000 or so messages per hour. Keep in mind you will also need to accept feedback in the form of bounced

messages—your outgoing speed shouldn't affect your ability to receive bounces.

5. **Accept bounces.** Some e-mail systems, especially older ones, have a nasty habit of rejecting bounce messages. These "bounced bounces" arrive at the receiving ISP and can raise red flags. Nothing irks an ISP more than sending a response that a recipient doesn't exist, only to have the notification rejected and the mailings continue.

6. **Validate HTML content.** One of the dirtiest tricks in a spammer's arsenal is invalid, broken, and malicious HTML code. If you use HTML in your messages, make sure your code is error-free and follows W3C HTML guidelines, as discussed earlier.

7. **Avoid scripting.** Security risks due to script vulnerabilities in e-mail browsers have increased over the years. The result is that most scripts are stripped out of messages. Some e-mail systems reject messages outright if scripting is detected. For greatest delivery success, avoid using any scripts in messages. Instead, direct your readers to your Web site, where use of dynamic scripting can be fully implemented.

8. **Understand content filtering basics.** Ignorance of filtering approaches is no excuse for not getting messages delivered. Read bounce messages, track which messages had high bounce rates and low open rates, and see if you can reverse-engineer offending content.

9. **Monitor delivery and bounce rates by ISP/domain.** After every delivery, run reports by major domain and ISP on your messages. Look for unusual bounce, unsubscribe, spam complaint, and open rates at specific domains.

10. **Monitor spam complaints.** Even the best permission marketers with world-class practices receive spam complaints, particularly if they have a high AOL subscriber base. Monitor the number of spam complaints for each mailing and establish

a benchmark average. Look for mailings with spam complaint percentages that vary from the norm. See if you can determine what may have caused the problem. Was it the subject line? Too many messages in too short a time? Remember, a high number of spam complaints may result in an ISP blocking current, or even future, messages.

Some resources you can use to monitor complaints are:

AOL Feedback Loop:
http://postmaster.info.aol.com/fbl/index.html
SpamCop: http://www.spamcop.net/fom-serve/cache/94.html
Abuse.net: http://www.abuse.net/addnew.html

Diagnosing the root causes of deliverability problems will help you prevent them. You must monitor your delivery rates religiously because the rules around delivery change every day! Don't make the mistake of understaffing or underfunding around this issue, as it undermines the overall effectiveness of your e-mail marketing program (and your company image at the same time).

Remember, to reach full delivery, you must:

• *Monitor:* Use a seed list–based monitoring system that tracks your true delivery rates across all major ISPs. Know when a problem occurs, and don't rely on your bounce-backs to give you all the information you need. Some mail just never gets delivered, or is put directly into "junk" folders or trash bins—and you'll never know without such a system in place.

• *Analyze:* When you're at less than 100 percent delivery, it's high time to find out why. You should look closely at the individual e-mail, as well as the e-mail program as a whole. There are lots of reasons for failed delivery—and early detection ensures smooth future deliveries.

• *Resolve:* Create strong relationships with ISP tech-support people to have a valuable resource to troubleshoot alongside your staff members. ISP relations should be a high priority.

• *Optimize:* Use information from all sources to solve your e-mail delivery problems. Small changes in creative copy, list, or server configuration can make a world of difference in your delivery rates.

Make sure you are tracking your deliveries, testing for ISP blocking and spam filtering before a large mailing, and react *quickly* to problems when they arise. Although complicated, it's imperative in the creation and maintenance of a truly successful e-mail marketing program.

## LONG VS. SHORT E-MAIL COPY

"What works best in e-mail marketing?" I got asked for the umpteenth time the other day. "Long copy or short copy?"

It's a quandary for direct marketers much more so than for general marketers. Here's why: There's a widely held viewpoint that, on the Internet, the less copy the better. Web marketing experts tell us that the Internet is faster paced than the "snail mail" world, that attention spans are shorter, and long messages get zapped into oblivion with the click of the mouse. "Keep it short!" they extol in countless advisory e-zines.

General advertisers, for the most part, also believe that when it comes to copy, the shorter the better. Often their print ads have large pictures and only a handful of words. So they have no trouble embracing the "people don't read" mentality that the Web marketing gurus say works best.

But traditional direct marketers whose products are typically sold with long-copy direct-mail packages and self-mailers—

newsletter publishers, seminar promoters, magazines, book clubs, insurance, audiocassettes—have a problem. It goes something like this:

"In print, I have to use long copy to make the sale . . . or I just don't get the order. We've tested short copy many times—who *doesn't* want a cheaper mailing piece with less ink and paper? But it has never worked for our product. Now my Web marketing consultant says the e-mail should be just a few paragraphs. If a few paragraphs won't convince people to buy offline, why should things be any different online?"

And they are right. Just because a person buys online doesn't change the persuasion process. If she needs the facts to make a decision, she needs them regardless of whether she is ordering from a paper mailing or a Web site.

Yet we also have a sense that the Web marketing gurus have at least a clue as to what they are talking about. We sense that our 4-page sales letter, if sent word for word as a lengthy e-mail, wouldn't work. People would click away long before they got to the end.

I think I have some sensible guidelines to answer this puzzle. First, we need to quantify what we mean by "short" versus "long."

When a Web marketing guru talks about "short" e-mail, he probably means only three or four paragraphs. So when he says long copy doesn't work, by "long" he means e-mails of more than a few paragraphs.

If I say "long copy *does* work," I mean long compared to the typical e-mail—not compared to the typical direct mail letter on paper. A "long" e-mail, which may fill several screens, is closer in length to a 2-page letter—short by direct-mail standards—than to a 4-page letter. And it doesn't even come close to an 8-page letter.

Second, we need to quantify how much shorter online copy

is than offline. Should you translate your entire package, word for word? Should you compress it to half its length? Less?

Kathy Henning, who writes extensively about online communication, says, "In general, online text should be half as long as printed text, maybe even shorter." Not a precise formula, but a good starting point for estimation.

Third, and most important, we need to remember that the copy for e-mail marketing campaigns is not wholly contained within the e-mail itself. It is really in two parts.

The first half of the message is in the actual e-mail. The e-mail contains a link to a page on a Web site or server. When you click on that link, you jump to the page, where the remainder of the message is presented, along with the online order mechanism.

In a traditional direct-mail package, the message is unevenly split. Consistently, 98 percent of the copy is in the letter and brochure, with the remaining 2 percent on the order form. In e-mail marketing campaigns, the division is less balanced and more varied.

The diagram on the next page of an e-mail marketing mode shows the various ways the total copy can be divided between the e-mail and the response page. There are four options, as shown in the box at the center:

1. *Short e-mail, landing page* (left upper quadrant)—Many marketers with simple lead-generating offers use short e-mails (the traditional three to four paragraphs) with a link to a "landing page." A landing page is a short Web-based form, usually with a headline, a couple of paragraphs explaining the offer, and a mechanism for the recipient to fill in his information and submit his response. This format is similar in length and style to the traditional one-page sales letter and business reply card used in lead-generating paper direct mail.

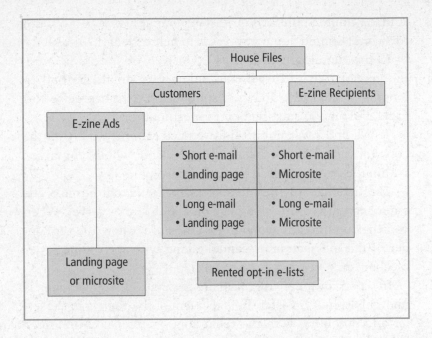

2. *Long e-mail, landing page* (lower left quadrant)—This is similar except the e-mail, by Internet marketing standards, is "long." For convenience, define a short e-mail as any e-mail that, when printed out, takes half a page or less. By comparison, any e-mail that takes more than a page when printed out is "long." This format is similar in length and style to a direct mail package with a 4-page letter and a simple 4- by 9-inch order card.

3. *Long e-mail, microsite* (lower right quadrant)—This format has a long e-mail and a long landing page. The microsite is a custom URL designed specifically for the offer. Unlike a landing page, which is usually a single screen, the microsite's lengthier copy requires many screens. The microsite can be broken into distinct pages (see www.hypnoticwriting.com) or it can be one continuous document through which the reader must scroll (see www.surefirecustomerservicetechniques.com). This long e-mail/microsite format allows for maximum copy,

and is ideal for translating lengthy mailings, such as magalogs (12- to 24-page, long-copy self-mailers that look like magazines), to the Web.

4. *Short e-mail, microsite* (upper right quadrant)—This format combines a short e-mail up front with a long-copy microsite on the back end. It is ideal for offers that require a lot of copy but are being transmitted to prospects who might not read a lengthy e-mail.

The bottom line: E-mail marketing can work without having e-mails competing with *War and Peace* in word count. By strategically splitting your copy between the front-end e-mail and back-end response page, you can get your message across without having time-pressured Web surfers fleeing in terror.

## WRITING AN ONLINE CONVERSION E-MAIL SERIES

"Online conversion" is a proven model for building an e-list of prospects and profitably marketing products on the Internet. Here's an oversimplified version of how online conversion works:

1. You create some free content.
2. You offer people the free content online.
3. When they accept, you then sell them products and services they have to pay for—again, online.

Let's break down each step, starting with creation of free content. This is the easiest step. Just repackage some of your content as an information premium. The content does not have to be long. Repurposing existing articles works fine for this purpose. So do special reports specifically written for the online conversion campaign. Or the same reports you offer as premiums in postal direct marketing.

The premium is typically offered as a "free special report." It is usually available as a downloadable PDF file. Some marketers prefer to post the report as a multi-page HTML document on the Web.

The second step is to collect e-mail addresses of prospects by offering them the free content online. There are many ways to attract potential customers to a Web page where they can download your free content. One way is to send e-mails to lists of prospects. The e-mail offers the content as a "free special report." To get the free report, the recipient clicks on an embedded URL in the message text.

If the content is a downloadable PDF file, the recipient is brought to a short transaction page. She enters her e-mail address, and is then allowed to download and print the PDF file.

If the content is a series of sequential HTML pages, the recipient is again brought to a short transaction page. She enters her e-mail address, clicks SUBMIT, and is brought to the first page of the microsite where the report is available to read as a posted HTML document.

Within the HTML report, put a number of links to a landing page or transaction page for your paid subscription product. Many readers may click on these links and order your paid product while they are in the middle of reading your free bonus report online.

Either way, the reader must give us her e-mail address to read the free report, which is the key to the online conversion method.

There are many other methods you can use to generate leads for your online conversion campaign. Some marketers have had great success with postcards. Others have used banners or online ads in e-zines.

Finally, you need to convert the leads to paid customers. So far, two things have happened. First, we have captured the prospect's e-mail address, so we can market to her as often as we like at virtually no cost. And second, we know that the prospect is interested in the topic of our content, because she at least requested a free article or report on it.

Since the content was free, we do not know at this point whether she will pay for products related to this topic. But she is a qualified lead in the sense that she is (a) interested in the topic and (b) responds to online marketing.

The next step is to send her a series of e-mails, known as the online conversion series, with the objective of converting her from a requester of free content to a buyer of our paid product.

While the online conversion process is still relatively new, experience so far shows that our online conversion series works best with between three to seven efforts.

Some marketers want every e-mail in the series to attempt to make a sale. That is, they all have a URL the reader can click to reach a page from which the product may be ordered.

Others like the first two e-mails to be simply goodwill, promoting the value of the information and encouraging the reader to actually read the free content—and in some cases, even giving her more free content. These are called "free touch" e-mails, because they touch the reader without asking her to purchase.

Subsequent e-mails in the series ask for the order; these are called "conversion e-mails." In a six-effort series, the first one or two e-mails might be free touch; the remainder, conversion e-mails.

When the reader clicks on the URL link in your e-mail, she may go either to a landing page or a transaction page. A landing page has a fair amount of descriptive copy about the product you are selling and your offer. It does a strong job of selling the reader on the value of the product. A transaction page has minimal description of the product. It is basically an online order form.

Some marketers always send the e-mail recipient who

clicks on the link in the e-mail to the landing page, on the theory that the more sales copy, the more sales made. Other marketers believe that if the conversion e-mail is long and has a lot of sales copy, there is no need to repeat this in a landing page; and so they just send the prospect to a short transaction page.

The best offer for an online conversion effort is a free 30-day trial of the product. If you can set up your site so that the recipient's credit card is not billed until after the 30-day trial period, that's the best choice. Then you are truly offering a free trial.

By comparison, if you charge recipients' credit cards as soon as they submit their orders, it is not really a free 30-day trial; it is a risk-free 30-day trial. The recipients are paying, but if they cancel within 30 days, they get a refund.

You can experiment with timing, number of efforts, and mix of efforts (free touch and online conversion) in your online conversion series. A typical series might go like this:

*Day 1*—e-mail #1, free touch. Thank the prospect for requesting your free content and reinforce its value.

*Day 2*—e-mail #2, free touch. Encourage the prospect to read the free content and highlight its value. Point out some especially good ideas, tips, or strategies it contains.

*Day 4*—e-mail #3, online conversion. Tell the prospect he can get more of the same content by accepting a free 30-day trial to your product. Sell him on the product and its value.

*Day 7*—e-mail #4. Remind the prospect that he can still become an expert on the topic by getting your product and accepting your free trial offer.

*Day 14*—e-mail #5. Tell the prospect the free 30-day trial is expiring, resell him on the content you are offering, and urge him to act today. Tell him after that, it's too late.

Write your online conversion series e-mails the same as you would write other online and offline promotions to sell your products. Use the same copy, content, and organization. Get attention in the lead, generate interest, create desire for your product, and ask for the order.

One key difference: In your lead, always acknowledge that they are hearing from you as a follow-up to the free report or article *they asked you* to send them. This has two benefits.

First, they may feel slightly more obligated to read your message; after all, you did give them a gift. And second, if they liked the free content, it automatically puts them in a receptive mood for more of the same—even if they have to pay for it.

Should you try online conversion? Every marketer who wants to market products and services online could probably benefit from testing an online conversion series.

Just renting an e-list of opt-in names and asking them to subscribe won't work; people who are online tend not to buy from strangers. But send those same names an offer of a free article or report, and they will take you up on it. After all, what's to lose?

If you have targeted the right audience, and the free content you provide is of high quality and value, then enough of the readers will want more of the same and be willing to accept a free 30-day trial of product related to the same topic.

And if your product is of high quality and value, a large percentage of the readers will not send it back and request a refund. You will have successfully converted free content requesters to paid buyers—your goal in online conversion.

## WRITING A MARKETING E-ZINE

For many marketers, the fastest way to build a house list of opt-in e-mail names and addresses—an important asset for online marketing—is with the offer of a free subscription to an online newsletter or "e-zine."

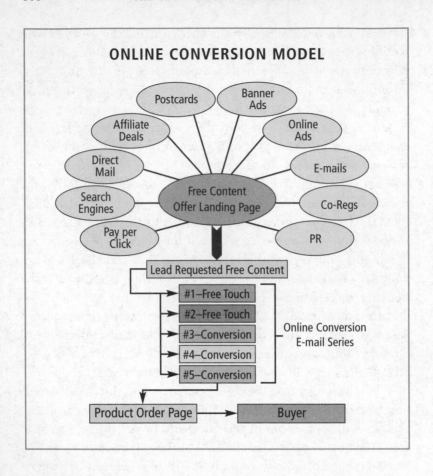

The free e-zine is the online equivalent of a company newsletter, except it is distributed electronically instead of printed and mailed. The cost and time savings are tremendous—an e-zine can be distributed at virtually no cost, almost instantaneously, to thousands of prospects and customers at the click of a mouse.

When you build a large subscription list for your e-zine, you can then send promotions to potential customers via the Internet whenever you want, generating thousands of extra dollars in incremental sales you might not otherwise have made. And you save thousands of dollars on printing and postage.

A variety of online marketing tools are used to drive potential customers to a Web page where they can sign up for a free subscription to your e-zine in exchange for giving you their e-mail address. You can also ask for their name, which allows you to personalize future e-mails you send to them.

These traffic-building methods include such things as contextual marketing, banner ads, online ads in e-zines reaching similar audiences, e-mail marketing, pay-per-click advertising, and search engine optimization of the e-zine sign-up Web site. The acquisition cost per subscriber can range from $1 to $5 a name, depending on the method used and the market targeted.

Generally, the larger and more targeted your subscriber list, the more profitable your online marketing will be. After all, a click-through rate (CTR) of one percent to a thousand e-zine subscribers will bring just ten visitors to your landing page; but if you have a million online subscribers, a 1 percent CTR will generate 10,000 visits.

But for your e-zine to work as an online marketing tool, subscribers must not only sign up; they must also open and read your e-newsletters. If they don't open the current issue, they can't respond to any of the ads or offers you make in it. And if they don't read it on an ongoing basis, they will eventually unsubscribe, and you will lose them as an online prospect.

In my experience, the best e-zines—those with the highest open, read, and click-through rates—are those that present useful how-to tips in short, bite-size chunks, the more practical and actionable, the better.

Your e-zine is not the place to pontificate on business philosophy or explain complex technology; you can send your subscribers to Web pages and downloadable white papers or special reports that cover those topics. E-zine readers love practical articles that tell them how to do something useful— and do so in just a few concise paragraphs.

News also can serve as effective e-zine content, but by itself, is not as potent as advice. The best way to use news is to link a tip or other advice to it. For instance, if you are a financial publisher talking about $50 a barrel crude, tell the reader which oil stocks he should own to profit from rising oil prices.

You don't need a news angle to make advice an effective content strategy for your free e-zine. However, if you can relate your tips to current events or news, do so; experience shows that it can potentially double your readership and response.

That being said, you never know what article is going to strike your e-zine reader's fancy. And it's often not the article you'd think. For instance, a manager for a company that sells information on safety to HR managers publishes a regular e-zine on safety and other HR issues. He reports that his best-read article of all time was "10 Ways to Reduce Eye Strain at Your PC."

The eye-strain article generated much more response than more specialized articles targeted to his HR audience. Go figure.

Here's what I've found makes the ideal e-zine article (many of these ideas are borrowed from my colleague, Ilise Benun, of www.artofselfpromotion.com):

1.  Think of yourself as a conduit. Your job is to pass useful information along to those who can use it.

2.  Pay close attention to questions, problems, and ideas that come up when you're doing your work or interacting with customers.

3.  Distill the lesson (or lessons) into a tip that you can share with your network, via e-mail or snail mail or even in simple conversation.

4.  State the problem or situation as an introduction to your tip. Distill it down to its essence.

5.  Give the solution. Tips are action-oriented. So make sure you give a couple of action steps to take. Readers especially love something they can use right away, like the 10 tips on how to reduce eye strain while working at a PC.

6. Describe the result or benefit of using these tips to provide some incentive to take the action. If there are tools readers can use to measure the results of your tip once they put it into practice, give them a link to Web sites offering these tools.

7. Include tips the reader can use without doing any work, phrases they can use verbatim, boilerplate clauses, checklists, forms, and so on.

8. List Web sites and other resources where readers can go for more info.

9. Put your best tip first, in case people don't read the whole thing—because sometimes even really short tips are too much.

Be aware that most e-zines have a dual audience consisting of: (1) prospects who get the free e-zine but are not your customers, and (2) subscribers who have bought products from you and get your free e-zine because they are on your customer list.

For reasons of economy of scale and simplicity of management, most publishers use one e-zine to serve both audiences. But you have to keep the different needs and perspectives of both groups in mind for your e-zine to be effective.

The first group of e-zine subscribers consists of people who have signed up for your free online newsletter. They have not yet bought products from you; and in fact may not even be aware of your products or even who you are.

Your goal with these subscribers is to (a) delight them with the free e-zine they are receiving; and (b) upgrade them to the next step—purchase of one of your products or services.

To accomplish these goals:

• Pack the e-zine with solid content. Nothing beats useful, practical, how-to tips.

• Put a 100-word ad in each issue of your e-zine offering a free 30-day trial for one of your products, with a link to a landing page where the reader can accept such an offer.

• Send at least one solo e-mail to subscribers between e-zine issues giving them a compelling reason to accept your 30-day free trial offer; this could be the offer of premium, such as a free gift or free content (e.g., a special report). If you offer free content, let them get the report as a downloadable PDF after they order your product on the landing page.

The second group of e-zine subscribers are customers: people who have already purchased one or more of your products. Your e-zine can do any or all of the following for your customers:

• Give them news updates, recommendations, and fresh ideas for using your products
• Highlight product upgrades, new accessories, or other product-related items of interest
• Bring them special discount offers on your other products and services

Can you stray from my formula of how-to advice and tips? Of course. My e-zine, *The Direct Response Letter* (available at www.bly.com), uses many different types of articles including book reviews, quotations, news items, and new product announcements.

But take a tip from me: When you're putting together your next e-zine issue, remember that nothing gains the reader's interest and attention like solid how-to tips.

# 13 ✐

# HOW TO GET A JOB AS A COPYWRITER

Advertising executive Fairfax Cone once remarked, "The inventory of an advertising agency goes downstairs in the elevator every night."

In other words, people are an ad agency's most valuable resource. And the copywriter ranks as one of the more important "people resources" in the ad agency business.

Copywriters write the words we read and hear in ads, commercials, and Web sites. Aside from the art director, no advertising or marketing professional's work has as much visibility as the copywriter's.

Many other people make equally significant contributions to the advertising campaign. Account executives help plan the advertising strategy. Market researchers delve into the mind of the consumer and come up with the real reasons why he or she buys your product. Media buyers buy the best space at the best price.

But this is all invisible to everyone save the client and the agency. The only thing the general public sees is the finished product: the ads and commercials.

This fact is to the copywriter's advantage in job hunting.

The copywriter can present a book of ad clippings or a film reel of TV commercials and say, "This is mine. I wrote it." The contributions of media planners, account executives, market researchers, print production managers, traffic managers, and other agency people are harder to pinpoint.

Writers who work at advertising agencies are more in the "mainstream" of advertising than freelancers. Staff copywriters write print ads for major consumer publications. They also write most of the television commercials.

Freelancers handle the leftovers: direct mail, radio commercials, trade ads, brochures. Freelancers almost never get to write TV commercials (and many people feel television is the most glamorous and prestigious advertising medium to work in).

As an ad agency writer, you have a wealth of resources at your fingertips. There are artists to sketch out your concepts. Creative directors to give you assignments and guidance in your work. Other writers to read your copy and to bounce ideas off. Account executives to handle client meetings and provide whatever background information you need.

Plus, there are all the resources of any large office: a nice desk, a fancy computer, a photocopy machine, free Internet access, free paper and pencils, maybe even a secretary and a plush private office.

The freelancer has no one but himself to depend on. Worse, he has to buy his own paper and pencils.

Agency copywriters get nice, steady paychecks. The freelancer can go months without seeing a dime.

Speaking of paychecks: Copywriters earn respectable salaries. According to research from the College of Business of Northern Illinois University, copywriters' annual earnings range from $45,000 to more than $135,000. *Advertising Age* says that the average hourly rate of staff copywriters in 2003 was $32.56, which translates into $67,730 a year.

The creative director is the person responsible for the production and coordination of all creative work in the agency—copy, art, print, and broadcast production. The surest way to reach six figures in annual compensation is to become a creative director. For many copywriters, the position of creative director is the next step up the corporate ladder. But, if you make the move, you'll spend more time supervising others and less time writing.

Agency writers are usually assigned to one or two accounts, and they stick with these accounts for a long time. Agency writers work on continuous ad campaigns, rather than one-shot projects, as freelancers do.

If you want to write "prestige" copy—major campaigns for large national consumer accounts such as Burger King, Pepsi, Ford, or AT&T—you can do it only by getting a job with the large agency that handles the account. This type of work is handled by agency staff writers 99.9 percent of the time; freelancers rarely get an opportunity to handle big campaigns for "blue chip" accounts.

Finally, if you want to be part of the advertising industry's "in" crowd, your best bet of making it is to work for a big-name agency handling a big-name account. For the most part, writers who work freelance, in the advertising departments of manufacturers, or for small, unknown agencies are outsiders in the business.

## WHERE THE JOBS ARE

Hundreds of job openings are advertised each week in the "Help Wanted" sections of dozens of national and regional advertising journals. Two excellent sources for job hunters are the help-wanted classifieds in *Adweek* and *Advertising Age*. (A list of advertising magazines appears at the end of this book.) Another source of job opportunities is the help-wanted section of your local paper. The help-wanted classified section of the Sunday *New York Times*, for example, lists dozens of ad agency openings in the New York/New Jersey area.

Help-wanted ads are a good place to start your job hunt. After all, when you respond to a help-wanted ad, you know for a fact that the company has a job opening they want to fill.

Job seekers reading help-wanted ads spend a great deal of time agonizing over whether they're qualified for the position being offered. They wonder, "Is the agency rigid about the job's qualifications? Or will they take a look at me even if I don't have the experience and background they ask for in the ad?"

The answer lies somewhere between these two extremes. The agency realizes that the "ideal" candidate is a rare breed and will interview people even if they lack some of the qualifications. On the other hand, an agency advertising for a top-level creative director is not going to hire a college graduate fresh out of Advertising 101.

Here are a few recent help-wanted ads, along with my analysis of what the agency is really looking for:

**HOW TO GET YOUR BEST ADS OUT OF THE AGENCY**
Send them to us.

   Right now we're looking for terrific writers and art directors. For starters, we'd like to see copies of your five best samples (product or spec). If it's what we're looking for, not only will your best work get out of your agency in one piece, so will you.

Comment: The key here is "product or spec." A "spec" ad is an ad you write on your own to demonstrate your copywriting skill. It's not an assignment from a real client.

By accepting spec work, the agency is in effect saying, "What's most important is that you're good and can prove it. We don't care whether you've had a lot of experience." This ad tells me the agency will hire a talented beginner. But if you respond to the ad with spec work, it had better be great.

### COPY CHIEF, DIRECT MARKETING/PROMOTION

X Company is looking for a Writer/Supervisor for package goods direct marketing accounts. A thorough knowledge of direct mail, promotion, and consumer writing is required. Min. 5 years experience. If you can handle a fast pace, lots of responsibility, and want to grow, send resume, salary requirement, and photocopy of your favorite sample.

Comment: They're looking for someone with experience in a highly specific field. To get the job you'd have to be a direct-marketing copy specialist with a portfolio full of projects done for major package-goods accounts. They're not going to settle for someone who has done mostly trade ads, product brochures, or business and industrial copy.

### WRITER

Expanding Connecticut Advertising/P.R. Agency with blue chip national accounts needs an experienced Writer or Writer/Creative Director. Print, collateral, some broadcast, audiovisual, P.R. Business-to-business experience essential; consumer background a plus.

Comment: By calling for a "Writer or Writer/Creative Director" the agency is saying, "We are looking for people who are solid writers, but we might also be interested in hiring someone who's a little more heavyweight, someone who can take on more supervisory responsibility."

They sound flexible about most of the requirements. For example, "some broadcast" means they'll probably overlook the fact that you haven't written TV commercials if you've done some other form of audiovisual work. I'd guess that a good writer with two to five years of experience could qualify for this job, yet someone with ten years experience could also be in the running.

### COPYWRITER WHO SHARES OUR CONCEPT OF CONCEPT

You're an advertising copywriter who already understands that concept is what it's all about. Sparkling, fresh, bold, daring, intrusive concepts.

Concepts that not only break through the clutter, but also get results by being on-target in terms of advertising and marketing objectives.

That means you use the wealth of computerized research and other data available to you, but you don't get bogged down with it. Because your striving for exciting creative product won't let you.

If that's your concept of concept, send samples of your work (spec or produced) that demonstrate that you're more than a writer. You're our new advertising copywriter. Salary commensurate with experience, employment commensurate on creativity.

Comment: The style of this copy and the emphasis on vague notions of "concept" and "creativity" have me worried. Instead of listing specific qualifications, the ad talks in glowing but general terms. It sounds as if they really don't know what they want—or if they do, they aren't telling you about it. As a hard-sell, straightforward copywriter, I'm not moved by this ad. But other writers may be excited and enthusiastic about it.

These critiques were designed to help you interpret help-wanted ads and get a feel for whether a position is right for you (and whether you're qualified for the job). When in doubt, write the letter and send the resume. It never hurts to ask, and you're only gambling a first-class stamp.

Keep in mind, though, that the majority of job openings are

never advertised. They are filled through contacts, through executive search firms, and through job seekers getting in touch with the right person at the right time.

Look through a copy of *The Standard Directory of Advertising Agencies*. See which agencies handle the types of accounts and specific clients you'd like to write for.

Write letters to the creative directors of these agencies. Tell them you'd like to write copy for them and give them reasons why they should take a look at your portfolio and give you an interview. (I'll give you some tips on how to write letters and resumes a little later on in the chapter.)

## WHAT TYPE OF AD AGENCY IS BEST FOR YOU?

Agencies come in many different varieties. The two basic types are large and small. You'll have to decide which type is right for you.

Big agencies have many advantages: They have the most opportunity for advancement. They handle the most prestigious accounts. They have different jobs, departments, and clients to choose from. And a few big agencies even have special training programs for entry-level copywriters.

What's more, big agencies pay better salaries than small agencies. According to an *Adweek* salary survey, copywriters at the country's biggest agencies earn about 46 percent more than writers at small (under $1 million in billings) agencies.

Big agencies let you concentrate on one account. If you land a job with IBM's agency and work on the IBM account, you may spend all your time planning and writing print ads for IBM personal computers.

At a small agency, you will probably work on many different accounts. And they'll be smaller in scope: everything from local auto dealers and restaurants to software firms and industrial manufacturers.

Big agencies tend to concentrate on print ads and commercials as well as online marketing. Small agencies attract clients by promising to do other tasks as well: direct mail, sales literature, technical publications, manuals, catalogs . . . even public relations work.

Big agency copywriters are somewhat insulated from clients, outside vendors, and other departments in the agency. The writers write and leave other tasks to specialists.

At a small agency, you become less of a specialist, more of a generalist, because the small agency can't afford to hire a separate person for every task. For instance, a copywriter at a small agency may also act as the account executive. (Such a copywriter is called a "copy/contact person" because, in addition to writing copy, he or she is the agency's contact with the client.) The copywriter might also be responsible for producing radio and TV commercials or working with outside artists and printers to produce ads and brochures.

Another choice is whether to work for a "creative shop" or a "marketing shop."

"Shop" is advertising slang for "ad agency." A creative shop is an agency whose strength lies in the ads and commercials it produces, rather than in the planning and strategy stage. Doyle Dane Bernbach was known as a creative shop because of the advertising it produced for Volkswagen, Polaroid, and other accounts. In the late 1980s Ally & Gargano was one of the hottest creative shops around because of its commercials for Federal Express and MCI Long Distance. Today, Donny Deutsch's ad agency, Deutsch Advertising, is known as the hot shop.

A marketing shop is an agency known for its marketing savvy—skill in market research, advertising strategy, business planning, media selection. Ted Bates was well-known as a marketing shop.

At creative shops, the creative department—copywriters, art directors, producers—reign supreme. At marketing shops, the account executives have more clout.

The ideal agency is probably a blend of both. It encourages fresh, original creative work but uses this creative talent to achieve the client's sales and marketing objectives. (Beware of agencies that care more about advertising's aesthetic qualities than the sales results it produces.) Choose an agency whose work environment you feel most comfortable with. Make sure their idea of what makes for good advertising is in sync with your own.

Finally, there's the choice of whether to go with a "general" agency—one that produces print ads and commercials for a broad range of consumer accounts—or to work for an agency that specializes in an area such as financial, retail, direct marketing, high-tech, industrial, or medical advertising.

The advantage of specialization is that specialists can command greater salaries when they switch agencies, because other agencies need their industry-specific experience to handle accounts in these areas. The danger is that once you become established in a specialty (such as automotive copy or package goods), you'll become tagged as an "automotive writer," "soap writer," "food writer," or whatever.

The longer you stay in a particular specialty, the harder it becomes to break out and work in new areas. One writer complained to me, "When I started in this business thirty-five years ago, I never thought about being a specialist or generalist. Now, after thirty-five years on hardware accounts, no one will hire me to do anything else."

Many writers avoid specializing because they like the variety of working on many new products and accounts. They don't want to be limited or stuck in one area.

Writers who want to be generalists would do best to go with

a general agency. At a general agency, you can get experience on a wide variety of accounts without getting pigeonholed as a product specialist.

Copywriters planning an eventual move to freelance life would be better off working for a specialty agency. The reason is that in freelancing, specialists are more in demand and command higher fees than generalists. And the quickest way of becoming a specialist is to do it writing copy for an ad agency with accounts in the specialty you are interested in.

This brief overview can only give you a general idea of what to look for in an ad agency. But remember: Each agency is unique. Each has its own character, its own personality, its own special environment.

When you go in for a job interview, you should check out the agency as thoroughly as they check you out. You want to be sure the job is right for you before you accept an offer. And so . . .

Start by looking over the agency's client list published in *The Standard Directory of Advertising Agencies*, known as the Red Book. Does the agency handle accounts that interest you?

Next, take a look at the ads they've produced for these accounts. You'll probably find framed reprints of these ads plastered all over the walls of the agency's lobby and hallway.

When you look over this work, do you see ads you admire? Or do you get the feeling that you and the agency have a different conception of what good advertising should be? You want to work at an agency whose "philosophy" and style are in tune with your own.

Get the creative director to give you a tour of the agency. Do the people look happy, energetic, productive, enthusiastic? Do they look like they are having fun? Are they people you would enjoy working with? They'd better be, because you're going to spend at least the next year or two of your life with them.

Here are some questions I'd ask of an agency I was considering working for:

• What type of assignments do your copywriters work on? What's the mix between print ads, TV and radio commercials, direct mail, brochures, public relations? What, specifically, will I be doing all day?

• What accounts will I be assigned to? What do these companies manufacture? Which products will I be working on? How do the billings (gross income) produced by these accounts rank with other accounts handled by the agency? (This tells you whether you're working on important accounts or minor business.)

• How many other people are assigned to the account? Am I the only writer or part of a team? Do I work with an account executive or handle client contact myself?

• What is the career path for copywriters in this agency? Can copywriters get promoted and still write copy? Or are senior copywriters, copy chiefs, and creative directors mainly supervisors?

• Which accounts did the agency gain in the last two years? Which did it lose?

• What will the agency's billings be this year? What were they last year and the year before?

• Will I be working in an open area? A partially enclosed "modular office"? Or will I have a real office with a door I can close? (Depending on how you like to work, this may be important to you.)

• Do you do online marketing as well as offline advertising? (If not, you risk not developing skill and a portfolio in online marketing, which can adversely affect your own marketability, whether freelance or in the job market, down the road.)

## TIPS ON RESUMES AND COVER LETTERS

"Advertising is a creative business," thinks the aspiring copywriter, "and so my best bet of getting an interview is to write the most far-out resume possible. It will stand out from the crowd and prove how creative I am."

Wrong. Advertising isn't just creativity for creativity's sake. It's the application of creative ideas to the selling and marketing of a product or service. Advertising is a serious business, and the executive who hires you wants a hardworking, talented professional—not a far-out wacko. Your resume should sell your experience, skill, and professionalism in a straightforward, persuasive manner.

"Don't submit a 'creative' resume," warns Hugh Farrell, president of Hammond Farrell, Inc., a New York advertising agency. "We don't read resumes to be entertained." The resume should be brief and simply state the facts. The cover letter should make it clear you know the nature of the agency you're applying to and, in brief form, why you think you're right for that company.

Unusual mailings may get attention but rarely result in an interview. Hal Riney, a senior vice president of Ogilvy & Mather, recalls receiving such "creative" packages as a poem, a cartoon, and a box containing a set of teeth and a note that said, "I'd give my eyeteeth to work for you."

Other than being brief (preferably one page, no longer than two) and neatly typed, there's really no standard format for resumes. Some people list their background in chronological order; others do it by the types of jobs or experiences they've had or by their skills in different areas.

What's important is that the resume gives the reader a quick and complete overview of who you are and what you do. The key to writing a successful resume, says Paula Green, head of her own ad agency, is "putting your resume together so that it reflects your accomplishments and skills, not just your height, weight, date of birth, etc."

Let's say you've held two positions in which you did some copywriting on the job. In listing these jobs on your resume, you should tell the name of the company you worked for, what business they were in, and the type of copy you wrote (product sheets, catalog listings, sales letters, trade ads).

Other items of interest to readers of your resume include:

• A statement of your objectives or your profession (e.g., "Objective: To write copy for major package goods accounts"). This statement should appear at the top of your resume.

• Experience in selling, marketing, graphic design, Web programming, and other facets of business.

• Freelance copywriting experience. Even one or two assignments count for something.

• Other writing experience: journalism, feature writing, books, public relations, proofreading, copyediting.

• Other responsibilities related to advertising, such as overseeing the production and printing of sales literature or coordinating trade show exhibits and seminars.

• Creative awards your copy has won, sales results your copy has produced.

You've already seen how, in a direct-mail package, "the letter sells, the brochure tells." And so it is with cover letters and resumes. The letter makes the sales pitch. It tells the reader, "You should give me a job. Here are the reasons why." The resume elaborates on these sales points and includes your complete background—details you don't have room to discuss in the cover letter. The resume tells the reader all about you. The letter sells the reader on giving you an interview.

A tip: Do not waste the reader's time telling him how interested and enthusiastic you are about the advertising field, or how you came to be that way. It's already assumed that you like advertising. Otherwise, why would you be asking for a job with an ad agency?

Let's take a look at a cover letter that was effective in getting interviews.

A few years ago, I considered getting a job with an ad agency. The problem was, a lot of the help-wanted ads I saw insisted that the writer have ad agency experience, which I did not. I decided to write a letter that would turn my lack of credentials into a plus for me and get me the interview. Here's what I wrote:

Mr. John Wilson
Box ABCD
New York, NY

Dear Mr. Wilson:

Your ADWEEK help-wanted ad says you're looking for a copywriter with agency experience.

Why?

I'm a writer on the client side. The product managers I worked for aren't interested in slick, pretty ads that win creative awards. They demand (and I give them) copy and concepts that generate leads, create awareness, and increase sales.

Rather than build a portfolio of splashy four-color advertisements, I've built campaigns that achieve marketing objectives within set budgets.

Now, the average agency copywriter may write more ads than I do. But my book will show you that I do first-rate work.

And if that's not enough, I challenge you to try me out on a few assignments and see if I don't top every agency-experienced writer that applies for this job.

Sincerely,
Bob Bly

I'm not saying this is a perfect letter or that there isn't a better way to write it. But, of three ads I responded to, all three agencies gave me an interview.

My letter was written in response to an ad. Here's a letter written to an agency that was not advertising for copywriters at the time:

Dear Mr. Carriello:

What do you look for in a copywriter? Is it skill in persuasive writing? The enclosed "spec" samples will give you a good idea of my ability to write hard-selling, attention-getting print ads.

Is it experience in writing? I've been a newspaper reporter, a proofreader, and a marketing communications writer for General Electric. The enclosed resume will give you the full story.

Is it experience working for an ad agency? That I don't have. And that's why I'm writing to you.

I'd like a job writing copy for your agency.

Salary and title are unimportant right now. I just want to get in the door, to prove myself to you. Once you see me perform I won't have to ask for more responsibility.

You'll want to give me all I can handle (and that's an armful!).

You know I can write. But can I sell?

I'm going to call you next week. Give me five minutes on the phone, and I'll do my best to sell you on giving me a half hour of your time in an interview.

You'll see me. And, you'll see a book full of first-rate spec copy. Then, I'll know how well I can write. And sell.

Thanks for your consideration. Talk to you next week.

Sincerely,
Brad Frankel

## HOW TO PUT YOUR BOOK TOGETHER

A "book" is a portfolio: a collection of ads and other promotions you've written.

You must have a book to get a job in advertising. Everybody who interviews you will ask to see it. They will judge you as much by the work in your book as by your cover letter, resume, and how you handle yourself in the interview.

The actual portfolio is a plastic or leather case with pages similar to those in a photo album. The pages are heavy paper or cardboard covered with clear plastic. Reprints of your ads are mounted on the cardboard and protected by the plastic covers.

The outside of the portfolio is usually plastic, vinyl, leather, or imitation leather. Most are black, some brown. Portfolios can be zipped shut and come with a handle for easy carrying.

You can buy a portfolio case at an art supply store. Many stores that specialize in leather products such as briefcases, handbags, and luggage also carry portfolios.

Portfolios come in many sizes. Choose one that is small enough to be carried conveniently, but with pages large enough to display your simple ads. For magazine ads, a 7- by 10-inch or 8½- by 11-inch page is big enough. But for newspaper ads, oversize brochures, or direct-mail packages with many pieces, you may need a larger size to display the material adequately.

The simplest way to display your ads is to mount them in a portfolio, one ad per page. Some copywriters also paste a descriptive label or index card beneath the ad. The label tells which agency produced the ad, where it ran, the sales results it produced, and the awards it won, if any.

You can organize your portfolio by type of assignment, putting all ads in one section, all brochures in another, all sales letters in a third.

You can organize your portfolio by campaign. Each section

contains the ads, commercial scripts, and collateral for a different ad campaign.

Or you can organize your portfolio by product area: package goods, consumer electronics, medical products, office equipment.

There's no "right size" for a portfolio. Two samples is probably too few. A hundred is probably too many. Somewhere between six and sixteen samples seems about right.

Experienced copywriters may have more. Novices will have fewer.

Portfolios can contain both "published" and "spec" work. Published ads are those that are actual assignments from real clients and have been published in magazines or newspapers. Spec ads, as you've seen, are assignments you make up on your own to demonstrate your copywriting skill.

Published ads are more impressive. There's something about a book filled with typewritten sheets of spec copy that says "amateur," just as a book filled with sharp-looking magazine tear sheets says "professional."

However, the real test is not whether the work is published or spec, but whether it's good, brilliant, or mediocre. Brilliant spec copy can make a creative director sit up and take notice of a novice writer. And a seasoned pro with a book of bland, unexciting, unoriginal work is not going to get a job with a top agency no matter how long he's been in business.

If you are just starting out, you have no published work to show, and so you will have to go about writing a portfolio of spec ads.

A good way to get started is to go through magazines and clip half a dozen or so ads you think you can improve on. Rewrite these ads. Then, in your book, put the original ads on left-hand pages with the rewrites facing them on the right-hand pages. This before-and-after technique can make a dramatic presentation of your copywriting skills.

Portfolios can—and should—be tailored for specific interviews. If you're interviewing with a direct-mail agency, begin your portfolio with some hard-selling sales letters. If you're going after a job with an agency known for its creative approach, make sure your ad copy reflects their level of creativity.

Put together a spare portfolio. That way you can go on interviews even if a creative director asks to hold on to your original portfolio for a few days.

## WINNING AT THE JOB INTERVIEW

How you look, act, and talk during an interview can decide whether you get the job. A great interview can, in part, make up for a so-so book. And a poor interview can eliminate a great copywriter from the running.

Here are some pointers for doing your best in the interview:

### 1. Be Sharp
Surviving a job interview takes a great deal of concentration, so you should be at your best. This means getting a good night's sleep the night before. And, if a big meal makes you groggy, don't eat or drink until after the interview.

### 2. Be on Time
Few things are as important in advertising as meeting deadlines. Make sure you show up for your interview on time. If you aren't on time for your interview, how will you meet your deadlines on the job?

Leave your house to go to the interview with plenty of time to spare. If you get there early, sit in the reception room or walk around the block until it's time. If you have to rush to get there on time, you'll be disheveled, sweaty, and flustered, and you won't be at your best for the interview.

### 3. Look Professional

Dress in business clothes: a three-piece suit for men, a conservative skirt or dress pants and blazer for women. Be well groomed, clean, neat. Short, clean hair is more appealing than long, unkempt, stringy hair. Like it or not, appearance makes a strong first impression, and you can blow your chance by dressing too casually or too "hip."

### 4. Bring Samples of Your Work

Always bring your portfolio. Also carry a file folder with other materials you might need: additional samples of your work, extra copies of your resume, reprints of articles you've written, letters of recommendation from clients and colleagues. You want to have these items handy in case the interviewer asks to see them.

### 5. Listen

Don't go into the interview with a memorized sales pitch. Let the interviewer ask questions. Listen. And give the best answers you can.

Keep your answers friendly but brief and to the point. If you start blabbing, you're bound to say the wrong thing and hang yourself with it. Which brings us to our next tip . . .

### 6. Let the Interviewer Do Most of the Talking

When the interviewer is doing most of the talking, it's a sure sign that the interview is going well. It means the interviewer is comfortable with you, doesn't need to be sold on your qualifications anymore, and is in fact trying to sell you on the agency and why you should work there.

One way to get the interviewer to do the talking is to ask a lot of questions about the agency, the clients, the work environment, the job, and even about the interviewer himself.

## 7. Be Aggressive

Don't be bashful about promoting yourself; no one else is going to do it for you. You don't want to lie or put up a false front. But you should apply "the 10 percent rule"—advertise yourself as 10 percent better than you really are.

For example, if you've written two or three press releases for a couple of clients, you can say, "Yes, I've handled public relations projects for a number of different firms." Don't be "redder than the rose" and volunteer the fact that the number is only two.

## 8. Don't Let Yourself Be Put on the Spot

Some interviewers may ask you to perform for them. They might ask you to write some copy on the spot, or critique some ads and come up with better headlines, or solve a hypothetical marketing problem. If you can come up with the answers right then and there, great! Show them your stuff.

But, if you don't feel comfortable being put on the spot, don't submit. Say, "I'll be glad to take these problems back to my office and come up with the ads in a day or two for you. But frankly, I don't write copy or come up with strategy without going off and carefully studying the problem. That's how I work best, and I know you wouldn't want less than my best." Don't submit to the test and blow your chances if you think you can't do well in a "quickie" quiz.

## 9. Don't Apologize

Every interviewer will ask you if you have background or experience in something that you don't. Most writers, being humble and insecure, will bow their heads, apologize for their shortcomings, and beg forgiveness and a chance to get the job anyway.

Don't beg, don't apologize. Instead, turn weakness to strength. For example, the interviewer says, "I see you don't have any experience in insurance. We handle a lot of insurance accounts. How do you expect to be able to jump in and take on the work?"

You reply, "Well, it's true that I don't have a lot of experience in the area. But I've done plenty of work in related areas— banking, personal finance, real estate. And I didn't mention it on my resume, but years ago I edited an in-house newsletter for Prudential Insurance. So I do know quite a bit about the industry and their products."

Or, suppose the interviewer says, "You're a medical copywriter. But we handle a lot of computer accounts, which are highly technical. You don't have any computer experience or training. How are you going to be able to learn it?"

You say, "You're right. I haven't worked on computers before. But I'm not a doctor, and I became a first-rate medical copywriter, and medical products are also highly technical. So you see, I have an aptitude for technical copy. It doesn't matter what the product is. With research and background material, I can quickly study and learn enough to write effective copy on any subject—including drugs and computers."

## SUCCEEDING ON THE JOB

With a great background, portfolio, resume, cover letter, and interview technique, you are bound to get a job in copywriting sooner or later.

Advertising is a highly competitive industry, so finding a job may take some time. I know one copywriter with seven years' experience who looked for three months before she was hired. I know another writer who is a beginner; it took her a year to get an offer.

When you show up for work, you'll be assigned a desk, an art director, a creative director, an account executive, and one or more accounts.

The art director is your creative partner. The two of you will spend much time working together, dreaming up concepts for ads and commercials.

You'll write the copy. The art director will design the layout.

Sometimes, you'll think of a better way to design the ad and the art director will use your idea. Sometimes, the headline for the ad will come from the art director, not the writer.

The creative director is your boss. He or she runs the creative department. The creative director supervises and works with the agency's writers, artists, TV producers, and print production department. The creative director's job is essentially quality control of print and broadcast advertising.

When a new campaign is launched, the creative director may work with the artist and writer to establish an overall direction for the campaign. Then the artist and copywriter go off to produce the ads and commercials.

The account executive is the marketing expert of the team. He works with the client to plan advertising and marketing strategies. Then he goes back to the agency and explains the strategy to the writer and artist so they can create ads that achieve the objectives of the plan.

In addition to being a business expert and planner, the account executive is the liaison between client and agency. The account executive gives the writer the background information he needs to write accurate, effective copy. If the background information is wrong, the copy will be wrong, no matter how skilled the writer is.

The "account" is the client. The client is the one who approves, disapproves, or asks for changes in the copy you've written.

If the client turns down work you feel strongly about, you will try to convince the account executive that you are right and that the work should run as is. If the account executive can be persuaded to see your point of view, he may go back to the client to defend your work and try to get approval for it.

However, the client is paying the bill and has final say over what is published and what is rejected.

Studies have been done to determine how much of an ad agency employee's time is spent doing billable work. "Billable work" is hours that can be billed to the client. A copywriter's billable work includes time spent on writing, editing, thinking, working with the art director, and meeting with the account executive, creative director, or client to discuss the client's campaign.

The results of the study may interest you:

- 62.5% of the copywriter's time is spent on billable work
- 11.5% is spent on days off—vacation, personal, sick days, and holidays
- 10% is spent in internal agency meetings
- 7% is spent on miscellaneous breaks (coffee, bathroom, staring out the window)
- 7% is spent working on presentations and speculative work to attract new business
- 2% is spent promoting the agency

## WORKING ON THE CLIENT SIDE

Not all advertising writers work at agencies. Many work for the advertisers: the companies that manufacture products or offer services. This side of the business is called "the client side."

Because of its glamorous image, most people would prefer to work on the agency side. As a result, the client side is less competitive, and it's easier to get a writing job on the in-house staff of a corporation than it is at an agency.

Working on the client side is excellent training for an agency career. Not only will you build a portfolio of published copy, but you'll gain an intimate knowledge of the client's business and of how people on the client side think and feel. Most copywriters without client-side experience have very little idea of what goes on inside the client's mind or how the agency's work is really reviewed and approved.

After a year or two with a client, you're ready to make the move to an agency. Don't wait too much longer than that. Older writers who have been on the client side their whole careers are viewed as second-rate talents by many big-agency creative directors.

Snobbery? Yes. But that's the way it is. So, if you plan an agency career, use your client job as a training period and a stepping-stone.

However, you may find that you enjoy the client side. Many people do, and they spend enjoyable, profitable, rewarding careers working for manufacturers, service firms, and retailers.

The following points of comparison between clients and agencies will help you decide which is right for you:

• *Agency life is more hectic*. Agency writers have more projects and tighter deadlines. It's an unfortunate fact of agency life that clients often don't give the agency a reasonable amount of time to complete their work. And the agencies take this abuse because they're afraid of losing the account.

Writers on the client side generally have fewer projects and more leisurely deadlines. They have a more secure relationship with the people they write for because they're all in the same office (or at least in the same company). So it's easier for a client-side writer to get a deadline extension or to set a deadline that gives plenty of breathing room.

All the agency writers I know complain of putting in several 10- or 12-hour days every week. When I was a writer on the client side, I rarely worked past five P.M., although today, hours are probably longer. And when I did, it was by choice, not because I had to.

• *Agency writers have more variety.* They work on many different accounts and many different products. The writer employed by an advertiser lives with the company's one product or product line day after day. And that can be boring, especially when you consider that client-side writers tend to change jobs less frequently than agency writers.

• *The client-side writer becomes a product expert.* Because they work for the company that makes the product they write about, client-side writers gain a far greater and more intimate knowledge of their product than any agency or freelance writer can. They have much more opportunity to chat with engineers and designers, tour the labs and the plant, visit conventions, hobnob with top-level marketing and product managers.

They also get to go into the field to see the product in operation and to accompany salespeople when they call on their customers. The client-side writer has the luxury of becoming a product expert, an enjoyable position for a writer to be in.

• *Client-side writers see the "big picture."* Client-side writers work side-by-side with the people who design, manufacture, and sell the product, as well as with the people who plan its marketing and advertising strategy.

Also, client-side writers are frequently responsible for the total communications campaign, which may include trade show exhibits, seminars, sales presentations, technical literature, instruction manuals, product labels, dealer promotions, and sales meetings in addition to advertising and publicity. Agency writers, on the other hand, usually write the major print ads and TV commercials only. They don't get to dig into the complete campaign the way in-house writers do.

• *Team spirit.* The in-house writer is part of the client's team, the corporate family. He or she is an insider, working in the office next door to the product manager or brand manager.

The writer and the product manager attend the same company picnics, shoot the breeze by the same water fountain, ride in the same carpool. They might drop by each other's office five or six times a day to discuss a project or have a friendly chat.

The agency writer is viewed as an outsider by the client—a hired gun, not part of the team. Some clients resent their agencies and would prefer to handle the advertising in-house. And even though most clients are on a friendly basis with their agency writer, there is rarely the close relationship that develops with the company's own writing staff.

## CLIENT SIDE: WHERE THE JOBS ARE

Corporations have many different departments that hire staff writers. These include:

### Advertising Department

The advertising manager in charge of this department works with the outside agency to develop major ad campaigns. The agency buys space and places ads according to a media plan approved by the ad manager. The ad manager also hires and supervises staff writers who produce trade ads, brochures, catalogs, trade show displays, and product data sheets. They might also write the company magazine and the annual report.

### The In-House Agency

The in-house agency is an advertising department that functions as a full-service advertising agency. The in-house agency buys space, places ads, and receives commissions from the media, just like a regular advertising agency. The in-house agency offers the advertiser a broader range of services than the advertising department (these include media planning and buying and television production). Some in-house agencies even take on outside clients whose businesses don't conflict with the corporation's.

## Marketing Communications

The marketing communications department produces communications that support a company's marketing efforts. They write industrial films, slide shows, sales brochures, easel presentations, and point-of-purchase displays. Marketing communications writers spend all of their time writing advertising support material; they rarely write the ads themselves.

## Public Relations

Many advertisers have a separate department that handles public relations. Writers in these departments turn out news releases, feature stories, and other publicity-related material, such as newsletters and fact sheets.

## Employee Communications

The writers in the employee communications department help top management communicate with the employees. As an employee communications writer, you may be asked to write a slide show used for recruiting new engineers and MBAs from universities, a film that gives plant workers an overview of the company, a series of booklets explaining the benefits programs, or the weekly employee newsletter.

## Audiovisual Communications

The AV department produces videotapes, films, and slide shows used by such departments as corporate, employee relations, marketing, sales, advertising, and training. Many AV departments hire full-time writers to write scripts for these films and presentations.

### Corporate Communications

Corporate communications is a service department that helps corporate management communicate. Corporate communications writers ghostwrite speeches and articles for busy executives. They may also be in charge of the annual report, the corporate ad campaign, and other communications aimed at stockholders, investors, and the general public.

### Technical Publications

The technical publications department is a team of technical writers, editors, and artists who produce reports, proposals, manuals, and other technical documents. They may also get involved in data sheets and product brochures.

# 14

## HOW TO HIRE AND WORK
## WITH COPYWRITERS

"The advertising business is neatly split down the middle between people who make and create things and the people who approve and disapprove things," writes *Adweek* columnist Ed Buxton. "There are the doers and the undoers, the builders and the destroyers, the white hats and the black hats."

This chapter is written to help these two warring factions—advertising professionals and their clients—work together more efficiently and more profitably and in relative peace and harmony.

If you are a client—someone with the power to approve or disapprove advertising—you will learn how to hire the best copywriters and how to work with them to get the best copy and ideas for your money.

If you are a copywriter (agency or freelance), you will learn how to get your copy reviewed and approved and how to avoid misunderstandings, arguments, and bad feelings between you and your clients.

## WHY SOME CLIENTS DON'T RESPECT
## THEIR COPYWRITERS

The copywriting business is full of horror stories about abominable clients who bully and insult their writers. One writer tells of a client who, displeased with a sales letter, sat the copywriter down at a PC and called in the entire office staff to stand over the writer as he rewrote the letter. Each time he typed in a new word, the office staff members would give their opinions on whether the word was acceptable and what should come next.

Another writer was hired to write a brochure for a pharmaceutical company. After submitting his copy, the writer never heard from the client again, even after repeated calls and letters to the company. Disgusted, he sent an invoice for his services. The firm sent back a note that said, "We decided to rewrite the copy ourselves. Enclosed is payment for your invoice minus our cost for rewriting your manuscript." Attached to the note was a check for only a small fraction of the agreed-upon amount.

Few murder suspects would tell their lawyers how to conduct their defense. And most sick people have faith in their physician's diagnosis. But almost every advertiser thinks he can write copy better than his agency, and most don't hesitate to take their editor's blue pencil to the copywriter's work.

Why do copywriters "get no respect"? I can think of two reasons.

First, writing is more subjective than most other fields. An accountant can point to a ledger and prove that the books balance. A lawyer can back up her case with legal precedents and logical arguments.

Writing copy is not so cut and dried. There may be dozens of ways of writing an ad, each with merit. The copywriter can say he thinks his way is best. But he can't prove his ideas are superior. The client has to take it on faith . . . and few do.

Of course, there are guidelines for effective copy, presented earlier in this book, among other places. Unfortunately, many clients and writers are not aware of these rules. And without a clear idea of what makes good copy, how can the copywriter defend his work and say that it's good?

The second reason clients don't respect writers is that, way down deep, many clients fancy themselves better writers than their copywriters.

Doctors, lawyers, accountants, plumbers, mechanics, and TV repairmen deal in areas so technical and complex that their clients don't know enough to interfere. But everybody can write. (Even parrots and mockingbirds use language!) So there is less mystery to the copywriter's work, and clients are more confident that they could write the ad or letter "if only I had the time."

What can you do to improve the situation? Here's a three-step recommendation:

1. Hire the right copywriter for the job: someone who fits in with the product and your company.

2. Work with the writer on a professional basis. Treat the writer with the same respect you would your lawyer, accountant, or doctor. Stand back, and let the writer do her job. Don't interfere.

3. Establish logical guidelines for reviewing copy. Base your review on these concrete standards, not on subjective or aesthetic judgments. And above all, be specific in your criticism.

Let's look at each step of the plan in more detail.

## HOW TO HIRE A FREELANCE COPYWRITER

How do you go about finding freelance copywriters? And how do you know which writer is right for your business? Here are 10 tips for finding and selecting the best copywriter for the job at hand.

### 1. Ask around

Need to find a writer? The best way to find one is through referrals. Ask your friends, colleagues, and acquaintances to recommend writers they have used in the past.

The people most likely to know the name of a good copywriter include:

- Local advertising agencies and PR firms
- Magazine space reps and editors
- Printers, photographers, graphic artists, design studios, and other outside vendors
- Communications managers of nearby manufacturing and service firms

Some copywriters advertise their services in advertising journals. *Adweek*, for example, publishes a weekly "Creative Services Guide" that contains a number of ads offering freelance copywriting services.

*Adweek* also publishes an annual *Adweek/Art Directors' Index USA*. The book contains a section listing freelance copywriters. Many copywriters advertise in the Yellow Pages under "copywriter," "writer," or "advertising agency." And a Google search will point you toward those freelance copywriters that have Web sites.

## 2. *Choose a writer with experience in your industry*

There are three advantages to using a writer who knows your business. First, you'll spend less time briefing her and bringing her up to speed in your technology and your markets.

Second, because the writer already speaks the jargon of your industry, your employees will accept her more readily than they would an "outsider" who didn't speak their language. This may be important if you want your managers and engineers to work closely with the writer.

Third, the writer may be able to criticize your strategy or suggest new ideas based on her experience working with clients whose products are similar to your own.

Clients have asked me, "Do you have to be a computer programmer to write copy on a computer account?" You don't, and many great computer ads have been written by writers who didn't know a minicomputer from a microcomputer when they started. On the other hand, a writer with programming experience does have a head start over the writer who has never touched a computer keyboard.

The writer you hire doesn't have to be an expert in your particular product. (She won't ever know as much about your business as you do.) But she should have a feel for your industry and a knack for writing the type of copy you need.

For example, if you need a writer to write a brochure on your new Caribbean cruise package, don't insist that the writer have a portfolio full of brochures on Caribbean cruises. Chances are you won't be able to find such an individual. But you should look for a copywriter specializing in travel rather than one who is more at home with subscription mailings, annual reports, or fashion advertising.

In other words, don't insist that the writer have specific experience in your product line. Do look for a writer who specializes in your general type of advertising, be it travel, high-tech, home furnishings, or pharmaceuticals.

### 3. Hire someone in your league

Not all copywriting assignments require the same level of skill. Writing a bulletin board notice to sell your 1992 Chevrolet doesn't take the same level of copywriting sophistication that writing a corporate ad campaign for Exxon does.

Copywriters also operate on different levels. There are high-paid specialists. Middle-level generalists. And beginners to handle the easy stuff. These writers charge according to their level of skill, and you can save money by not overhiring for the job.

An advertising manager at a small industrial firm needed a cover letter to accompany a new brochure he was mailing to customers, sales reps, and regional offices. When he called a direct-mail specialist, the copywriter said, "I'd be glad to do the job, but my specialty is doing large mass mailings for big-name publishers and direct marketers. Because my letters are successful for these firms, I charge accordingly—$2,000 minimum for a short letter. I'm saying this not to brag, but to suggest that the job you have in mind doesn't require an experienced—and costly—top direct-mail writer. Hiring me to do this letter is like nuking a house to kill a mouse."

The direct-mail writer recommended an industrial writer who was willing to do the letter for only $750. The ad manager hired the industrial writer and was pleased with the copy he received.

### 4. Pick a writer whose style is in sync with your own

The conservative company, thinking that it's time to improve their image, hires the most creative agency in town.

The first ads come in. They're what you'd expect from a

creative agency—creative. "A little too far out for us, though," says the conservative client. "Can you come up with something a little more dignified. We're just not sure about the dancing chemical drums . . ."

"You're stifling our creativity!" screams the agency. They pick up their presentation, stamp out of the conference room, send a bill, and refuse to work with the barbaric client anymore.

Moral of the story: An ad agency or freelancer is unlikely to convince the client to make a radical change in their way of doing business. So clients would do well to select copywriters whose approach and style are in tune with their own.

If you like hard-sell ads—ads with coupons, with benefits in the headlines, with price and where-to-buy information, with straightforward body copy that sells the features and benefits of the product—you probably won't like the ads you get from a copywriter trained on splashy "image" campaigns for national brands. After all, this writer probably believes an ad should have a "clever" headline, a glossy color visual, and that people "don't read long copy."

Well, he's not going to convert you to his point of view. And you're not going to waste your hard-earned ad dollars so he can win creative awards. The best bet is to stay away from each other in the first place. Hire a writer whose portfolio is full of your type of fact-filled ads. Let a company who wants "showplace" ads hire the creative guy.

Do you like long-copy ads or short-copy ads? Fancy color photos or plain-Jane graphics? Informational copy or emotional copy? Plain language or purple prose? Choose a copywriter whose style and "advertising philosophy" fit in with your own. You'll both be happier with the working relationship—and with the copy it produces.

## 5. Taking the first step

Let's say you have the name of a copywriter you want to hire. The first step is to phone or write her and ask to see background material on her copywriting services.

At the very least, you want to see samples of her work, a resume or capsule biography, and a list of clients. Experienced copywriters already have a standard package prepared that contains all this and more. Novices have to be told what to send you.

Here are the things to look for when evaluating the freelancer's package:

• *Is it well written?* If the freelancer can't promote himself effectively, how can he write copy for services and products with which he's not intimately familiar?

• *Do you like the sample work?* The samples represent what she considers to be her best ads. If you don't think they show promise, keep looking. This isn't the right writer for you, and asking to see more samples isn't going to change anything.

• *Look at the client list.* Make sure the copywriter has experience in your industry or in related fields. Don't hire a straight technical writer to write your new perfume ad. Find a writer who likes doing perfume ads and is good at it.

• *Did the copywriter include information on his fee rate and structure?* A true professional will give you his rates up front. He doesn't want to waste your time—or his—if you can't afford to pay him.

• *What related writing and communications experience does the copywriter have?* A well-rounded copywriter does more than write copy. What else has your copywriter written? Any books? Articles? Papers? Speeches? Seminars? Teaching experience?

• *What overall feeling do you get from the whole thing?* You've looked over the writer's material and chatted with her over the phone. Do her package and presentation say "professional" or "amateur"? Do you feel comfortable with the writer and confident that she can handle the job? Gut feelings are important. Go with your instincts.

### 6. *Don't expect something for nothing*

An amazing number of smaller companies will call me up and say, "We're a small manufacturer in South Jersey. We don't do much advertising, but we saw your ad and may need a one-page press release to announce our president's retirement next month. We'd like to meet with you to check you over. Can you come over this afternoon? Get a pencil and I'll give you directions . . ."

I have news for you. Unless you're a major advertiser or ad agency with a large project in hand or the promise of a lot of business for me, you are not going to see me. Ever. And why not? Because if I jumped in that car and spent the better part of the day visiting every small business that wanted a $750 press release, I'd have no time to write copy for my dozens of paying clients.

My point is: The copywriter, like a lawyer or doctor, is a professional. If you want his time, you must be willing to pay for it. Few copywriters give free house calls these days.

You may object, "But I want to hire you! Isn't a meeting the next step?"

It doesn't have to be. We can handle the assignment by mail and phone.

"But I want to meet you!"

Fine. Come to my office and there is no charge. If I have to leave the office, though, I have to charge you for my time—if it's just an exploratory meeting. If you have an assignment for me, I'll include the meeting as part of my fee, provided we've already agreed that I'm going to handle the project for you.

As I've said, I may make an exception if you're a big advertiser or agency or if you're dangling an attractive project in front of my nose. But it's unreasonable for most clients—smaller companies with infrequent copywriting assignments—to expect the copywriter to come running without compensation. The few projects they have to offer don't justify the time spent in travel and meetings.

Most copywriters will be glad to chat with you at length over the phone or in their office. But don't expect the copywriter to make an out-of-office trip to your plant or office unless you're willing to pay for a consultation. A writer who earns $800 or $1,500 a day isn't going to spend half a day chasing down a $500 assignment.

In the pre-Internet days, the major reason for copywriters to visit clients was to drop off their portfolio case of copywriting samples. But today many copywriters, me included, post our samples on our Web sites (mine is www.bly.com), where anyone can see them at the click of a mouse.

## 7. Discuss fees up front

There's no point in talking if you can't afford the writer's rates. Save yourself a lot of time and find out fees up front.

Most writers can give you rough estimates of what they charge for different jobs: so much for an ad, so much for a sales letter, more for a brochure. Ask to see the copywriter's fee schedule, if she has one.

These estimates are "ballpark" figures only. The exact fee depends on the specific assignment. But the ballpark figures give you a good idea of what you'll pay for the copy you need.

If the copywriter charges by time instead of project, find out her rate for a week, day, half-day, or hour. Ask how long she thinks your project will take. Multiply the number of days by the day rate to get the total cost estimate.

Also discuss deadlines up front. The top copywriters are often booked weeks in advance and cannot always handle rush jobs. Some prospects are shocked to learn that I can't write their ad overnight. They don't realize that I already have six jobs on my desk, all due in a week or so.

Find out how much time the writer normally takes to do small projects (ads, letters) and large ones (brochures, catalogs). If your deadlines are short, say so, and ask the writer if she can meet them.

Copy revisions should also be discussed up front. Are they included in the copywriter's initial fee or do they cost extra? How many drafts are included in the basic project price? How quickly can the writer make revisions? What happens if there is a change in the nature of the assignment? Are revisions still included? Is there a time limit in which revisions must be assigned?

Make sure you understand the writer's policy toward revisions. Otherwise, it can become a problem area later on.

### 8. Provide complete background information on the project

Send the writer all the background information you can. With this material in hand, the writer can give the most accurate estimate as to what the job will cost. Without it, he is "flying blind" because he doesn't know how much research is involved, and his high estimate will reflect this degree of uncertainty.

You'll get the best price by giving the writer whatever information he needs to make an informed, accurate estimate of what the copy will cost.

### 9. Get it in writing

Put the fee, terms, deadlines, and a description of the assignment in a purchase order or letter of agreement and send it to the copywriter.

A written agreement eliminates confusion and spells out what the client is buying and what the writer is selling. Too many buyers and sellers in all fields of business have gone to court because they made their deals orally. Don't you make the same mistake. A written agreement protects both the client and the writer. So don't just shake hands on it. Put it in writing.

### 10. Stand back

Once you've hired the writer and given her the background material, stand back and let her do her job. Don't interfere, don't ask to "take a look at the first few pages," don't badger the writer with constant "how's it going?" phone calls.

You've hired a professional. Now let the professional work. You'll get your copy by the deadline date or sooner. And it will be copy that pleases you and is effective in selling your product. If you need changes, the writer will make them. After all, that's what you're paying for.

## TIPS ON WORKING WITH YOUR COPYWRITER

The best way to work with your writer is to leave him alone during the first-draft stage of the project. He knows what he's doing, and you trust him. Otherwise, you wouldn't have hired him in the first place.

But, even though the copywriter is working at a distance, it's important that the two of you start off with a comfortable, mutually agreeable working relationship. Copywriting is a partnership: You provide the information and direction, the copywriter provides the persuasive writing, and together you sell more of a product or service.

If one or both partners isn't happy, someone won't be doing his job with enthusiasm. And a job done without enthusiasm is a job done poorly.

Here are some suggestions for maintaining a good working relationship between client and copywriter:

## 1. Pay fairly

Pay fair rates for copywriting services performed. Remember, an underpaid worker is an unhappy and unproductive worker. Writers writing for slave wages rarely produce exciting prose.

Everything in life is negotiable, but only so far. A good writer with a steady business may take 10 or 20 percent off the price if your assignment interests her. But she can't afford to— and probably won't—go much below that.

A writer who needs the work may come very cheaply. But even if you sense you can get it for less, pay a fair wage. If you force the writer down to the bargain-basement price, she's not going to feel very good about your project. And you want your writer to be enthusiastic, not apathetic.

## 2. Pay on time

There are few things as unpleasant in business life as trying to collect an unpaid invoice. Unfortunately, it's not unusual for clients to be four, six, even eight weeks or more behind in their payments to their freelancers.

Pay on time—in 30 days—and the freelancer will get a warm glow inside whenever you call. Better still, get a check out in ten days or less, and the freelancer will try to perform miracles for you on your next ad or campaign.

Agencies feel pretty much the same way, and although the agency writer doesn't get paid by you directly, accounts that pay their bills on time get special attention and love.

## 3. Cooperate

Provide complete background information on the product, your audience, and your objectives. Be available to answer questions or give direction. Review outlines and rough drafts in a timely fashion.

One person from the client organization should be the

contact between the company and the copywriter. It is inefficient for the copywriter to have to track down executives from half a dozen different departments of your firm.

### 4. Don't waste time

Avoid unnecessary meetings. Maybe a meeting or two will be needed, but most of the writing and revision can be handled by e-mail and phone.

Don't feed information or revisions to the writer one piece at a time. Give him the background information or the instructions for the rewrite in one shot.

It is good manners not to keep people waiting when they have an appointment with you. This applies to copywriters, too.

To the copywriter and the ad agency, time is money. If you do not waste their time, your account will be profitable to them, and they will gladly devote themselves to giving you the best advertising possible.

On the other hand, the more you waste the writer's time, the less profitable the project becomes. The writer will either devote less time to writing your copy or she will drop your account.

In general, writing copy should not require a great deal of contact between client and copywriter. The fewer number of contacts, the better. Meetings should never be more than two hours and should follow a tight agenda. Phone conferences should be brief and to the point.

Not only will the writer save time (and possibly charge you less as a result), but you will save time, too.

### 5. Let them hear from you

The copywriter mails his copy and never hears from the client until the next project. His insides are twisted with worry: Did the client hate the copy or did they love it? Probably they loved it—no news is good news—but the writer doesn't know.

A kind word from a client—a quick phone call, a brief, one-line note of praise—can do wonders for the copywriter's ego. Writers seldom receive feedback on their work, even when the reaction is favorable.

A thank-you note will be much appreciated by the writer starved for praise and ego gratification. Sincere flattery can quickly put you at the top of the writer's "favorite clients" list. And the benefits of this—better service, better copy—are far in excess of the effort involved.

### 6. Critique copy rationally

"I don't like it" is a meaningless critique and a frustrating response for the copywriter to deal with.

The key to reviewing copy is to give specific, objective criticisms. Subjective and vague comments don't give the writer any guidelines for revision and often lead to hurt feelings, defensiveness, and a gradual collapse of the client-copywriter relationship.

Below are nine rules for reviewing and approving copy. They will eliminate bad feelings and misunderstandings and give the copywriter the guidelines he or she needs to rewrite the copy so that it will be acceptable and effective.

## HOW TO REVIEW AND APPROVE COPY

Reading and reviewing copy is as much as an art as writing copy. Here are some guidelines to help you review copy in such a way that you end up with the strongest promotion possible:

### 1. Be specific

Make your critique of the copy factual and specific. Show the copywriter where he went wrong—and how you want him to fix it.

Some examples of nonspecific versus specific criticisms:

| *Nonspecific:* | *Specific:* |
| --- | --- |
| "Not enough pizzazz." | "Our product is the only one that offers these features. The copy should stress its uniqueness more strongly." |
| "The copy doesn't 'position' the product." | "Our process is 20% more efficient than the competition's. That should be in the headline." |
| "The ad is dull and boring." | "Put in less about the technical features and more about what the product can do for people." |
| "It doesn't tell the story we want to tell." | "Here are the four consumer benefits the copy should cover." |
| "I don't like it." | "This is a good start. But there are some changes I'd like to see. Let me tell you what I have in mind." |

The copywriter is not a mind reader. It is not enough to say you want changes in the copy; you must specify what those changes are.

This does not mean that you should do the copywriter's job and rewrite the copy yourself. It does require that you write down specific, factual changes and corrections you want made and give them to the copywriter so he can rewrite your copy to incorporate these changes.

And be sure to give these instructions in writing, not orally (unless they are very brief and very minor). The act of writing out your comments forces you to be more specific. Use Word's Track Changes feature to mark up the electronic draft with your comments; this makes your edits easier to read and eliminates the need for the copywriter to struggle with your hand-written comments.

## 2. *The fewer levels of approval, the better*

Who should have approval authority? The marketing expert—usually a product manager. A technical expert, usually an engineer or scientist. The advertising manager. And the company president. But certainly no more than that.

Everybody has a different opinion of what should appear in an ad. By trying to please a committee, you end up with an ad that is too spread out, one that is weak and watered down, with no strong selling message or point of view.

Four reviewers or less is ideal. Six should be the maximum. Any more, and you are writing ads by committee—and committees cannot write effective ads.

When I write for small companies, my copy is usually approved by one person: the company owner or president. Some of my best copy has been published this way. If others in your organization want to see the copy before it is published, put them on a "cc" list of people who receive informational copies. These people can give you their opinion if they want to, but they have no right of approval or disapproval. Only a handful of high-level managers should have a say over what the final content of the ad will be.

Clients and prospects frequently ask me, "Do you find that your copy is improved once it has gone through the approval process?"

Occasionally, a revision will sharpen and improve the copy. But honesty compels me to admit that 99 out of 100 times the original version is better than the copy published after that ad has gone through the numerous layers of corporate approval. The fewer revisions made, the better.

### 3. Attach an approval form to the copy

When you route the copy for approval, attach a standard approval form to it. The form lists the reviewers in the order they'll review the copy. The reviewer of least authority sees the copy first, the person with final say sees it last.

List each person's name along with the date by which he or she should sign off on the copy and send it to the next reviewer. Ask each reviewer to initial the approval sheet and to date their initials (this will speed the approval process).

Any discrepancies in reviewers' comments should be reconciled by the advertising manager before the copy is returned to the writer for revision.

### 4. What about legal?

Lawyers can ruin good copy. Don't allow the legal department to rewrite copy. If there's a legal problem with the copy, the lawyers should point it out so the copywriter can make the necessary revisions. But lawyers don't understand the nature of salesmanship in print, and they can ruin a good piece of copy by changing strong, sharp language into weak, vague, lawyerlike prose.

One advertiser experienced a 56 percent drop in response to their mailings after the legal department changed the order form. The change was minor—the words "annual subscription" were replaced with "12-month lease"—but the editing had a devastating impact on sales. As consultant Shell Alpert explains, "The monumental difference lies not in the meaning of the words, but in their connotation. The perceived risk that the word 'lease' almost viscerally evokes is far more intimidating than 'subscription.'"

On the other hand, there are some situations in which it can be dangerous not to show the copy to your lawyer. For instance, the FDA ruled that Pfizer's campaign for Procardia, a heart medication, was "false and misleading." They ordered Pfizer to revise its promotional materials, send letters to all physicians who might have received the original literature, and run "remedial ads" in two issues of each medical magazine that carried the original ads. My guess is that this cost Pfizer hundreds of thousands of dollars.

Not every ad has to be run by legal. But you should show copy to the lawyers when:

- You're advertising a highly regulated product such as ethical drugs or financial services (an "ethical drug" is one that can only be purchased with a prescription from a medical doctor)
- The promotion involves a sweepstakes or contest
- You're running comparative advertising that names the competition
- There is a question as to whether you might be violating a trademark or copyright
- You are making product claims that are difficult to prove
- The market is highly competitive, and there's a chance a competitor might take legal action to stop your ads from running
- You're promoting products in heavily regulated industries, such as nutritional supplements, commodities trading, or stock market newsletters

### 5. Be civil

Some clients love to tear apart a writer's work. Others are merely insensitive. They don't realize that writing is a highly personal act, and writers take criticism on a personal level.

Amil Gargano says that some people "take delight in browbeating creative people. These are people who have a very fragile ego and a difficult time handling rejection. You should comment on their work in a way that is thoughtful, considerate, and articulate."

You don't have to baby writers. Just remember they're people. And, like your own employees, they are quick to respond to praise and to insult.

Be tactful when you have to tell a writer that his work doesn't meet your standards. Don't say, "The copy isn't very good, and we need a total rewrite."

Rather, start with praise, then get to the defects. Say, "Overall you've done a good job in putting this together. Let me show you our reactions and the changes we'd like you to make."

Companies spend a great deal of money motivating employees. Outside vendors also respond to the motivators of praise, kindness, courtesy, and decency. Treat your copywriters well, and they'll give you their best.

### 6. *Let writers write*

"Good clients don't write copy," says Malcolm MacDougall, president of SSC&B. "Good clients know in their hearts that nobody from Harvard Business School ever wrote a great ad campaign. That is why they have an agency."

Let your writers do their job. Don't write or rewrite copy. If you want changes made, write out what these changes are. But don't make them yourself. Give them to the copywriter and let him redo the words.

Don't play schoolteacher or amateur grammarian. The copywriter is the expert on how to use language as a selling tool.

If you think the ad doesn't reflect your strategy and objective, say so. If there's a wrong fact, point it out. But don't change commas to semicolons or dot *i*'s and cross *t*'s. Leave writing to the writer.

### 7. Don't take opinion polls

One of my clients had me come up with two versions of a brochure cover. He made his selection by asking his mother, his father, his wife, his wife's parents, his grandfather, and several friends which they liked best. Cover "B" got more votes and that's the one he went with. Don't make the same mistake as my client. Ad copy should be judged by professional businesspeople, not by friends, relatives, and neighbors.

When viewing an ad layout or reading a piece of copy, amateurs judge the ad by aesthetics. Not by whether it would move them to buy the product. They'll pick the pretty layout, the flowery, poetic-sounding copy every time. So, nice as these folks may be, their opinion of your ad shouldn't play a part in your approval process.

### 8. Read copy as a customer, not as an advertiser or an editor

I worry when the client reads copy with pen or pencil in hand. It tells me he's reading the ad as an editor, and not as a buyer.

Instead, read the copy from the customer's point of view. Ask, "If I were my customer, would this ad get my attention? Does it hold my interest strongly enough to get me to read or at least skim the body copy? Would I remember the ad, want to buy the product, or be moved to clip the coupon and respond?"

Don't worry if the ad doesn't show a picture of the company president or talk about the new conveyor belts in the Kentucky factory. If the customer doesn't care, then you shouldn't either.

### 9. Develop and publish guidelines for copy review

As I said, the copywriter can't read your mind. He can't know your corporate guidelines, your company's likes and dislikes, unless you tell him what they are.

Develop a set of rules and guidelines for your writers to

follow. These rules should contain both mandatory stylistic requirements (for example: "The company name is to be set in all caps and followed by a registered trademark symbol") and suggested guidelines.

The suggested guidelines clue copywriters on the way you're used to doing things. (For example, you might prefer long, informative subheads in brochures rather than short, snappy ones.) However, the copywriter should consider these guidelines as suggestions only. Rules can be bent and broken to make the copy more effective.

You can enlist the aid of your freelance copywriter, advertising consultant, or ad agency in developing these rules and guidelines. Together you may decide to add new rules or delete those guidelines that serve no real purpose.

Of course, the wisest thing you can do is to forget about your prejudices and tastes and give the copywriter total freedom to write the best copy he or she can.

# 15

# GRAPHIC DESIGN FOR COPYWRITERS

This is going to be one of the shorter chapters in the book. The reason is that it deals with a simple question. The question is: "What does the copywriter need to know about designing an ad layout?" And the answer is: "Probably not as much as you might think."

This is a relief to those of you who can't draw. But it may puzzle readers who do ads in which the words are strongly tied to a visual concept.

Let's see how involved the copywriter gets with the design side of advertising.

## DRAWING VS. VISUALIZING

The copywriter is not a graphic artist. It's not his or her job to design ad layouts, select photographs, specify type style and size, or select paper stock. These tasks are handled by art directors.

The copywriter's job is to come up with selling ideas. Most of the copywriter's ideas can be expressed primarily with words. The layout serves only as a framework to contain the words.

The visual supports, enhances, and explains the ideas in the copy, but the copy doesn't depend on the visual and can stand on its own.

Some concepts, however, can be expressed only by a strong combination of words and pictures. A classic Volkswagen ad showed a cartoon of a man holding a gas pump to his head as if he were shooting himself with it. The headline underneath the cartoon reads, "Or buy a Volkswagen." Obviously, this idea depends on a combination of words and images to get its point across. The copywriter who dreamed it up could not have presented it to the client without a rough sketch of the layout.

There are times when you, as a copywriter, need more than copy to get your ideas across. You may need to describe your visual in words, or sketches, or in a mock-up of the final version.

However, these need not be elaborate or well drawn. Stick figures, scribbles, and crudely drawn lines, boxes, and lettering will do. No one expects the copywriter to be an artist; clients understand that your drawing is a rough sketch only.

In fact, the term *copywriter's rough* is used to describe ad layouts and brochure dummies drawn by copywriters (a "dummy" is a paper mock-up of the brochure as it will be printed in its final form). See the diagram on following page for an example of a copywriter's rough.

I draw my copywriter's roughs in Microsoft Word, so I can easily insert them into the Word documents containing my copy. I also keep a subdirectory of files containing copywriter's roughs on my PC. Often the copywriter's rough for one project can be reused as is or with minor modification, saving me time and effort.

Some prospective clients ask, "Do you do the artwork also?" I reply, "I don't do mechanicals or comps. If my concept depends on a visual, I'll either write a description of the visual in the copy or provide a copywriter's rough." Although I'm a writer, I know something about graphic art and its jargon. Here are a few basic terms you should be aware of:

**Art.** A drawing or photograph used in advertising.

**Comp.** Short for "comprehensive." A comp is an artist's drawing of a layout. It is used for review purposes and as a guide for the printer.

**Dummy.** Mock-up of a brochure, catalog, or other piece of printed literature. The dummy is used to indicate the layout, look, weight, and feel of the finished piece.

**Four color.** Printed material reproduced in full color.

**Layout.** The positioning of the elements of a printed piece. These elements include the headline, subheads, body copy, coupon, logo, photos, and illustrations.

**Mechanical.** A paste-up of the type and visual elements of the layout. The mechanical is used by the printer to make reproductions of the ad or brochure.

**Rough.** An artist's crude sketch of the layout, used for showing the basic idea. If the rough is approved, the next step is a comp, then a mechanical.

**Thumbnail.** Small sketch (about the dimensions of a wallet-size photo) used to give a quick impression of a layout or visual idea.

**Two color.** Ad or printed promotion reproduced in two colors, usually black and a second color such as blue, red, or yellow.

**White space.** Blank area on a page.

A freelance copywriter submits a copywriter's rough to the client, whether the client is an ad agency or an advertiser.

An agency writer turns his copy and copywriter's rough over to the art director for polishing. A good art director enhances the writer's visual concept by adding his own ideas and creativity to it.

The art director may do a series of thumbnail sketches. These sketches can present a number of different visual concepts in rough form.

The writer, art director, and account executive review the thumbnails and choose the ones they want to develop into full-size artist's roughs. These roughs, along with the copy, are submitted to the client for approval.

Some agencies submit two or three versions of the layout so the client can select the one he likes best. To me, this is like having my lawyer say, "Which defense do you think I ought to use?" I believe the agency should select the version it thinks is best and submit this to the client. After all, the client is paying the agency to make judgments in the creative area.

Once the rough is approved, the agency may submit a more

polished drawing—the comp—before photos are taken and type is set.

Why do agencies go through the process of submitting roughs? Because of the cost of revisions. It is relatively inexpensive to make changes to a rough. It is costlier to redo mechanicals, set new type, or retouch or reshoot a photo if the client requests changes in the later stages of ad production.

## ART DIRECTION FOR COPYWRITERS

Agency copywriters know they have staff artists who can put their layout ideas in polished form.

Freelancers don't. They can either hire a graphic artist, or draw their own crude copywriter's roughs.

There is no need for the freelancer to hire an artist; just let your clients know that you will be providing copywriter's roughs, not finished comps. If the client demands comps, and if you're willing to provide this service, you can hire an artist.

In return for supervising the artwork, you add an extra charge for artwork to your bill. This charge can be based on a percentage of the cost of hiring the artist. Or it can be whatever fee you think is reasonable.

If all this talk of drawing and art has you, as a "pure" writer, a bit worried—stop worrying.

On nine out of ten projects I do not do a copywriter's rough or any other type of sketch. It's not necessary: Either my concept doesn't depend on a visual or, if it does, the visual can easily be described in words in the manuscript I submit.

Only one out of ten of my ads is so visually complex or dependent upon a visual that I need to sketch it out. And doing the crude sketch never takes more than ten minutes.

The computer has helped with this enormously. Reason:

Not every promotion needs an original layout. So the layout I draw for one project can often be recycled, as is, or with minor modification for other projects—saving me an enormous amount of time.

As mentioned earlier, I keep all the layouts I do for my various copywriting assignments in a folder on my PC labeled "layouts." They are all drawn in Microsoft Word, making them easy to incorporate into the Word documents I submit as copy to my clients.

Below is another sample layout from this folder. As you can see, a copywriter's rough is truly rough—this is a layout for a postcard. The copywriter does not design the finished piece; the layout is to show position of copy elements only.

Teaser!

Indicia

Label or Ink Jet

FRONT

HEADLINE
Subhead

800-XXX-XXXX
www.xxx.com

Here are a few of my projects and how I handled the visual element:

• *Four-page brochure for a bank*. The client told me, "We'll have the headline on the cover, the logo and address on the back cover, and the copy in the inside two-page spread. Our design studio will come up with the appropriate graphics." Since my description of the bank's service did not need to be illustrated visually, I submitted a typed manuscript of copy only, with no rough layout or descriptions of visuals.

• *Brochure for a software firm*. The firm needed a folded pamphlet to fit in a #10 business envelope. Such a brochure can be folded in several different ways, and the manner of folding affects the order in which the reader sees the sections of copy.

To make sure my copy would be read in sequence, I submitted a dummy of the brochure that indicated the manner of folding and which sections of copy would be printed on each panel of the brochure. I wrote in headlines and subheads and used squiggly lines to indicate body copy.

• *Annual report*. A graphic design studio hired me to write an annual report for one of its clients. Since the studio would do the actual design and the text was not tied to specific visuals, I did not submit a dummy or rough.

I did include a list of suggested visuals: charts, graphs, tables, and photos that I knew would enhance the message of the copy. The design studio, not being as familiar with the company's story as I was, needed this guidance to come up with the subject matter for appropriate visuals. However, the style and execution was all theirs.

• *Eight-page brochure for a radar system*. I attached a detailed list of suggested visuals and photo captions. After all, there are a lot of things to show in a brochure on radar:

transmitters, receivers, control panels, the antenna, the scope, interior circuitry, results of test flights, the manufacture of the components.

• *One-page sales letter for a producer of corporate videos and multimedia presentations.* No need for any layout: I typed the manuscript for the letter single-space, exactly as it would be printed on the client's stationery in its final version.

• *Series of full-page ads.* An ad agency hired me to write three ads, each on a different piece of industrial equipment. The agency had already come up with layouts and rough headlines, so there was no need for me to do a sketch or come up with a visual.

• *Full-page ad for a software firm.* Although the ad contained no visual (it was an all-copy ad), I did a rough sketch to indicate the positions of the headline, logo, and the coupon. (The company had not used coupons in its ads before, and mishandling the design of the coupon—making it too small or placing it in a position other than the bottom right-hand corner—can drastically reduce reader response.)

• *Feature article.* I submitted a typed manuscript only. Most articles don't require visuals. If yours does, you can attach a list of suggested photos at the end of the manuscript.

## MORE DESIGN TIPS FOR COPYWRITERS

The writer doesn't design the ad or brochure. But the writer should know what works in design and what doesn't. Ad agencies, graphic design studios, and large corporations have their own resources for producing print material. Smaller companies may not have a graphics expert to guide them. They look to the copywriter for advice on how to put together print promotions.

Here is a miscellany of graphic arts tips, rules, and techniques that every copywriter should know:

• First, there's the magic of the "Basic A" ad layout. This is the simplest, most standard layout: Large picture at the top, headline underneath, body copy in two or three columns under the headline, logo and address in the bottom right-hand corner.

• Basic A is not spectacular, and some art directors consider it "old hat." But it's sensible, it draws the reader into the copy, and it's easy to read.

• You may want something different. Fine. But at least consider Basic A before going on to a more "creative" design.

• A layout should have a single "focal point" where the eye goes to first. This is usually the visual; it can also be the headline.

• A layout should pull the eye from headline and visual through the body copy in logical sequence to the signature and logo. Subheads and bullets can help accomplish this.

• Setting the headline in big, bold type helps draw attention to it. A powerfully written headline, splashed across the page in large letters, can be a real stopper in an ad.

• If you want the reader to respond to your ad, use a coupon. The coupon should appear in the lower right-hand corner of the ad; the ad should be run against the outer edge of the right-hand page. If a coupon borders the "gutter"—the fold running down the middle of a magazine or newspaper—people will not tear it out.

• If you want people to respond to your ad by phoning, set the phone number in large type at the end of the body copy. A toll-free number gets more calls than a pay number—even if you invite the reader to call on your pay number "collect."

• Photos make better visuals than drawings. They are more real, more believable, than illustrations.

• Full-color gets more attention and gives a better impression than black and white. But full-color is much more expensive to produce and to run.

• In the hands of a skilled graphic artist, a second color can add to a brochure or ad's effectiveness. In the hands of an amateur, it can look chintzy and cheap. Be careful when using a second color in your layout.

• The simpler the layout, the better. Ads with too many elements—small pictures, graphs, tables, charts, sidebars—have a complex look that discourages people from reading the copy. It takes a highly skilled graphic designer to produce a multi-element ad that doesn't look cluttered and ponderous.

• The most important factor in selecting type is its readability. Type should be clear, easy on the eye, friendly, and inviting. Style is important—the choice of font is one of many elements that contributes to the image conveyed by the ad—but readability comes first. Always.

• Photos should be sharp, clear, and simple. If you have to choose between using a photo of poor quality or no photo, don't use a photo. Professional photography is expensive but necessary in advertising. Few amateur shutterbugs are capable of producing ad-quality photographs, although they may think otherwise.

• The best photos demonstrate a product benefit or make you think, "That looks interesting. I wonder what is going on here?" The latter type of photo has story appeal but doesn't tell the whole story; it leaves something to the imagination and arouses curiosity so that you will read the body copy to find out what the photo is about.

An example of this type of story-telling photo is one used in an ad for Paco Rabanne cologne. The photo shows a handsome young man lying in bed in his artist's studio. He is talking on the phone and, although covered by sheets, has obviously been sleeping in the nude. Who is he talking to? What happened in that room last night? You want to read the copy to find out.

• Never do anything to make the copy difficult to read. Type should be set in black against a clear white background: not a tint, not white on black, not in color. I just saw an ad in which the copy was printed on a tablecloth and shot as a photo! Naturally, it was quite difficult to read.

Some ads, of course, are strongly driven by visuals, but even then, the visuals must complement the copy. One recent example is an ad for United Technologies. The headline reads, "If you could punch this hole in a Sikorsky Black Hawk helicopter's gas tank, it would seal itself. In flight."

The visual is stark: a black circle five inches in diameter. To make the demonstration more dramatic, the ad is printed as an insert in the magazine on card stock.

The circumference of the black is perforated with a dashed line. Push on the black circle, and it pops out of the page, leaving the hole talked about in the headline.

## PARTING THOUGHTS

Here are a few opinions I've developed on copywriters, art, and art directors:

Some copywriters try to add to their value in the marketplace by taking on a second skill. There are copywriter-photographers, copywriter–art directors, copywriter-narrators, and copywriter–television producers.

The logic makes sense. By hiring the dual-function copywriter, the client gets two services for the price of one.

In reality, the best copywriters are those who write copy exclusively. People who do two jobs are usually not very good at either one. I know of only one or two exceptions, if that.

For example, all the copywriter-photographers I know are mediocre writers and mediocre photographers. The reason may be that a skilled writer is so in demand that he has no time for picture taking, just as a skilled photographer commands such high fees that there is no need to develop a secondary talent.

But whatever the reason, I've rarely met a "combination copywriter" who was a truly first-rate writer.

Successful copywriters—at least, the ones I know—are good at visualizing their ideas, but their visual concepts and layouts are always simple in design. The reason may be that copywriters don't have the drawing skills needed to express complex visual concepts on paper. So they stick to layouts they can illustrate with stick figures and squiggly lines.

Art directors, on the other hand, have the ability to do elaborate sketches, and so their layouts tend to be more sophisticated and complex.

A good art director can take a writer's simple concept and add graphic elements that enhance its selling power.

A clear-thinking copywriter can look at an art director's layout and see ways to make it cleaner, simpler, easier to read, and easier to respond to.

Designing ads is not the complex, mysterious task some people make it out to be. Laypeople believe, and artists encourage this belief, that there is some arcane formula of color combinations, type styles, photography, illustration, graphic elements, and positioning that creates ads with magical selling power.

The truth is, design has a mostly minor effect on sales compared with the nature of the product (its appearance, function, features, and benefits), the consumer's needs, the price, the availability of the product (how it is distributed), the seller's reputation, and the sales pitch made in the copy of the ad.

So, much of the fuss and bother clients and art directors make over the ad's graphic design don't make much difference one way or the other.

Simple layouts are the best layouts. They are easier to conceive and cost much less to produce. Yet, they are often the most effective.

A copywriter friend of mine wrote a small (6½- by 4⅞-inch) black-and-white ad selling a home-study foreign language course. The ad's layout is undistinguished: all copy except for a small line drawing of the study kit in the bottom right-hand corner. Yet, this plain-Jane ad has produced sales of more than $5 million!

Words, not pictures, are the most important way of communicating great ideas. The Bible contains many thousands of words and not a single picture.

# GLOSSARY OF ADVERTISING TERMS

**Account**—An advertising agency's client.

**Account executive**—An advertising agency employee who serves as the liaison between the agency and the client.

**Advertisement**—A paid message in which the sponsor is identified.

**Advertising manager**—A professional employed by an advertiser to coordinate and manage the company's advertising program.

**Art**—A photograph or illustration used in an advertisement.

**Art director**—An ad agency employee responsible for designing and producing the artwork and layout for advertisements.

**Audiovisual presentation**—A presentation involving both pictures and spoken words. TV commercials, slide shows, videotapes, and films are all audiovisual presentations.

**AV**—Audiovisual.

**B&W**—Black and white.

**Billings**—The fees an ad agency charges its clients.

**Bleed**—An illustration that goes to the edge of the page. Bleed artwork has no borders or margins.

**Blue chip**—A highly profitable company or product.

**Boilerplate**—Standard copy used because of legal requirements or company policy.

**Book**—See *portfolio.*

**Bounceback**—Second mailing sent to a prospective customer who responded to an ad. Bouncebacks are designed to increase response to the initial mailing of product information.

**Brand**—The label by which a product is identified.

**Brand manager**—A manager employed by an advertiser to take charge of the marketing and advertising of a brand.

**Broadside**—A one-page promotional flyer folded for mailing.

**Brochure**—A booklet promoting a product or service.

**Budget**—The amount of money the advertiser plans to spend on advertising.

**Bulk mailing**—The mailing of a large number of identical pieces of third-class mail at a reduced rate.

**Bullet**—A heavy dot used to emphasize lines or paragraphs of copy.

**Buried ad**—An ad surrounded by other ads.

**Business-to-business advertising**—Advertising of products and services sold by a business to other businesses.

**Buzz**—Excitement about a product generated primarily by PR (see *public relations*) and word of mouth.

**Campaign**—A coordinated program of advertising and promotion.

**Client**—A company that uses the services of advertising professionals.

**Clio**—Advertising industry award given for the best television commercials of the year.

**Collateral**—Printed product information such as brochures, flyers, catalogs, and direct mail.

**Considered purchase**—A purchase made after careful evaluation of the product.

**Consumer**—One who buys or uses products and services.

**Consumer advertising**—Advertising of products sold to the general public.

**Consumer products**—Goods sold to individuals rather than to business or industry.

**Contest**—Sales promotion in which the consumer uses his or her skill to try and win a prize. Some contests require proof of purchase.

**Copy**—The text of an ad, commercial, or promotion.

**Copy/Contact**—An ad agency copywriter who works directly with the client instead of through an account executive.

**Copywriter**—A person who writes copy.

**Creative**—Describes activities directly related to the creation of advertising. These include copywriting, photography, illustration, and design.

**Creative director**—Ad agency employee responsible for supervising the work of copywriters, art directors, and others who produce advertising.

**Demographics**—Statistics describing the characteristics of a segment of the population. These characteristics include age, sex, income, religion, and race.

**Direct mail**—Unsolicited advertising material delivered by mail.

**Direct response**—Advertising that seeks to get orders or leads directly and immediately rather than build an image or awareness over a period of time.

**Downscale**—Consumers on the low end of the social scale in terms of income, education, and status.

**Editorial**—Those portions of a magazine's or newspaper's reading matter that are not advertisements—articles, news briefs, fillers, and other material produced by the publication's editors and writers.

**E-zine**—An online newsletter. Also called an e-newsletter.

**Farm out**—To assign work to an outside vendor rather than handle it in-house.

**Feature story**—A full-length magazine article.

**Fee**—The charge made by an agency or advertising professional to the client for services performed.

**Four A's**—American Association of Advertising Agencies, an industry trade association.

**Four color**—Artwork reproduced in full color.

**Fractional ad**—An ad that takes less than a full page in a magazine or newspaper.

**Freelance**—A self-employed copywriter, photographer, artist, media buyer, or other advertising professional.

**Full-service agency**—An ad agency that offers its clients a full range of advertising services including creative services, media buying, planning, marketing, and research.

**General advertising**—Advertising that seeks to instill a preference for the product in the consumer's mind to promote the future sale of the product at a retail outlet or through a distributor or agent. This is the opposite of direct response advertising.

**House organ**—A company-published newsletter or magazine.

**HTML**—Hypertext markup language. The programming language in which many Web site pages are coded.

**Hype**—Highly promotional, sensationalized, "over the top" marketing and promotion.

**Image**—The public's perception of a firm or product.

**Impulse buy**—A purchase motivated by chance rather than by plan.

**Industrial advertising**—Advertising of industrial products and services.

**In-house**—Anything done internally within a company.

**Inquiry**—A request for information made by a potential customer responding to an ad or promotion.

**Inquiry fulfillment package**—Product literature sent in response to an inquiry.

**Jingle**—Music and lyrics used in a commercial.

**Landing page**—When you click on the hyperlink in an e-mail marketing message, you land on a Web page that provides additional selling copy on the product along with a mechanism for ordering the product online.

**Layout**—A drawing used to get a rough idea of how a finished ad, poster, or brochure will look.

**Lead**—See *sales lead*.

**Letter shop**—A business that reproduces sales letters and other advertising literature.

**Lift letter**—A second letter included in a direct-mail package; the lift letter is designed to increase response to the mailing. Also known as a publisher's letter because it is primarily used in mailings that solicit magazine subscriptions.

**List broker**—A person who rents mailing lists.

**Listserv**—Used for software for managing e-mail transmissions to and from a list of subscribers.

**Logo**—The name of a company set in specially designed lettering.

**Lottery**—In a lottery, winners are chosen by chance and must make a purchase to enter.

**Madison Avenue**—The mainstream of the New York City advertising community. Madison Avenue is a street that runs along the East Side of Manhattan, but used in the advertising sense, the term "Madison Avenue" refers to agencies located in the heart of Midtown Manhattan.

**Market**—A portion of the population representing potential and current customers for a product or service.

**Marketing**—The activities companies perform to produce, distribute, promote, and sell products and services to their customers.

**Marketing communications (marcom)**—Communications used in marketing a product or service. "Marketing communications" includes advertising, public relations, and sales promotion.

**Mass advertising**—Advertising aimed at the general public.

**Mechanical**—Type and artwork pasted up on a board for reproduction by the printer.

**Media**—Any method of communication that brings information, entertainment, and advertising to the public or the business community.

**Merchandising**—Activities designed to promote retail sales.

**Microsite**—A long-copy Web site dedicated to selling a single product.

**On speculation**—Work that the client will pay for only if he or she likes it and uses it.

**Package goods**—Products wrapped or packaged by the manufacturer. Package goods are low in cost and typically sold on store shelves.

**Per diem**—Fees charged by the day.

**PI**—Per inquiry advertising. Advertising for which the publisher or broadcast station is paid according to the number of inquiries produced by the ad or commercial.

**Portfolio**—A presentation folder containing samples of your work. Shown to prospective employers when you are interviewing for a job.

**Premium**—Gift offered to potential customers as motivation for buying a product.

**Press release**—Written news information mailed to the press.

**Product manager**—Employed by an advertiser to supervise the marketing and advertising of a product or product line.

**Promotion**—Activities other than advertising that are used to encourage the purchase of a product or service.

**Prospect**—A person with the money, authority, and desire to buy a product or service; a potential customer.

**Psychographics**—Data relating to the personalities, attitudes, and lifestyles of various groups of people.

**Pub-set**—Ads designed and typeset by the publication in which they will appear.

**Public relations (PR)**—The activity of influencing the press so that they print (and broadcast) stories that promote a favorable image of a company and its products.

**Publisher's letter**—See *lift letter*.

**Puffery**—Exaggerated product claims made by an advertiser.

**Pull**—The response generated by an advertisement.

**Red Book**—Refers to both *The Standard Directory of Advertising Agencies* and *The Standard Directory of Advertisers*.

**Reel**—A reel of film or videotape containing sample commercials written by the copywriter.

**Reply card**—A self-addressed postcard sent with advertising material to encourage the prospect to respond.

**Research**—Surveys, interviews, and studies designed to show an advertiser how the public perceives his or her product and company or how they react to the advertiser's ads and commercials.

**ROI**—Return on investment.

**Sales lead**—An inquiry from a qualified prospect.

**Sales promotion**—A temporary marketing effort designed to generate short-term interest in the purchase of a product. Coupons, sales, discounts, premiums, sweepstakes, and contests are all examples of sales promotion.

**Space**—The portion of a magazine or newspaper devoted to advertisements.

**Split-run test**—Two versions of an ad are run in different copies of a publication to test the effectiveness of one version against the other.

**Storyboard**—Rough series of illustrations showing what a finished TV commercial will look like.

**Sweepstakes**—A sales promotion in which prizes are awarded by chance and the consumer does not have to make a purchase to enter.

**Teaser**—Copy printed on the outside envelope of a direct-mail package.

**Trade advertising**—Advertising aimed at wholesalers, distributors, sales reps, agents, and retailers rather than consumers.

**Two color**—An ad or sales brochure printed in two colors, usually black and a second color such as blue, red, or yellow.

**Type**—Text set in lettering that can be reproduced by a printer.

**Universe**—The total number of people who are prospects for your product.

**Upscale**—Prospects at the upper end of the social scale in terms of income, education, and status.

**Vertical publication**—Magazine intended for special interest readers.

# PERIODICALS

**PRINT PUBLICATIONS**

**Advertising Age**
711 Third Avenue
New York, NY 10017-4036
Tel: 212-210-0100
www.adage.com
Contains in-depth coverage of newsworthy events in the advertising
business, with a strong focus on ad agencies.

**Adweek** (Eastern Edition)
770 Broadway
New York, NY 10003
Tel: 646-654-5421
Fax: 646-654-5365
www.adweek.com
Offers readers a blend of advertising news, features, how-to articles,
and columns.

**B-to-B**
360 North Michigan Avenue
Chicago, IL 60601
www.btobonline.com

Covers advertising, sales, and marketing of products and services sold to business and industry. It's a "must read" for industrial, high-tech, medical, and financial copywriters.

**Direct**
http://directmag.com
Monthly tabloid covering the direct response industry.

**Direct Marketing**
224 Seventh St.
Garden City, NY 11530
Tel: 516-746-6700
www.dmcny.org
For readers involved in direct-response marketing—direct mail, mail order, telemarketing, Internet marketing. Published monthly.

**DM News**
Editorial and Advertising Office
100 Avenue of the Americas
New York, NY 10013
Tel: 212-925-7300
Fax: 212-925-8752
www.dmnews.com
A newspaper-style tabloid, published weekly. Coverage is similar to *Direct Marketing*, but articles are briefer and more oriented toward late-breaking news rather than general information. But *DM News* also publishes several helpful how-to articles in each issue.

**Public Relations Journal**
33 Maiden Lane, 11th Flr.
New York, NY 10038-5150
Tel: 212-460-1400
Fax: 212-995-0757
www.prsa.org
This is the official monthly magazine of the Public Relations Society of America, a society of public relations professionals. Copywriters just getting into public relations can learn a lot from this magazine on how to write material that editors will read and publish.

**Sales and Marketing Management**
770 Broadway 7th Flr.
New York, NY 10003
Tel: 800-641-2030
Fax: 646-654-5355
www.salesandmarketing.com
A monthly magazine for sales managers and marketing managers, *Sales and Marketing Management* runs informative articles on all facets of marketing, including advertising. Most of the articles are brief and instructive.

**Target Marketing**
1500 Spring Garden Street, Suite 1200
Philadelphia, PA 19130
Tel: 215-238-5300
Fax: 215-238-5270
www.targetonline.com
Monthly magazine covering direct marketing.

ONLINE NEWSLETTERS

**Bencivenga's Bullets**
www.bencivengabullets.com
Master copywriter Gary Bencivenga's can't-miss e-zine based on his decades of tested results.

*The Copywriter's Roundtable*
www.jackforde.com
John Forde's superb e-newsletter on copywriting.

*The Direct Response Letter*
www.bly.com
My monthly e-newsletter on copywriting and direct marketing.

**Early to Rise**
www.earlytorise.com
Daily e-zine on business success, wealth, and health by marketing guru Michael Masterson.

**Excess Voice**
www.nickusborne.com/excess_voice.htm
Nick Usborne's e-newsletter on online copywriting. Informative and
great fun.

**Marketing Minute**
www.yudkin.com/markmin.htm
Weekly marketing tip from consultant Marcia Yudkin.

**Paul Hartunian's Million-Dollar Publicity Strategies**
www.prprofits.com
Great marketing e-newsletter focusing on publicity.

**The Success Margin**
www.tednicholas.com
Ted Nicholas's must-read marketing e-zine.

# WEB SITES

**American Writers and Artists Institute (AWAI)**
www.awaionline.com
Home-study courses and conferences on copywriting.

**Monthly Copywriting Genius**
www.monthlycopywritinggenius.com
Regular reviews of winning promotions and interviews with the copy-writers who wrote them.

**The Small Business Advocate**
www.smallbusinessadvocate.com
Radio show and Web site dedicated to small business.

**The Advertising Show**
www.theadvertisingshow.com
Radio show on advertising.

**Mailbox Millionaire**
www.agora-inc.com/reports/700SCBMO/W700D643/
Home-study course on how to start and run a profitable direct re-sponse business.

# APPENDIX D
## BOOKS

*How to Write a Good Advertisement* by Vic Schwab (Wilshire Book Company, 1962).

A commonsense course in how to write advertising copy that gets people to buy your product or service, written by a plain-speaking veteran mail-order copywriter in 1960.

*My First 50 Years in Advertising* by Max Sackheim (Prentice-Hall, 1970).

Another plain-speaking, commonsense guide that stresses salesmanship over creativity, and results over awards. The author was one of the founders of the Book-of-the-Month Club.

*The Robert Collier Letter Book* by Robert Collier (Robert Collier Publications, 1937).

How to write sales letters with numerous examples of classic mail-order letters.

*Reality in Advertising* by Rosser Reeves (Alfred A. Knopf, 1961).

The book in which Reeves introduced the now-famous concept of the USP (Unique Selling Proposition).

*Breakthrough Advertising* by Eugene Schwartz (Boardroom, 2004).

A copywriting guide by one of the greatest direct-response copywriters of the twentieth century.

*Tested Advertising Methods, 5th ed.*, by John Caples, revised by Fred Hahn (Prentice-Hall, 1997).

An updated edition of John Caples's classic book on the principles of persuasion.

*Confessions of an Advertising Man* by David Ogilvy (Atheneum, 2004). Charming autobiography of legendary ad man David Ogilvy, packed with useful advice on how to create effective advertising.

*Scientific Advertising* by Claude Hopkins (Bell Publishing, 1920). A book on the philosophy that advertising's purpose is to sell, not entertain or win creative awards—and how to apply this philosophy to create winning ads.

*Method Marketing* by Denny Hatch (Bonus Books, 1999). How to write successful direct-response copy by putting yourself in the customer's shoes. Packed with case histories of modern direct-response success stories, including Bill Bonner of Agora Publishing and Martin Edelston of Boardroom.

*Advertising Secrets of the Written Word* by Joseph Sugarman (DelStar, 1998). How to write successful advertising copy by a modern master of the space ad.

# ORGANIZATIONS

**American Consultants League**
www.americanconsultantsleague.com

**Business Marketing Association**
www.marketing.org
Association for business-to-business marketers

**Direct Marketing Association**
www.the-dma.org

**Newsletter and Electronic Publishers' Association**
www.newsletters.org

# SOURCES

**1. AN INTRODUCTION TO COPYWRITING**

1. Luther Brock, "Put the Spotlight on Benefits, Not Gimmicks," *Direct Marketing*, May 1983, p. 108.

2. Hank Seiden, "The Delivery Doesn't Fly," *Advertising Age*, October 31, 1983, p. MM–66. Reprinted with permission from the October 31, 1983, issue of *Advertising Age*. Copyright 1983 by Crain Communications Inc.

3. Alvin Eicoff, *Or Your Money Back* (New York: Crown Publishers, Inc., 1982), pp. 1–3.

4. Keith V. Monk, "Consumers Care Little for Creativity," *Advertising Age*, August 1, 1983, pp. 3–4. Reprinted with permission from the August 1, 1983, issue of *Advertising Age*. Copyright 1983 by Crain Communications Inc.

5. Howard G. Sawyer, *Business-to-Business Advertising* (Chicago: Crain Books, 1978), p. 266. Lewis Kornfeld, *To Catch a Mouse, Make a Noise Like a Cheese* (Englewood Cliffs, NJ: Prentice-Hall, Inc., 1983), pp. 56–58.

6. Robert M. Snodell, "Why TV Spots Fail," *Advertising Age*, July 2, 1984, p. 18. Reprinted with permission from the July 2, 1984, issue of *Advertising Age*. Copyright 1984 by Crain Communications Inc.

7. Flora Carlin, "Interview: Richard Kirschenbaum," *Psychology Today*, April 5, 2005, p. 4.

8. Joe Vitale, *The Seven Lost Secrets of Success* (VistaTron, 1992), p. 87.

9. Maxwell Sackheim, *My First Sixty Years in Advertising* (Prentice-Hall, 1970), pp. 19–22.

**4. WRITING TO SELL**

1. "Brain Teaser: What Makes You Spend?" *Kiplinger's*, July 2004, p. 23.

2. Andrew J. Byrne, "Long Copy Increases Chances of Making Sale," *Direct Marketing*.

3. Russell H. Colley, *Defining Advertising Goals for Measured Advertising Results* (New York: Association of National Advertisers, 1961), p. 39.

4. Malcolm D. MacDougall, "How to Sell Parity Products," *Adweek*, February 13, 1984, p. 30.

5. Donald J. Moine, "To Trust, Perchance to Buy," *Psychology Today*, August 1982, p. 52.

6. Jack Trout and Al Ries, "The Positioning Era" (reprinted from *Advertising Age*, April 24, May 1, and May 8, 1972).

**5. GETTING READY TO WRITE**

1. Betsy Sharkey, "Krone's Back Home," *Adweek*, August 29, 1983, p. 24.

2. Dorothy Hinshaw Patent, "Interviewing the Experts," *The Writer*, May 1983, p. 20.

3. Don Hauptman, "The Art of Creative Capitalism: Eleven Ways to Dream Up Profitable Business Ideas," *Success Unlimited*, May and June 1978.

4. John Caples, *How to Make Your Advertising Make Money* (Englewood Cliffs, NJ: Prentice-Hall, Inc., 1983), pp. 25–37.

**6. WRITING PRINT ADVERTISEMENTS**

1. "Total Recall: Sloganeering," *BusinessWeek*, October 25, 2004, p. 16.

2. Robert F. Lauterborn, "Never Underestimate the Power of the Printed Word," speech presented at the February 2, 1984, meeting of the New York Chapter of the Business/Professional Advertising Association; *Publishers Weekly*, June 26, 1987.

3. Jakob Nielsen, "The Most Hated Advertising Technique," *Metalworking Marketer*, March 2005, p. 1.

4. "Go, Gargano!" an ad for the *Wall Street Journal*, published in *Business Marketing* (April 1984). Copyright Dow Jones & Company, Inc., 1984, all rights reserved.

7. WRITING DIRECT MAIL

1. "From the Test Tube: To Tease or Not to Tease," *Test Patterns* 11 (newsletter published by Bloom & Gelb, Inc.), no. 1, Spring 1984.

2. Sources for these tips include: *Direct Marketing: Strategy, Planning, and Execution* by Ed Nash (McGraw-Hill, 1982); "How to Create and Produce Successful Direct Mail" (Cahners Publishing); "The How Not to Mail Booklet" (Hayden Direct Marketing Services); "444 Begged, Borrowed, Stolen & Even a Few Original Direct Response Marketing Ideas!" (Rockingham/Jutkins Marketing); "Direct Mail Editor's Checklist" (*Adweek*, December 13, 1982, p. 32).

8. WRITING BROCHURES, CATALOGS, AND OTHER SALES MATERIALS

1. Howard G. Sawyer, *Business-to-Business Advertising* (Chicago: Crain Books, 1978), p. 139.

9. WRITING PUBLIC RELATIONS MATERIALS

1. Alan Caruba, "Public Relations: What Is It?" *New Jersey Business*, November 1982, p. 70.

2. B. Beda, speech presented at Sephardic Bikur Holim fundraiser.

3. Carol Rose Carey, "A New Image for an Old Product," *INC.*, June 1982, p. 93.

4. "Lawpoll: Big Firms Favor P.R.; Little Firms Like Ads," *American Bar Association Journal*, 1983, p. 892.

5. Len Kirsch, "Press Releases: Format, Content . . . Dos and Don'ts," Kirsch Communications.

6. Pamela Clark, "Running in Place," *Popular Computing,* July 1984, p. 6.

7. Nancy Edmonds Hanson, *How You Can Make $20,000 a Year Writing (No Matter Where You Live)* (Cincinnati: Writer's Digest Books, 1980), pp. 186–87.

7. Ron Huff, "That Speaking Invitation: It Sounds Flattering, But—," *Advertising Age,* September 4, 1978, p. 40.

## 10. WRITING COMMERCIALS AND MULTIMEDIA PRESENTATIONS

1. Ed McMahon, "TV's Greatest Censored Commercial Bloopers," NBC, November 7, 1983.

2. Richard Morgan, "Public to 4A's: We Still Don't Like Advertising," *Adweek,* May 16, 1983, p. 2.

3. Donahue transcript #09032, copyright 1982, Multimedia Program Productions, Inc., Cincinnati, Ohio.

4. Malcolm D. MacDougall, "No Big Mistake," *Adweek,* June 4, 1984, p. 14.

5. Sid Bernstein, "Maybe We Are Too Creative," *Advertising Age,* June 18, 1984, p. 16.

6. David Campiti, "Writing Radio Commercials," *Writer's Digest,* November 1983, pp. 30–33.

7. Reprinted with permission of the Masonry Institute of St. Louis, copyright 1978, The DOCSI Corporation.

8. John Baldoni, "The Vision Translated into Words: An Overview of Script Writing," Audio-Visual Directions, October 1982, pp. 36–41.

## 11. WRITING FOR THE WEB

1. Beth Viveiros, "GM Uses Web to Give Itself a Voice," *Direct Marketing,* May 2005, p. 16.

## 12. WRITING E-MAIL MARKETING

1. Christine Blank, "More E-Mails Blocked," *DM News,* March 28, 2005, p. 12.

2. Kim Stacey, "E-Mail Marketing: Breaking Down the Barriers," privately published memo, April 25, 2005.

**13. HOW TO GET A JOB AS A COPYWRITER**

1. Barrington Boardman, "Ad Agencies' Biggest Neglect: Their People," *Adweek*, December 6, 1982, p. 28.

2. Robert W. Bly and Gary Blake, *Dream Jobs: A Guide to Tomorrow's Top Careers* (New York: John Wiley & Sons, Inc., 1983), pp. 8–9.

3. ———, "Tips on Top Job Hunting Tactics," *Advertising Age*, February 23, 1981, p. S–15, p. S–4.

4. George Tibball, "An Agency's Message to Clients," *Business Marketing*, September 1983, p. 95.

**14. HOW TO HIRE AND WORK WITH COPYWRITERS**

1. Ed Buxton, "Doers vs. Undoers on Ad Row," *Adweek*, January 16, 1984, p. 24.

2. Shell R. Alpert, "In Direct Marketing Testing, Details Can Be Everything," *Business Marketing*, February 1984, p. 84.

3. Dr. Adweek and Betsy Sharkey, "How to Manage Creative People," *Adweek*, February 1984, p. C.R. 28.

4. Malcolm MacDougall, "Just Deserts: Why Clients Get the Advertising They Deserve," *Adweek*, April 1984, p. B.W.C. 4.

# INDEX

# ABOUT THE AUTHOR

ROBERT W. BLY is a freelance copywriter specializing in business-to-business, high-tech, and direct marketing.

He has more than twenty-five years of experience writing ads, brochures, direct mail packages, sales letters, publicity materials, e-mail campaigns, white papers, booklets, special reports, newsletters, landing pages, and Web sites for more than 100 clients including Grumman, AlliedSignal, AT&T, IBM, Lucent Technologies, Medical Economics, McGraw-Hill, Phillips Publishing, Forbes, KCI, Agora Publishing, Ken Roberts Company, and EBI Medical Systems.

He has won a number of industry awards including a Gold Echo from the Direct Marketing Association, an IMMY from the Information Industry Association, two Southstar Awards, an American Corporate Identity Award of Excellence, and the Standard of Excellence award from the Web Marketing Association.

Robert W. Bly is the author of more than sixty books, including *The Complete Idiot's Guide to Direct Marketing* (Alpha Books) and *Internet Direct Mail: The Complete Guide to Successful E-Mail Marketing Campaigns* (NTC Business Books).

His articles have appeared in such publications as *Cosmopolitan, Chemical Engineering, Computer Decisions, Business Marketing, New Jersey Monthly, The Parent Paper, Writer's Digest, City Paper, Early to*

*Rise, Successful Meetings, Sharing Ideas, DM News, Amtrak Express,* and *Direct Marketing.*

Robert W. Bly has taught copywriting at New York University and has presented sales and marketing seminars to numerous corporations, associations, and groups including the American Marketing Association, Direct Marketing Creative Guild, Women's Direct Response Group, American Chemical Society, Publicity Club of New York, and the International Tile Exposition. He has been a guest on dozens of radio and TV shows including CNBC and CBS's *Hard Copy,* and has been featured in periodicals ranging from *Nation's Business* to the *Los Angeles Times.*

He is a member of the Business Marketing Association, Newsletter and Electronic Publishers Association, and the American Institute of Chemical Engineers. His e-zine, *Direct Response Letter,* goes to more than 70,000 subscribers monthly.

For more information, contact:

Robert W. Bly
Copywriter
22 E. Quackenbush Avenue
Dumont, NJ 07628
Phone: 201-385-1220
Fax: 201-385-2238
E-mail: rwbly@bly.com
Web site: www.bly.com